COACHING FOR ADAPTIVE EXPERTISE

This exciting new book strikes at the heart of what's missing in much teacher professional development – coaching that strengthens teachers' decision-making. It introduces the Adaptive Expertise Framework, an approach that supports teachers in continuously developing their expertise, allowing them to respond intelligently to the complex lesson environment.

Drawing on research from cognitive science, complexity theory, and studies of expert decision-making, the book outlines four areas every teacher must develop to grow their adaptive expertise that form the basis of the coaching framework. Part 2 then examines each stage of the coaching process including:

- The purpose of each stage of coaching so you know what you're aiming for
- Common pitfalls and how to avoid them
- Codified coaching techniques that coaches can practise and use flexibly
- Rich annotated coaching examples to illustrate the techniques at work
- Sequence and sentence stems to help you apply the techniques straight away in your coaching

Written by leading experts and part of the Teacher CPD Academy series from InnerDrive, *Coaching for Adaptive Expertise* provides a timely blueprint for schools seeking to cultivate reflective, responsive educators who can adapt skilfully to any teaching situation.

Sarah Cottinghatt is the research lead at Steplab and works with schools designing and delivering effective professional development. Sarah is the author and chapter author of books on teaching and professional development as well as part of the research team for the EEF's guide to professional development.

Haili Hughes is an Associate Professor of Educational Innovation and Impact at La Trobe University in Melbourne. She was a school and trust leader for 20 years and has written ten education books.

Adam Kohlbeck is Director of Teacher Quality at Chiltern Learning Trust. He is also a doctoral student, researching teacher decision-making in complex environments and is a proud council member at the Chartered College of Teaching.

The Teacher CPD Academy

Series editors: Bradley Busch and Edward Watson

The Homework Conundrum
How to Stop the Dog From Eating Homework
Jovita M. Castelino

Do I Have Your Attention?
Understanding Memory Constraints and Maximizing Learning
Blake Harvard

Creativity for Teachers
A Cognitive Science Approach
Claire Badger and Jonathan Firth

The Scaffolding Effect
Supporting All Students to Succeed
Rachel Ball and Alex Fairlamb

Evidence Informed Wisdom
Making Better Decisions in Education
Bradley Busch, Edward Watson, and Matthew Shaw

Unlocking Oracy
Enhancing Student Learning and Personal Development
Nikki Sullivan, Kelly Heaton, and Lucy Lowde

Demystifying Adaptive Teaching
How to Teach to the Top
Jade Pearce

Fail Better
How Teachers can Help Students Overcome Failure, Perfectionism, Procrastination, Impostor Syndrome and Test Anxiety
Mark Roberts

Coaching for Adaptive Expertise
Developing Teachers Who Make Better Decisions
Sarah Cottinghatt, Haili Hughes, and Adam Kolhbeck

If you are a leader or a coach supporting teachers to be reflective and adaptive experts in the classroom, then this excellent book is for you. The book is written with great attention to detail and is beautifully supported by snippets of coaching conversations which really bring the text to life and guide you to see how this framework can support teachers to flourish.

– **Rachel Ball**, *Coaching Development Lead, StepLab*

If you aim higher when developing teachers, you have to go deeper - and that is exactly what this book does superbly well by surfacing hitherto tacit mental models the better to analyse and improve them.

– **Oliver Caviglioli**, *Director of WalkThrus*

This book will make you a better coach. It covers many big ideas in coaching, adaptive expertise, agency, mental models, and coaching excerpts. All written in a clear, practical way by people who live and breathe coaching in schools. I wish it had existed 10 years ago.

– **Dr. Mark Dowley**, *Associate Head,*
Staff Development at Birghton Grammar, Melbourne Australia

A masterclass in coaching on coaching. This book models the very process it teaches - guiding you through insights, models, and rehearsal to elevate your practice. A must-read for all coaches!

– **Cat New**, *ASLT Lead Coach,* Pilton Community College

In my work, I read a lot of books on coaching. This is one of the best! The mental models framework makes sense of what good coaches do instinctively, and the focus on decision-making puts teacher professionalism at the centre. What more do you want from a coaching book?

– **Shane Learning**, *Organisational Coach*

Coaching for Adaptive Expertise is the book I've been waiting for - absolute gold - hooking me from the introduction, which nails the core challenge in teaching today: improving instruction isn't just about changing what teachers do - it's about reshaping how they think.

– **Lindsey Bennett**, *Head of Teacher Development,*
Astrea Academy Trust

I love this book. It gets to the heart of the challenge of teaching adaptively and provides a wonderful guide to coaching teachers which acknowledges the complexity of the process but keeps things simple. It reminded me of a Year 6 pupil I met recently, who praised her teacher because in maths she teaches them 'hard sums but easy methods.' I recommend this book to any school leader who is serious about improving their school through supporting teachers to be intentional, deliberate classroom practitioners . . . and that should be every school leader!

– **John Tomsett**, *Educational consultant and author*

Coaching for Adaptive Expertise is an exceptionally well-crafted and evidence-informed contribution to the field of effective teacher coaching. The authors achieve a rare balance: they ground their ideas in clear, robust theory while offering practical, actionable strategies that coaches can use immediately.

There is a great deal of value here for anyone looking to strengthen their coaching practice or deepen their understanding of how to help teachers refine and extend their craft. Whether you are a coach, a coach-trainer, or a leader responsible for teacher development, this book provides insightful guidance that feels both relevant and usable. Most notably, it presents a compelling case - and offers practical, thoughtful solutions - for supporting teachers to make better instructional decisions: in the moment, with precision, and for the right reasons. It is a timely and important resource for anyone committed to improving classroom practice.

— **Jon Gilbert**, *Professional Learning and Improvement Director at The Two Counties Trust*

This book is an outstanding resource for developing a coach's ability to guide teachers toward making more effective classroom decisions. Packed with practical strategies and evidence-based insights, it's an invaluable tool for school leaders committed to driving sustained improvement in teaching and learning.

— **Caroline Sherwood**, *Education Partner, Woodwater Academy*

COACHING FOR ADAPTIVE EXPERTISE

Developing Teachers Who Make Better Decisions

Sarah Cottinghatt, Haili Hughes,
and Adam Kohlbeck

Routledge
Taylor & Francis Group
LONDON AND NEW YORK

Designed cover image: Courtesy of InnerDrive

First published 2027
by Routledge
4 Park Square, Milton Park, Abingdon, Oxon OX14 4RN

and by Routledge
605 Third Avenue, New York, NY 10158

Routledge is an imprint of the Taylor & Francis Group, an informa business

British Library Cataloguing-in-Publication Data
A catalogue record for this book is available from the British Library

Library of Congress Cataloging-in-Publication Data
Names: Cottinghatt, Sarah author | Hughes, Haili author | Kohlbeck, Adam author
Title: Coaching for adaptive expertise : developing teachers who make better decisions / Sarah Cottinghatt, Haili Hughes, and Adam Kohlbeck.
Description: Abingdon, Oxon ; New York, NY : Routledge, 2026. | Series: The teacher CPD academy | Includes bibliographical references and index.
Identifiers: LCCN 2026003552 (print) | LCCN 2026003553 (ebook) | ISBN 9781032739779 hardback | ISBN 9781032739793 paperback | ISBN 9781003465850 ebook
Subjects: LCSH: Teaching—Vocational guidance | Teachers—In-service training | Mentoring in education | Teacher effectiveness
Classification: LCC LB1775 .C7375 2026 (print) | LCC LB1775 (ebook)
LC record available at https://lccn.loc.gov/2026003552
LC ebook record available at https://lccn.loc.gov/2026003553

ISBN: 978-1-032-73977-9 (hbk)
ISBN: 978-1-032-73979-3 (pbk)
ISBN: 978-1-003-46585-0 (ebk)

DOI: 10.4324/9781003465850

Typeset in Interstate
by Apex CoVantage, LLC

CONTENTS

FOREWORD FROM THE EDITORS

Teaching has always been a profession that demands both knowledge and judgement, relying on the ability not only to know what to do, but also when and why to do it. *Coaching for Adaptive Expertise*, by Sarah, Haili, and Adam, tackles this challenge head-on. It explores what it means to develop teachers who can navigate the complex, ever-changing reality of the classroom with confidence. As a result, it offers a way to help teachers make the right decision, at the right time, for the right reasons.

Coaching for Adaptive Expertise sits within InnerDrive's Teacher CPD Academy series, which is a collection dedicated to helping educators grow through an evidence-informed approach. The series draws on the best of educational research and translates it into clear, practical guidance that teachers can immediately apply.

Previous books, including *The Homework Conundrum*, *The Scaffolding Effect*, *Do I Have Your Attention?*, *Demystifying Adaptive Teaching*, *Unlocking Oracy*, *Evidence-Informed Wisdom*, and *Fail Better*, each address a key aspect of teaching and learning and do so in a way that bridges the gap between research and real-world practice. If these books provide 'the what' this book provides 'the how' in helping teachers coach each other to improve and hone their craft.

What makes *Coaching for Adaptive Expertise* such a vital addition to this series is its focus on professional judgement. As classrooms evolve and expectations rise, the need for adaptive expertise has never been greater. Teachers are asked to make countless decisions every day: when to step in and when to hold back, when to re-teach and when to move on, when to challenge and when to support. This book provides a framework for coaching conversations that help teachers better understand those moments, reflect thoughtfully, and act purposefully to drive positive change.

By combining rigorous research with engaging examples, *Coaching for Adaptive Expertise* offers a roadmap for growth that feels both inspiring and achievable. It reminds us that expertise is not about having all the answers, but about learning how to keep asking better questions. In that sense, this book represents what great professional learning should be: grounded in evidence, rich in insight, and deeply practical in helping teachers become the best version of themselves for the students they serve.

We at InnerDrive are proud to welcome *Coaching for Adaptive Expertise* into the Teacher CPD Academy series. We know it will make a positive impact on the lives of thousands of teachers for years to come.

Bradley Busch, Edward Watson, and the whole InnerDrive team

FOREWORD

Dear Reader,

It is an honour and a pleasure to write the foreword to this book. I am excited by the impact it can have across the sector and by the reflections and practical learning it will spark for every reader who spends time with these pages.

As an academic and practitioner, I have spent more than twelve years working at the intersection of complexity (a way of understanding how organisations and systems actually behave), decision-making, and psychology in education and leadership. Over that time, interest in this intersection has grown – not only within academia and practice, but also among those who operate in the vital space between the two.

This growth is welcome because complexity helps us see education as it is, not as we wish it to be. It reminds us that schools are not predictable machines with linear inputs and outputs. They are knotty, deeply interconnected, often counter-intuitive systems where causes and effects are hard to trace. Yet, whether through accountability pressures, wishful thinking, or what I have elsewhere called the 'thought architecture' of adults, we still find a persistent pull towards simplification: the belief that schooling can be reduced to single variables, silver bullets, or a relentless focus on actionable strategies (at a cost of understanding). I have seen these assumptions shape decisions from the boardroom to the classroom. In their wake, the crucial processes of sense-making and decision-making risk being displaced by blueprints and flowcharts, and by the uncritical transplantation of ideas without adaptation.

Talk to teachers, however, and you hear a different story – one that bears the marks of complexity. It is the story of days that defy prediction by 8:06 a.m.; of puzzling attainment patterns that resist easy explanation; of how information travels through a building at astonishing speed. The lived reality of the typical, hardworking teacher is not evidence of personal failure. Classrooms are not unpredictable because teachers are incapable; they are unpredictable because they are emergent, interactive, evolving systems. Adult developmental psychology helps us appreciate just how demanding that reality can be.

Until now, much of the conversation about complexity in education has centred on leadership decision-making. What excites me about this book is that it takes the next step: it brings complexity and decision-making into the heart of classroom practice – through coaching.

Crucially, the authors have not simply transplanted complexity theory into the classroom. They have thought carefully about how complexity manifests differently for teachers and learners, and they have placed decision-making as the fulcrum of professional growth. The book refuses the temptation to unveil complexity only to offer a seductively simple fix. Instead, it equips coaches to hold complexity with teachers – to inquire, notice, and iterate alongside them over time. This is how teachers build warranted self-efficacy in their judgement and deepen their willingness to make decisions on behalf of their pupils and school communities. In other words, to acquire the agency that is so essential to the work of practitioners in complex contexts.

The implications of this book stretch into how we support the most vulnerable and how we marry up teacher and leadership decision-making. First, I can see how this will be an important aide to those questioning how we support the most vulnerable in our schools. By virtue of the task, those who present with the most complex of needs require us to think about how we adapt, and in doing so unpack the step-by-step process in which we have arrived at a decision. I believe this emphasis will be a key supporting approach in advancing truly universal provision, where teachers need to adapt and where transferable solutions are not readily available. Second, as a scholar exploring complexity and leadership decisions, I am fascinated by how this classroom-centred approach complements complexity-informed work in leadership decision-making

Finally, this book provides a supporting frame for those who aspire to make decision-making the centre of the intellectual engine of teaching. It will support those working in classrooms to go beyond the implementation of a rigid flowchart, and develop their decision-making in such a way that they can embrace, wrestle, (and even have fun!) with the complex and knotty reality of infusing knowledge, context, and practice at the chalk (or white) board. It is through this sort of coaching where teachers will further develop their capacities to deliver for communities they serve – the sort of agency which will only become more central to our profession if we are prepared for the teaching challenges of both today and tomorrow.

I hope you enjoy and learn from the wisdom and thought of the authors as much as I have.

Dr Neil M Gilbride, CPsychol.

ACKNOWLEDGEMENTS

This book began when Haili contacted Sarah to write a straightforward book on coaching. Fast forward two years and it became something else entirely: more of a research project into new and compelling techniques, underpinned by a rethinking of the ultimate goal for teachers: adaptive expertise. Which, as you'll discover in these pages, is a bit of an oxymoron, since there is no end to adaptive expertise!

Along this journey, we've had peaks and troughs - often dictated by bursts of field testing, reworking ideas, and training other coaches. Momentum truly built though when we convinced our third author, Adam Kohlbeck (our coaching muse), to join us. He has helped us get to the finish line with smiles on our faces.

Here, we want to acknowledge some of the brilliant thinkers, coaches, academics, and friends who have supported and spurred on this work. We're grateful to you all.

Oliver Caviglioli, Director of WalkThrus, our wisest thought-partner and relentless pursuer of clarity who has pushed our thinking in directions we could never have reached alone. His extensive work on mental models, schema, and the visual communication of complex ideas has shaped many of the book's most important concepts.

Dr Neil Gilbride (who kindly authored our foreword), whose research into complexity theory helped make sense of so many of our early, half-formed ideas. His work provided the theoretical justification for much of what follows. Without his work, this book wouldn't exist in its current form.

Josh Goodrich, co-founder and CEO of Steplab, for his tireless work supporting coaching across schools in the UK and beyond and to the incredible team at Steplab who set the bar for high-quality professional development. Josh's book *Responsive Coaching* is cited in these pages, as is Steplab's ongoing work, both of which have had a profound influence on our practice and thinking. (Sarah, one of our co-authors, also has the privilege of working with Steplab as Research Lead.)

To Caroline Sherwood and Cat New who have baked this coaching approach into their everyday work and been kind enough to share their work along the way. We have learned so much.

For the female coaching experts Haili has stood on the shoulders of: Rachel Lofthouse and Rachel Ball. Haili has learnt so much from you both.

For our friend and champion, Chris Passey for helping to draw out these ideas and for all the coachees Adam has worked with, particularly Olly Cakebread and Liam Bannister whose openness and authenticity has enabled this approach to develop as it has.

Finally, a huge thank you to all of those leaders, coaches, and teachers who have supported this work along the way, testing ideas, providing feedback and, of course, for doing the absolute best for the students in their care. We hope this proves useful for the vital work you do every day.

Introduction

The problem

Teaching is the best job in the world but it is also a profession in crisis. In 2024, the government in England was expected to miss its 2024-2025 teacher recruitment targets by 40% at the secondary level and 17% at the primary level.[1] While teacher leaving rates increased in 2021/22, and in 2022/23, 44% more teachers said they intended to leave teaching than in the previous year,[2] which suggests that leaving rates may continue to rise. This isn't just a problem in England. Teacher shortages are a global issue, prevalent not only in developing nations but also in high-income regions such as Europe and North America. This is worrying, as teaching is arguably one of the most important professions since it is the profession which makes all other professions. Teachers are true professionals and we have to preserve this.

But what does this mean? It means they deserve training that supports the development of expertise rather than (unwittingly) strips it away. In recent years, there has been much research on what the active ingredients of effective professional development (PD) are. This has included the Education Endowment Foundation's 2019 research, which identified 14 mechanisms that can help those designing PD for teachers to ensure that teachers then use their learning to actually improve their practice.[3] This understanding has likely supported our work to close the knowing-doing gap[4] (where teachers know what to do but struggle to put it into practice).

In addition, teachers are much more engaged with evidence than perhaps ever before. Many also understand what strategies to use linked to evidence. However, to instruct teachers on how to execute these strategies, we have often taken a top-down approach. This approach may mean that in our efforts to close the knowing-doing gap, we may have perhaps opened up a knowing-*deciding*-doing gap – where teachers know what to do, but not when or why, which means they are not doing the right things, at the right time, for the right reasons.

The good news is that coaching, a tool being used to develop teacher expertise worldwide, could be harnessed to close both gaps. But it's not necessarily being used as flexibly as it could be. Coaches (and the school leaders who often train or arrange their training) may not have the right goal in mind yet or the understanding of how to harness coaching in this way.

In this book we explain why the end goal of professional development should be *adaptive expertise*. Adaptive expertise encompasses both efficient techniques and their appropriate usage. It

DOI: 10.4324/9781003465850-1

also entails a mindset of continuous improvement. If a coach is simply spending time diagnosing a teacher's challenges and problems and telling them how to solve them, we risk over-scaffolding the thinking behind teaching. Instead, we must coach teachers to develop their decision-making, rather than outsource the thinking. Why is this important?

The current reality in schools

Collectively, we (the authors) visit many schools each year and observe or conduct many coaching conversations. There is so much brilliant practice, but some lethal mutations have crept in too. The term 'lethal mutation' was coined by Ed Haertel[5] and it refers to research and frameworks being adopted by schools that then contextualise them so much that they are too far removed from the original concept. Of course, schools should contextualise research and frameworks but the danger is that if teachers do not understand the essential principles, they may modify ideas and techniques to such an extent that they are no longer effective, or even counter-productive.

One of the biggest lethal mutations in coaching is that *instructional* coaching means always telling people what to do. This is a fundamental misunderstanding of the word 'instruction,' which refers not to how to coach but to the content of the coaching, i.e., it is about teacher instruction. It also ignores research on how people learn as their expertise develops. As a teacher develops more expertise in a domain, they may be able to use their rich mental models and episodic memory, which contains banks of previous lesson episodes, to make decisions. A coach's role here might be to ask probing questions which prompt the teacher to do this, rather than telling them what to do.

Instead, popular coaching frameworks can sometimes be used as an opportunity for coaches to talk *at* teachers for most of the coaching session. They do not give the teacher the opportunity to speak at all, let alone to develop their decision-making.

In some schools however, there is excellent, responsive practice. Coaches using dialogue to adapt their coaching support, by finding out what their coachee already knows and tailoring their precise questions to help them reflect on the deeper reasons behind the decisions they made. They also aren't afraid to share their expertise in the joint pursuit of problem solving.

Techniques alone are not sufficient

Just collecting strategies is not enough. No matter how well some approaches have worked before, they may not work in a different situation with its own contextual features, so teachers need a reservoir - a pool of ideas and knowledge - that they can draw upon to help them make sense of and inform their choices. As Brooks adds, "part of this distinction is situated judgement"[6] and coaching needs to help develop the mental models that feed into teachers' situated judgement and decision-making if we want to develop their adaptive expertise.

Teacher expertise

Studies of teacher expertise reveal that inexperienced teachers are fairly rigid rule-followers, easily overwhelmed by unexpected situations and poor at adapting the approaches taken to meet the needs of pupils and the subject matter.[7] By contrast, more experienced and effective teachers are often able to adapt their lessons flexibly in response to formative assessment and also anticipate issues of learning and behaviour before they occur. Effective teaching for them is almost instinctive and automatic, yet also flexible. Teachers will be unable to move from the rigidity of being a novice to the flexibility of being an expert if they are always told what to do by a coach. Indeed, if a coaching approach just focuses on drilling technique and telling teachers what to do, without developing decision-making, then we suggest it is unlikely to work. By contrast, forms of coaching that only permit the coach to ask questions rather than share expertise at pertinent moments are unlikely to provide enough support to develop teacher expertise. Therefore, a one-size-fits-all approach to instructional coaching just isn't good enough. This book acts as a guide to coaching teachers at all levels – an approach which includes developing techniques *and* how to use these flexibly at the right time for the right reasons.

Yet, in the busy school environment, where some coaches get mere minutes with their coachees, how do we help to move teachers from being routine experts to adaptive experts? A focus on decision-making may be the answer and this book is your comprehensive guide to doing just that.

Our vision for the future of coaching in schools: putting decision-making at the heart of coaching

Giving teachers the opportunity to examine their decision-making is a crucial part of coaching and indeed, developing adaptive expertise. This involves surfacing their mental models. What are mental models?

Our mental models act as our internal representations of external reality and guide our perceptions and actions in the classroom. By expressing these models, we can reflect on and adjust our teaching practices. A paper which many cite when espousing the virtues of instructional coaching is Kraft, Blazar, and Hogan's (2018) metaanalysis, where they looked at 60 causal studies and found that teacher coaching positively impacts instructional practice and student achievement.[8] In this study, they emphasise that effective coaching involves a sustained professional dialogue, which is focused on developing specific teaching skills. We believe this kind of dialogue requires teachers to articulate and examine their mental models. Recent research and frameworks suggest the importance of coaching that highlights key aspects of mental models such as cause and effect.[9]

If we focus on developing teachers' decision-making by improving their mental models through dialogue, modelling, rehearsal, and implementation of the step we may be more likely to see a move towards adaptive, flexible expertise. But there's another reason to focus on teacher decision-making: it is also at the heart of what it is for teachers to achieve *agency*.

Coaching for teacher agency

Teacher agency has become a bit of a buzzword, but what does it mean? One thing it *doesn't* mean is teachers choosing their own adventures, i.e. doing whatever they want. A school is a complex ecosystem and unless everyone shares the same vision and swims in the same direction, it can be a recipe for disaster. Agency involves the ability to make intentional decisions and take action in response to professional challenges and opportunities. It encompasses aspects such as self-efficacy, reflective practice, and professional autonomy.[10]

Teachers with high levels of agency are more likely to engage in innovative practices and adjust to diverse student needs, as well as remain resilient in the face of external pressures such as policy changes or curriculum reforms.[11] Teachers who are given more agency also remain in the profession longer.[12] Clearly, these are attributes we want in our teaching workforce.

Coaching for adaptive expertise

So, the question is: how do we coach to improve teachers' expertise rapidly and sustainably, while preserving their professionalism? With the worldwide teacher retention crisis, this is a question on everyone's lips. We believe that, by getting on the same page about the end goal - adaptive expertise - and taking a systematic approach to learning how to develop it in our teachers, we will make strides in the right direction. Our Adaptive Expertise Framework and codified coaching techniques offer coaches and those leading teaching and learning comprehensive and practical guidance for training a community of effective, evidence-informed and agentic teachers.

Let's get started.

Notes

1 NFER (2024) *Teacher Labour Market in England: Annual Report 2024*. Available online at: https://www.nfer.ac.uk/media/hqdglvra/teacher_labour_market_in_england_annual_report_2024.pdf

2 Department for Education (2023) School workforce in England, reporting year 2022. Available at: https://explore-education-statistics. service.gov.uk/find-statistics/school-workforce-in-england

3 Education Endowment Foundation (2021) *Professional development guidance report*. Available online at: https://educationendowmentfoundation.org.uk/education-evidence/guidance-reports/effective-professional-development.

4 Pfeffer, J. and Sutton, R.I. (2000) *The knowing-doing gap: How smart companies turn knowledge into action*. Boston, MA: Harvard Business Press.

5 Brown, A. L. and Campione, J. C. (1996) 'Psychological theory and the design of innovative learning environments: On procedures, principles, and systems.' In: R. Glaser (Ed.), *Innovations in learning: New environments for education*. Mahwah, NJ: Erlbaum, pp. 289–325.

6 UCL (2021) 'The Core Content Framework and the fallacy of the teacher training curriculum.' Available online at: https://blogs.ucl.ac.uk/ioe/2021/09/02/the-core-content-framework-and-the-fallacy-of-a-teacher-training-curriculum/

7 Berliner, D. C. (2004) 'Describing the behavior and documenting the accomplishments of expert teachers.' *Bulletin of Science, Technology & Society*, 24(3), pp. 200–212; Hogan, T., Rabinowitz, M., and Craven, J. A. (2003) 'Representation in teaching: Inferences from research of expert and novice teachers.' *Educational Psychologist*, 38(4), pp. 235–247.

8 Kraft, M. A., Blazar, D., and Hogan, D. (2018) 'The effect of teacher coaching on instruction and achievement: A meta-analysis of the causal evidence.' *Review of Educational Research*, 88(4), pp. 547-588.

9 Boguslav, A. (2024) 'Parsing coaching practice: A systematic framework for describing coaching discourse.' *AERA Open*, 10, pp.1–65.

10 Biesta, G., Priestley, M., and Robinson, S. (2015) 'The role of beliefs in teacher agency.' *Teachers and Teaching*, 21(6), pp. 624–640.

11 Ibid.

12 Koerber, N., Marquez-Mendez, M., Mensah, A., Fasching-Varner, K., and Schrader, P. G. (2023) 'Sustaining teacher needs: A systematic narrative review exploring teacher retention, attrition, and motivation.' *Literature Reviews in Education and Human Services*, 2(2), pp. 1–20.

References

Berliner, D. C. (2004) 'Describing the behavior and documenting the accomplishments of expert teachers.' *Bulletin of Science, Technology & Society*, 24(3), pp. 200–212.

Biesta, G., Priestley, M., & Robinson, S. (2015) 'The role of beliefs in teacher agency.' *Teachers and Teaching*, 21(6), pp. 624-640.

Boguslav, A. (2024) 'Parsing coaching practice: A systematic framework for describing coaching discourse.' *AERA Open*, 10, pp. 1–65.

Brown, A. L. and Campione, J. C. (1996) 'Psychological theory and the design of innovative learning environments: On procedures, principles, and systems.' In: R. Glaser (Ed.), *Innovations in learning: New environments for education*. Mahwah, NJ: Erlbaum, pp. 289–325.

Department for Education (2023) School workforce in England, reporting year 2022. Available at: https://explore-education-statistics. service.gov.uk/find-statistics/school-workforce-in-england

Education Endowment Foundation (2021) *Professional development guidance report*. Available online at: https://educationendowmentfoundation.org.uk/education-evidence/guidance-reports/effective-professional-development.

Hogan, T., Rabinowitz, M., and Craven, J. A. (2003) 'Representation in teaching: Inferences from research of expert and novice teachers.' *Educational Psychologist*, 38(4), pp. 235–247.

Koerber, N., Marquez-Mendez, M., Mensah, A., Fasching-Varner, K., and Schrader, P. G. (2023) 'Sustaining teacher needs: A systematic narrative review exploring teacher retention, attrition, and motivation.' *Literature Reviews in Education and Human Services*, 2(2), pp. 1–20.

Kraft, M. A., Blazar, D., and Hogan, D. (2018) 'The effect of teacher coaching on instruction and achievement: A meta-analysis of the causal evidence.' *Review of Educational Research*, 88(4), pp. 547–588.

NFER (2024) *Teacher labour market in England: Annual report 2024*. Available online at: https://www.nfer.ac.uk/media/hqdglvra/teacher_labour_market_in_england_annual_report_2024.pdf

Pfeffer, J. and Sutton, R. I. (2000) *The knowing-doing gap: How smart companies turn knowledge into action*. Boston, MA: Harvard Business Press.

UCL (2021) 'The Core Content Framework and the fallacy of the teacher training curriculum.' Available online at: https://blogs.ucl.ac.uk/ioe/2021/09/02/the-core-content-framework-and-the-fallacy-of-a-teacher-training-curriculum/

PART 1
Adaptive expertise

1 The case for adaptive expertise

Why is adaptive expertise so important in teaching?

When you started your teaching career, you probably planned a lot of lessons in detail. How soon did your detailed plan become redundant? Probably within the first 5–10 minutes of the lesson. Predicting in detail with any certainty beyond the short term is almost impossible in lessons. Because of this unpredictability, we also can't guarantee a certain teaching technique will have the effect we want. What is it about teaching that creates this uncertainty?

Complexity[1] hampers predictability

The lesson environment can be characterised as a complex system for teachers.[2] Complex systems are difficult to predict beyond the short term. What makes prediction hard? The key is the interactions that occur. Interactions lead to various, uncertain outcomes, or what we will call *emergence*.[3] For example, when students pay attention to their teacher, they are processing the teacher's words through the lens of their varied prior knowledge (*interactions*) leading to various 'meanings' made (*emergence*). A teacher asks questions to understand what meanings students made from their explanation (*interactions*) and this leads to students articulating their understanding, which changes it in the process (*emergence*) and so on . . .

Interactions and emergence mean that lessons can go down many different paths, and this uncertainty requires flexibility on the part of the teacher.

Plus, in complex environments, it is tough to explain cause and effect. This is because of the interactions and emergence we just described but also because complex systems have histories that cannot be erased or forgotten.[4] For example, teachers generally teach classes of students who were taught by other teachers. Students' knowledge is shaped by their experience with their previous teachers, their feelings about each subject, the group dynamic, etc. These histories go on to affect all the interactions in their current teacher's lessons. The point being that these histories make it hard to determine causal relationships. For example, if most students do not grasp an explanation a teacher gives, is it because they were taught it in a different way last year and are finding this new explanation confusing? Is the teacher assuming strong prior knowledge when it isn't there? Did students just lose focus half way through? If so, why? It is difficult to say for sure which factor(s) caused the lack of understanding.

DOI: 10.4324/9781003465850-3

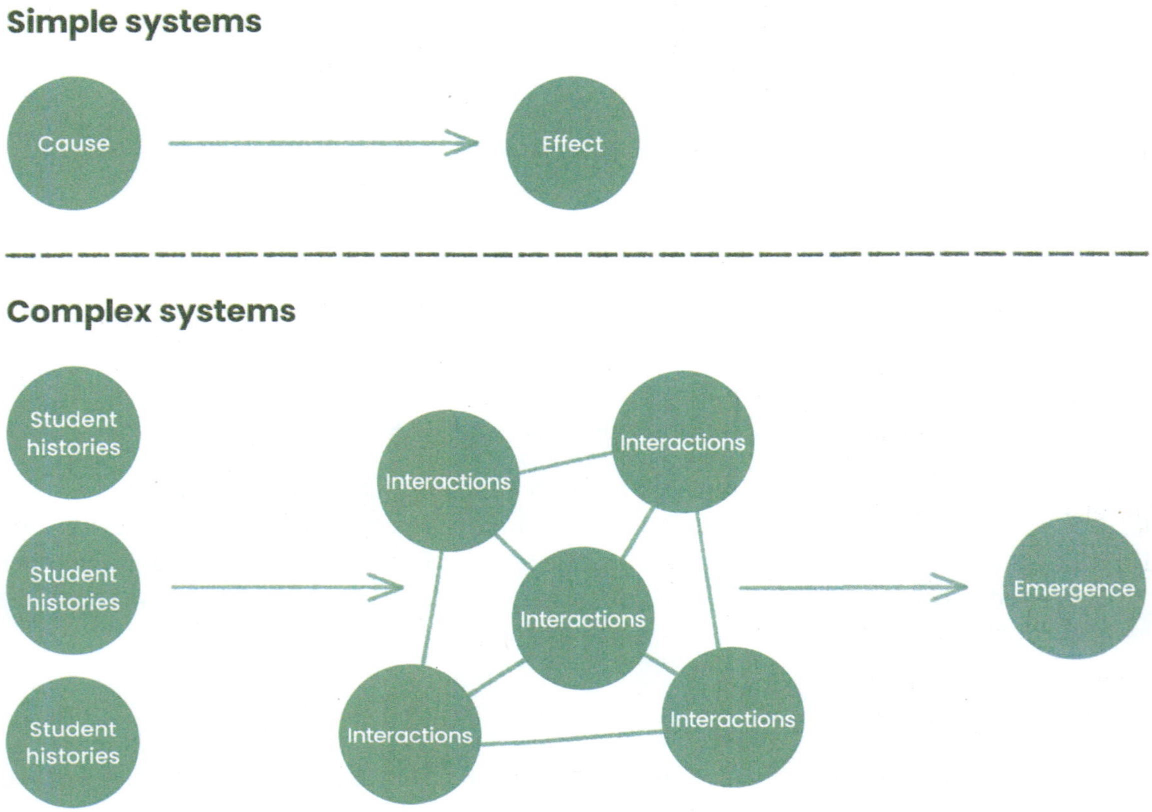

Unpredictability makes it challenging to stick to a plan or to learn from the teaching environment to perform better next time. A simple toolbox of techniques rolled out in the same way each lesson is therefore not going to adequately address the situations teachers will find themselves in.

In addition to unpredictability, there's another aspect of complexity that demands adaptive expertise: change.

Complexity is characterised by change

The demands on teachers are constantly changing. Teachers are required to have knowledge across a lot of different domains and to adapt their knowledge as domains change. Depending on how we slice it, we could say teaching involves knowledge of students, the subject, pedagogy, curricula, the context the teacher is teaching in, and how people learn . . . plus their knowledge must converge across domains so the teacher can best adapt their communication of important ideas to their students.[5] We could dice domains even smaller into different topics in subjects, different teaching techniques, etc. And, these domains are constantly changing: every year, teachers are often called upon to change year groups, topics, methods of teaching (e.g. when research is debunked and replaced), and at the very least, change students or teach students who themselves have changed!

All this change makes uncertainty the only certainty. Think about what this means for teachers: they can't just develop one way of doing things and stick with it. Constant change means they must keep learning to keep up.

It's important to note though, that uncertainty, and therefore complexity, is a relationship between the person and the environment.[6] Teachers experience the lesson environment in a uniquely complex way. Because their goal is to support many students to learn, they need to perceive environmental cues in meaningful ways and act accordingly. Their coach, at the back of the room observing, experiences complexity in a different way. Their goal is to infer what might be supporting or hindering student learning, but they don't have to actually teach the students. This means they apply a different lens to the environment and therefore experience it differently. It's this different experience of complexity that means coaches are well-placed to support their coachees to develop.

So, let's take a closer look at what it takes for teachers to thrive in this complex environment.

The goal: adaptive expertise

Jonas knows a lot about his students, the curricula he teaches, his school's context and teaching and learning in his subjects. He is a teacher who does the basics of the role efficiently and effectively – he has strong routine elements of his practice such as entrance and exit routines, delivering clear instructions and gaining students' attention. He is sensitive to conditions in the lesson and can adapt his practice accordingly. For example, he responds to students' answers to best support their learning and he even makes micro adaptations to routine elements of his practice when necessary such as changing the length of his countdown (his signal for getting students' attention) when they clearly need a little more time to finish their discussion or written work.

When it comes to improving his practice, Jonas understands the complexity of teaching. His school is careful to send the right messages to staff: they train them to build a repertoire of efficient approaches but to develop an understanding of how to use them at the right time for the right reasons. They emphasise the importance of context and never present techniques as silver bullets. Jonas' school ringfences time and support for their staff so they can focus on improvement.

Jonas understands that complexity makes it hard for him to change his practice for the better. He works hard with his coach to hypothesise about problems he's facing, test new approaches and evaluate them as best he can. He knows also that he must harness certain approaches to make sure he changes his practice, since changing his old habits is hard. He also understands that complexity, driven by unpredictability and change, means he will never be *an expert* teacher and therefore done with learning. In fact, he thinks expertise in teaching is characterised by the ability to continuously adapt and deal with change.[7] This mindset motivates him to be a constant learner.[8]

The characteristics Jonas displays here are encapsulated in the concept of *adaptive expertise*. While adaptive expertise is not a clear-cut concept, we aim to make it more useful and concrete for busy teachers and leaders. Based on what we've just described, we can say that those with adaptive expertise have the following qualities in these categories:

- **Knowledge:** rich, organised knowledge of relevant domains.[9]
- **Action:** a repertoire of useful and efficient teaching techniques.[10]
- **Decision-making:** sensitive decision-making that leads to appropriate use of techniques.[11]
- **Mindset and metacognition:** understanding of the need to improve and how to do so.[12]

Comparing adaptive and routine expertise

We can understand adaptive expertise even better by contrasting it with routine expertise. Routine expertise is when a person performs the core parts of their role with efficiency but struggles to adapt appropriately in more novel situations (they may not even notice the novelty).[13] In teaching, this might look like a teacher who executes the core competencies well but treats techniques as blunt instruments to be used for their own sake. They lack an understanding of the purpose of the technique[14] and are insensitive to the conditions where it does and does not work well. For example, they have learned that it is good to model processes for students. They model processes in the same way each time regardless of how much support students' answers suggest they need. This teacher views the lesson environment as highly predictable and tame: they believe that their role is to routinely use the 'best' teaching techniques for all their students. The problem with training teachers to be routine experts is that it doesn't equip them for their terrain: the environment is not tame or perfectly predictable. You can't teach really well if you think and behave like a routine expert.

But it's important not to romanticise the idea of adaptive expertise. At the heart of their practice, those with adaptive expertise have efficient, effective routine practice just like routine experts.[15] Routines are crucial for helping us embrace complexity. After all, 'innovation and adaptability favor the prepared mind.'[16] However, teachers with adaptive expertise *also* notice when to change course and know how to respond appropriately to students' unfolding needs whilst still achieving their goal.[17] They can 'go off plan but stay with intent.'[18] Think of it like someone who sets out on a trip but finds the road they need to go down is closed. It doesn't matter since they can work out another route to their destination, going off plan but still reaching their goal.

So, we are not saying adaptive expertise is about being a maverick, blindly trying new things out. Those with adaptive expertise look to solve important problems in their practice, but they still have their feet firmly in the core competencies of the role.[19] They work from a secure base of routine and structure[20] and it is this that enables them to notice and respond adaptively when necessary – what we could call *grounded* innovation. For example, they have a set entry routine into their lessons: students line up, the teacher issues short instructions, stands by the door and welcomes them in. However, even this well-honed routine is subject to minor adaptations: if a student is visibly upset, the teacher may check in with them individually as soon as everyone is settled; if students seem particularly unsettled when lining up, the teacher may narrate all the positive behaviours they see as students enter the room to encourage everyone to follow this productive norm. Indeed, it's argued that even within seemingly routine areas of their practice, teachers still have to vary what they do to best meet the needs of the situation.[21] So, we can say that teachers with adaptive expertise have all the efficiency of routine expertise but can adapt to the more novel cues in order to best support student learning. They engineer efficiency and adapt appropriately not as mavericks but as *masters of their contexts*.

To be clear, we think it's unlikely any teacher will be 'a routine expert' who never flexes their practice appropriately. Rather than a dichotomy, we see it as a continuum: some teachers are likely to have greater adaptive expertise and it's likely to vary by teaching area. Our (and now your) interest is in how to coach to *accelerate* development towards the goal of teacher adaptive expertise.

Developing adaptive expertise

When it comes to training teachers, it's tempting to think we should aim to build routine expertise before adaptive expertise. We think this misses the point. Adaptive expertise encompasses all the benefits of routine expertise (efficient core competencies) but is also a different mindset about the role of the teacher and a different understanding of what it takes to develop.[22] It is *qualitatively different* from routine expertise. Teachers with adaptive expertise have a different mindset about their role or what Gilbride (2025) refers to as 'thought architecture.'[23] That is, they have the cognitive structures to appreciate, capture and navigate complexity. They also recognise that this means the teacher's role is to be a continuous learner.[24] They recognise that, due to complexity, the goal for them is the continuous development of adaptive expertise, since things don't stay the same. In a sense, to them, adaptive expertise is simply . . . *expertise*.[25] To operationalise this mindset, they have developed certain habits of mind. They think in ways that support them to overcome barriers to behaviour change and to develop their decision-making. They do this by being metacognitive.[26] Together, this mindset and metacognitive awareness make adaptive expertise qualitatively different from routine expertise.

What does this mean for those who train teachers? Coaches and leaders need to see their role as gradually inducting teachers into the complex system they work in. Doing so will support them to cope with the complexity of their role and in future roles. Of course, we have to be mindful of the teacher's current level of expertise: they must learn routines so that they can embrace complexity and to give them something to adapt from. But the good news is, adaptive expertise appears to be something people can learn and be taught, with a 'version' they can grasp straight away.[27]

But, we cannot hope to develop teachers' adaptive expertise in unsupportive school environments. Teachers must be able to achieve agency if they are to iterate their practice outside of coaching, where they must implement new strategies and monitor the impact on student learning. To achieve agency, teachers need to believe they have the ability to make changes that will support student learning.[28] But it's not just about what a teacher knows or can do that fuels this belief; it also depends on the environment they're in. Supportive systems, time, and trust all matter. Agency is something teachers *achieve* when their skills and their context combine to make change possible. This means that developing adaptive expertise in teachers will only work in environments where teachers are supported to intelligently experiment with implementing potentially useful practices and are encouraged to take calculated risks.

To sum up . . .

Adaptive expertise isn't a clearly defined concept. However, we aim to harness it usefully to explain how to train teachers able to navigate and thrive in complexity. It's crucial to note that adaptive expertise is rooted in efficient core competencies of the role (similar to routine expertise) and yet those with adaptive expertise also notice and know how to adapt appropriately. We warn against attempts to develop routine expertise first and then adaptive expertise because adaptive expertise is a different way of thinking about teaching: a different mindset and different metacognitive processes. These can be developed from the get go alongside core competencies. This means adaptive expertise should be at the heart of how we coach teachers, no matter their current level of expertise in the area. But adaptive expertise requires implementation when the coach is not around and this means intelligently experimenting with potentially useful approaches. Teachers must work in an environment with conditions conducive to calculated risk taking and not one that punishes innovation.

Before we show coaches how they can train teachers for adaptive expertise, we need to understand the concept in greater depth so we know what we are trying to develop. We do this by going under the hood of adaptive expertise. We ask, cognitively, what underpins adaptive expertise?

Notes

1 We are indebted to the work of Dr Neil Gilbride for supporting us to apply a complexity lens to teaching. See Gilbride, N. M. (2025) 'The challenges of teaching complexity sciences to novice learners in public administration,' *Teaching Public Administration*, 43(2), pp. 143-156.

2 Davis, B. and Sumara, D. (2007) 'Complexity science and education: Reconceptualizing the teacher's role in learning,' *Interchange*, 38, pp. 53-67.

3 Hawkins, M. and James, C. (2018) 'Developing a perspective on schools as complex, evolving, loosely linking systems', *Educational Management Administration & Leadership*, 46(5), pp. 729-748.

4 Hawkins, M. and James, C. (2018) 'Developing a perspective on schools as complex, evolving, loosely linking systems', *Educational Management Administration & Leadership*, 46(5), pp. 729-748.

5 Shulman, L. (1987) 'Knowledge and teaching: Foundations of the new reform,' *Harvard Educational Review*, 57(1), pp. 1-23.

6 Spiegelhalter, D. J. (2024) *The Art of Uncertainty: How to Navigate Chance, Ignorance, Risk and Luck*. London: Pelican.

7 Ward, P., Gore, J., Hutton, R., Conway, G. E., and Hoffman, R. R. (2018) 'Adaptive skill as the *conditio sine qua non* of expertise,' *Journal of Applied Research in Memory and Cognition*, 7(1), pp. 1-9.

8 Timperley, H. (2013) *Learning to practise: a paper for discussion*. Wellington: Ministry of Education.

9 Schwartz, D. L., Bransford, J. D. and Sears, D. (2005) 'Efficiency and innovation in transfer,' *Transfer of Learning from a Modern Multidisciplinary Perspective*, 3(1), pp. 1-51.

10 Carbonell, K. B., Stalmeijer, R.E., Könings, K. D., Segers, M. and van Merriënboer, J. J. (2014) 'How experts deal with novel situations: A review of adaptive expertise,' *Educational Research Review*, 12, pp. 14-29; Timperley, H. (2013) *Learning to practise: A paper for discussion*. Wellington: Ministry of Education.

11 Kavanagh, S. S., Metz, M., Hauser, M., Fogo, B., Taylor, M. W., and Carlson, J. (2020) 'Practicing responsiveness: Using approximations of teaching to develop teachers' responsiveness to students' ideas,' *Journal of Teacher Education*, 71(1), pp. 94-107.

12 Kua, J., Teo, W., and Lim, W.S. (2022) 'Learning experiences of adaptive experts: a reflexive thematic analysis,' *Advances in Health Sciences Education*, 27(5), pp. 1345-1359; Lin, X., Schwartz, D. L., and Hatano, G. (2018) 'Toward teachers' adaptive metacognition.' In: *Computers as metacognitive tools for enhancing learning*. Abingdon: Routledge, pp. 245-255.

13 Hatano, G. and Inagaki, K. (1984) 'Two courses of expertise,' *Annual Report of the Centre for Clinical Developmental Psychology*, 6, pp. 27-36.

14 Kennedy, M. (2016) 'Parsing the practice of teaching,' *Journal of Teacher Education*, 67(1), pp. 6-17.

15 Anderson, J. and Taner, G. (2023) 'Building the expert teacher prototype: A metasummary of teacher expertise studies in primary and secondary education', *Educational Research Review*, 38, p. 100485.

16 Schwartz, D. L., Bransford, J. D., and Sears, D. (2005) 'Efficiency and innovation in transfer.' In: Mestre, J. P. (ed.) *Transfer of learning: From a modern multidisciplinary perspective*. Greenwich, CT: Information Age Publishing, p.30.

17 Crawford, V. M., Schlager, M., Toyama, Y., Riel, M., and Vahey, P. (2005) 'Characterizing adaptive expertise in science teaching,' *Paper presented at the Annual Meeting of the American Educational Research Association*, Montreal, Quebec, Canada, pp. 1-26.

18 Ward, P., Gore, J., Hutton, R., Conway, G. and Hoffman, R. (2018) 'Adaptive skill as the *conditio sine qua non* of expertise', *Journal of Applied Research in Memory and Cognition*, 7(1), pp. 35-50.

19 Gube, M. and Lajoie, S. (2020) 'Adaptive expertise and creative thinking: A synthetic review and implications for practice,' *Thinking Skills and Creativity*, 35, p. 100630.

20 Lampert, M. and Graziani, F. (2009) 'Instructional activities as a tool for teachers' and teacher educators' learning,' *Elementary School Journal*, 109(5), 491-509.

21 Hu, Y. (2024) 'Reconceptualizing teacher adaptability: the teacher adaptive-cognition theory,' Doctoral dissertation. Michigan State University.

22 Timperley, H. (2013) *Learning to practise: A paper for discussion*. Wellington: Ministry of Education.

23 Gilbride, N. M. (2025) 'The challenges of teaching complexity sciences to novice learners in public administration,' *Teaching Public Administration*, *43*(2), 143-156.

24 Darling-Hammond, L. and Bransford, J. (eds) (2007) *Preparing teachers for a changing world: What teachers should learn and be able to do*. San Francisco, CA: John Wiley & Sons.

25 Ward, P., Gore, J., Hutton, R., Conway, G. E., and Hoffman, R. R. (2018) 'Adaptive skill as the *conditio sine qua non* of expertise,' *Journal of Applied Research in Memory and Cognition*, 7(1), pp. 35-50.

26 Walsh, M. E. and Schunn, C. D. (2025) 'Reconceptualizing framing theory for adaptive teaching expertise: the role of strategic and expansive framing,' *Educational Psychologist*, 61(1), pp. 1-18.

27 Grotzer, T. A., Forshaw, T., and Gonzalez, E. (2021) *Developing adaptive expertise for navigating new terrain: An essential element of success in learning and the workplace*. Cambridge, MA: The Next Level Lab at the Harvard Graduate School of Education, President and Fellows of Harvard College.

28 Hardman, M., Taylor, B., and Daly, C. (2023) 'An inquiry into teacher agency and professional development: The introduction of the Early Career Framework in England.' In: I. Menter (Ed.), *The Palgrave handbook of teacher education research*. Cham: Palgrave Macmillan.

2 What underpins adaptive expertise?

In this chapter, we look at the cognitive constructs that may underpin adaptive expertise. Why? Because understanding this will support us to coach our teachers to develop them. To understand these cognitive constructs a little better, let's zoom in on a teacher's thought process.

Jessica is a teacher and has just asked a question to the class and chosen a student, Crystal, to answer:

Jessica hears Crystal's answer and she notices Crystal has a misconception about the concept and it's a misconception Jessica has never encountered before. She knows there are various actions she could take:

1. Correct Crystal and move on.
2. Ask another student for the answer and loop back to Crystal to see if Crystal can explain why her answer was wrong.
3. Ask the rest of the class to write down their answers to the question to see how prevalent the misconception is.
4. Assume the misconception is prevalent across the class and re-explain the idea to everyone.

In a split second, her knowledge of the curriculum and how learning happens gives her the sense that this idea is too important to skirt over, her knowledge of her students tells her that if Crystal is confused, others are likely to be too, so she decides to see how prevalent the misconception is. Now she has made this decision, she kickstarts the slick whiteboard routine she's developed with her class and phrases the question so just a two-word answer is needed from students. This enables her to scan their whiteboards and infer whether the misconception is prevalent. She sees that many students are also getting it wrong.

After the lesson, Jessica is bothered by what happened. She tries to trace back the causes of the problem and hypothesises that it may be due to her explanation. She decides to ask how others in her department explain the same concept and work out a better way to test out explaining it next lesson.

DOI: 10.4324/9781003465850-4

There is a deceptive amount going on under the surface that allows Jessica to size up the situation usefully, exercise her judgement to make a decision, execute the appropriate action and improve for next time. In this chapter we'll explore what might be happening in the minds of those, like Jessica, who display this adaptive expertise. We can organise this into four categories:

1. **Knowledge:** rich knowledge of relevant domains organised around problems.[1]
2. **Action:** a repertoire of useful and efficient teaching techniques.[2]
3. **Decision-making:** sensitive decision-making that leads to appropriate use of techniques.[3]
4. **Mindset and metacognition:** understanding the need to improve and how to do so.[4]

Let's begin with the knowledge of those with adaptive expertise.

Knowledge:[5] rich, relevant and organised around problems

In which domains do teachers with adaptive expertise have knowledge? To begin with, they have a *rich* understanding of all the *relevant* domains to their role: subject(s) they teach, pedagogy, relevant curricula, how people learn, their students and their context.

But teachers with adaptive expertise do not necessarily know more than other teachers - they appear to know *better*.[6] The difference between those with routine and adaptive expertise is said to be related to the quality of their knowledge. They don't just know sets of procedures (teaching techniques); they have a conceptual understanding[7] of the principles underpinning the use of these techniques, i.e, they understand *why* they are likely to work. This may contribute to the ability to act flexibly because a conceptual understanding means knowledge is not tied to a specific situation and can be used across similar situations.[8] For example, a teacher with a conceptual understanding of 'working memory' knows that it has limited capacity and instruction must be tailored to the likely capacity of the learner so as not to overload them. They understand that the teaching technique of breaking down complex material into small steps can be useful for managing students' cognitive load but will be unnecessary as their expertise grows. A conceptual understanding provides the 'why' behind the technique and helps the teacher use it adaptively and appropriately.

We believe a strong understanding of how people learn based on cognitive science can provide this conceptual underpinning. For example, a teacher who has a rich conceptual understanding of the importance of attention for learning adjusts how they teach to minimise distractions across contexts and uses their voice to create a sense of curiosity and vary pace.

But 'knowing better' is not just about the quality of knowledge. Those with adaptive expertise may also have knowledge that is better *organised*.[9] Better organisation means a greater depth of understanding (ideas are linked together) and easier accessibility: just as it is easier to find something in a tidy cupboard, it is easier to access organised knowledge.[10] So, how is knowledge organised for those with adaptive expertise?

We suggest that knowledge is organised around the *persistent problems*[11] teachers face when trying to support students to learn. Persistent problems are problems that all teachers grapple with and work to solve in their teaching, e.g. 'How do I ensure I have the attention of my students?' – teachers are always working to find a better way to address this problem (whilst knowing it will never be fully solved!).

The term 'problem' can have negative connotations. However, we use 'problem' as in 'problem-solving,' which is an interesting and useful endeavour people use in many domains to develop their expertise.[12] Therefore, when we use the term 'problems' we are not implying a deficit on the part of the teacher but suggesting that all teachers are working constantly to solve a set of common problems. These problems are universal to the profession. Put simply, teachers don't have problems because they are bad teachers but simply because they *are* teachers.[13] This view lends itself neatly to the notion that coaching is the ongoing problem solving between coach and teacher.[14]

What persistent problems should teachers know about? There are different taxonomies of these problems. We think Goodrich's parsing is useful because it covers multiple areas of teaching and gives us an order of priority, i.e., problems with attention should be tackled before those around communication, etc:[15]

- Ensure attention: problems related to students paying full, sustained, and visible attention.
- Optimise communication: problems around the way ideas or processes are communicated to students, e.g., managing cognitive load, modelling thought processes, using visuals, etc.
- Drive thought: problems related to how hard students have to think about the key ideas and how supported they are to do so.
- Gather and give feedback: problems related to checking for understanding at the right time and in the best way and responding appropriately.
- Ensure consolidation: problems related to supporting long-term learning.

What are the benefits of knowledge organised around problems? We think there are powerful benefits:

1. Problems provide purpose: rather than thinking mainly about teaching techniques, teachers will focus on the purposes they serve in relation to student learning.
2. Access and application: organised knowledge is easier to recall when needed and organisation around problems keeps the focus on real-world application rather than just theoretical understanding.
3. Focus for development: leaders can organise training around these problems and coaches and teachers can look for manifestations of these problems in lessons.
4. Shared language: persistent problems provide the basis for a language to discuss teacher development. This supports rich and expedient conversations between professionals.
5. Life-long learner: in-keeping with the mindset of those with adaptive expertise, persistent problems can never be definitively solved in a complex environment. Teachers must be life-long learners.

Now we know the qualities of the knowledge of those with adaptive expertise, we turn our attention to their actions.

Action: a repertoire of efficient techniques

Those with adaptive expertise will have a repertoire of techniques they can execute relatively automatically. They don't have to think explicitly about each action they are taking (or step of a thought process). For example, a teacher with adaptive expertise need not think about putting a student's name last when cold calling[16] – this is automatic. This creates efficiency and frees up cognitive capacity to notice significant cues that signal the need for flexibility. Without these automatic routines, teachers become overloaded and lose sight of their goals.[17]

What makes those with adaptive expertise different is that their use of techniques is sensitive to cues that suggest *when* they should be deployed and they know *why* they are useful.[18] This sensitivity prevents these relatively automatic techniques becoming entrenched habits that are used at the wrong time and for the wrong reasons. What underpins this sensitivity to context and purpose in those with adaptive expertise? We think it is the situation-sensitive mental models that drive their decision-making. Let's delve into this next.

Decision-making: situation-sensitive mental models in action

Teachers with adaptive expertise make rapid, effective decisions. Take Jessica, the teacher at the beginning of this chapter, responding to a student's misconception. She has several options but quickly evaluates the importance of the concept, assesses how widespread the misconception is, and selects a targeted response. We suggest that her *mental model*[19] guides what she notices, interprets, predicts, and decides.

What do we mean by 'mental model'? Put simply, mental models are our internal representations of 'how situations and systems work.'[20] They are a construct, i.e. not a physical thing we can point to in our brains. For example, we have mental models of how to interact with our friends, how to behave in restaurants, how to operate a car, etc. Teachers have mental models of all sorts of lesson situations: how students should enter the room, how to hold a class discussion with different year groups, how to do independent practice with their classes, and so on.

But why do we have mental models? The systems and situations we operate in (the school environment, social settings, etc.) are complex. Take teaching: a teacher's goal is that all thirty of her students learn what she is teaching. When she plans her lessons, delivers them and reflects on them after, there's too much information from the environment to consider it all. Mental models simplify situations so we can operate efficiently rather than becoming paralysed by incidental details.[21] In a sense, a mental model is a bit like a map:[22] a map simplifies an area by omitting details of the terrain or infrastructure. Maps are useful *because* they are simplified. We have mental models to simplify situations enough that we can operate.

What information does a mental model represent? Mental models contain causal relationships, i.e., our understanding and representation of cause and effect in a situation.[23] A simple example is to think of your mental model of crossing a road. You imagine standing by the kerb, looking both ways, automatically judging if there's enough time to cross between cars, and deciding to cross at the appropriate time. You know implicitly, 'if I step out too soon, I may get hit by a car or cause an accident.' This is cause and effect. If it's raining, you know not to stand too close to the kerb for fear of getting splashed - cause and effect again! For teachers, they may sense 'students are starting to glaze over, so I should reset the class and change pace' or 'students are going off task in this group work perhaps I need to remind them of the goal' or 'students are likely to form this common misconception, so I'll teach them explicitly to avoid it.' All of this thinking is reliant on the cause-and-effect associations in these teachers' mental models.

What do mental models help us do? First of all, mental models guide what teachers *notice*. Like lenses in those strange glasses opticians make us wear, mental models blur some things and sharpen others.[24] A good mental model filters irrelevant information and focuses teachers' attention on what is deemed important, which, for teachers with greater expertise, is usually information that helps them make useful instructional decisions to aid student learning.[25] For example, a teacher with expertise in holding class discussions is planning one for her next lesson. Her mental model blurs incidental information such as how enthusiastic students are. Instead, her mental model represents the relationships between her questions and students' possible answers.

But, mental models do not just affect what teachers notice. They also allow teachers to *interpret* cues more meaningfully, e.g. the teacher with the great mental model of running discussions with her class notices subtle cues of restlessness and interprets these as meaningful: these cues suggest the class is about to lose focus and she must act. It's hard to pull apart noticing and interpreting, but we can say, in the first instance, that those with adaptive expertise *notice* important cues (important for gauging where they are in relation to powerful instructional goals) and *interpret* these cues as meaningful and significant[26] such that they guide future actions.

What else do mental models do? As well as guiding what teachers notice and interpret, mental models help teachers *predict* what might happen next and therefore *decide* what to do. This is because the causal relationships in our mental models are dynamic and can be 'run,' like pressing play on a situation in our minds. This is called *mental simulation*[27] and it helps us reason about situations. Here's an example of a teacher mentally simulating in order to predict what might happen if she asks a particular question to a student:

> If I ask this question to this student, they will probably not know how to answer it because I'm using a tricky word I doubt they understand yet. If I change the way I word the question, I'll likely get a better answer from them, which is what I want.

This ability has been described as a mental 'sketchpad for us to explore possibilities and draw inferences.'[28] It is incredibly useful when planning lessons, teaching lessons, and reflecting on lessons:

- Planning: for example, a teacher planning a lesson can simulate an activity to see how it might land with the class. They make adjustments based on the results.
- Teaching: for example, a teacher can simulate the effect of asking a question to a particular student. They can adjust how they ask the question or who they direct it to as a result.
- Reflecting: a teacher can simulate a situation that occurred to try and understand what happened. They can also test what might have happened if they had done something differently. This helps them take better actions next time.

These examples show how mental simulation can affect teachers' decision-making and actions by allowing them to learn both from the future and the past. Just think for a moment how much better a teacher's decision-making would be if they were using accurate mental models like a crystal ball to test and select the best course of action.

Moreover, simulation is a powerful tool for learning beyond our immediate experience, i.e., to 'creatively reconfigure' our knowledge.[29] A useful analogy that illustrates the benefits of simulation to learn beyond the now is safeguarding. We can't wait for teachers to come across safeguarding issues before we train them on what to do because the stakes are too high: a child will be at risk. To learn to safeguard children well, we must live in the 'what if?'.[30] This gives teachers and leaders a chance to develop their mental models about what to do without having to wait for the experience to arise. The same can be achieved during coaching for teachers' classroom practice.

So to sum up, we can say that mental models can help us do four things:

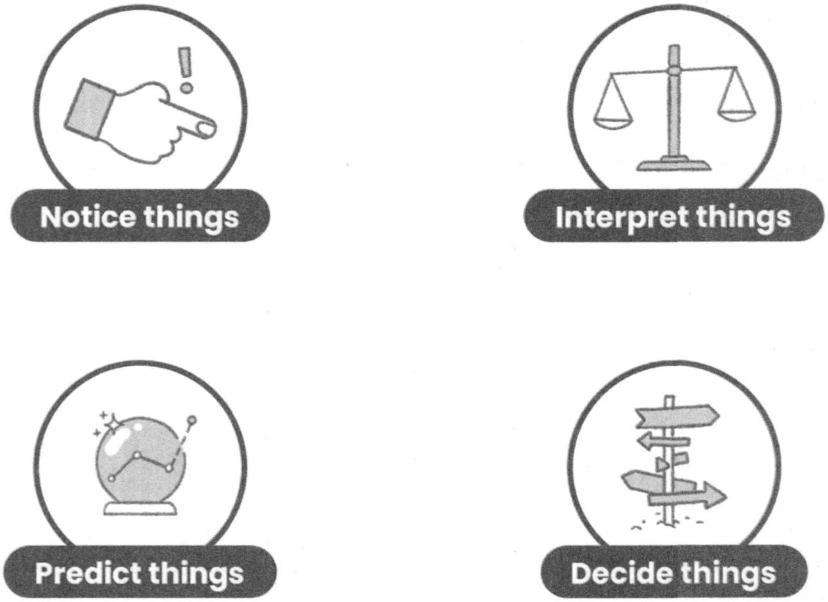

Now we know what a mental model is and what it enables us to do, we can ask, what do we mean by *better* mental models? We need to know this if we are to help teachers develop them. First of all, mental models are the interface between our knowledge and the environment. They are fuelled by our knowledge and experience.[31] Richer, more relevant and organised knowledge will therefore support teachers to form better mental models.

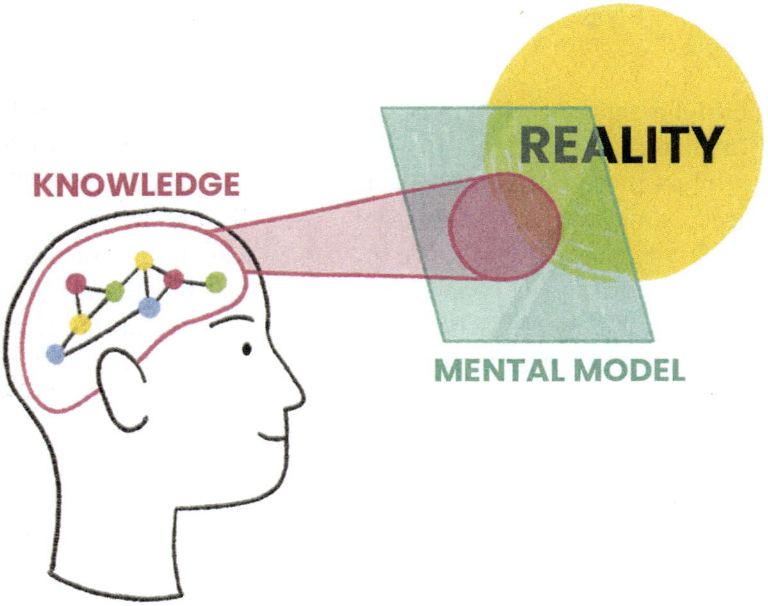

Secondly, since mental models are made up of cause-and-effect relationships, mental models that enable people to make more expert and adaptive decisions contain more useful (accurate and pertinent) causal relationships[32] that aid noticing, interpreting, predicting, and deciding. For example, a teacher may have a mental model of how to deliver an explanation about covalent bonding in chemistry. They have thought carefully about how to build on students' prior knowledge and believe if they tap into this, their explanation is likely to be successful (cause and effect). Their mental model does *not* contain incidental details about how the room is set out because these details are unlikely to play a role in this situation. This is an example of a mental model filtering irrelevant information to help the teacher focus. The teacher has taught this topic many times and carefully assessed how it has landed with their classes. They know the common misconceptions that can occur and why (cause and effect) and carefully phrase their explanation to avoid these. In contrast, a teacher new to teaching believes they just need to be accurate in their explanation and students will pick it up. Their prediction is simple and linear, lacking in the complex cause-and-effect relationships of the more expert teacher.[33]

This example shows us that more expert mental models are simplified representations (as all mental models are) but contain more useful complexity (in the form of cause-and-effect associations). This enables the teacher to be *situation-sensitive*[34] in their decision-making.

A good example of situation sensitivity is the different ways teachers support students' special educational needs. A less expert teacher in this area may pick a strategy they've been advised to try. A more expert teacher understands why the strategy might work (i.e. they have better knowledge), and takes into account the way the need manifests for each student (contextual details) in order to predict whether the strategy may work (cause and effect). They understand when and why the strategy is likely to be effective and can be more situation-sensitive in their decision-making.[35] It is these situation-sensitive mental models, fuelled by well-organised rich and relevant knowledge, that enable those with adaptive expertise to appear as the masters of their contexts.

We've noted how useful mental models can be in helping teachers make decisions, but what are their downsides? The first downside is that they are tacit. Just like when we wear a pair of glasses all the time we can forget they are there, we fail to notice our mental models. Our view becomes *the* view. This is because mental models lie silently beneath the surface, making them hard to describe or examine.[36] This means it is possible to have mental models that allow teachers to run on autopilot so they do not pick up on mental ruts they've fallen into. If given some attention, their mental models (through examining their decision-making) may reveal themselves to be suboptimal. This is one reason why coaching can be so powerful: it can 'interrupt' automatic thinking and help teachers examine their otherwise tacit mental models. Indeed, experts in their fields appear to be good at examining their mental models and looking at where adopting different viewpoints might be more beneficial.[37]

The second important downside is actually related to the very reason we think mental models exist in the first place: they are simplified representations. It's therefore easy to *oversimplify* our understanding of a situation and make poor decisions as a result. For example, a teacher might believe that 'more modelling means better learning.' But without recognising when students are already secure, over-scaffolding, wasting time, and disengaging learners who are ready to move on. In this case, the teacher's mental model of modelling needs refining to include cues for when it's necessary and when it's not.

In summary, our assumption is that teachers construct simplified mental representations of teaching situations called mental models. Mental models are thought to contain causal relationships and guide what teachers notice, interpret, predict, and decide.[38] Better mental models are fuelled by better knowledge and contain more accurate and pertinent cause-and-effect relationships, helping teachers to be more situation-sensitive in their decision-making and actions. But, mental models are hidden from us and therefore not regularly examined and deliberately developed. This compounds another issue: mental models can be oversimplified and therefore teachers can be trapped in sub-optimal ways of thinking and making decisions.

But those with adaptive expertise don't just have the knowledge, repertoire of actions, or situation-sensitive mental models to act efficiently and adaptively. As we said in the previous chapter, there's something qualitatively different about teachers with adaptive expertise: they understand the need to be a continuous learner and they know how to navigate complexity to keep improving. We describe this in terms of their mindset and use of metacognition.

Mindset and metacognition: knowing how to keep improving

Adaptive expertise isn't just about making decisions and taking action - it's about continuously improving in a changing environment. To do this, teachers need to know how to get better at getting better.[39] This is what those with adaptive expertise have figured out - it's as if they have an internal user manual that enables them to accelerate learning.

We believe this comes from developing an *adaptive mindset* and *adaptive metacognition*. These form the bridge between routine and adaptive expertise.[40]

- **Mindset** is the belief that a teacher's role is to keep improving and continuous improvement is possible.
- **Metacognition** is the awareness and monitoring of one's own thinking to ensure that improvement actually happens.

If we adopt a journey metaphor, mindset is the reason for the journey and metacognition is the means of getting there.

These two qualities form the backbone of adaptive expertise and must be cultivated by coaches and the wider school environment. They shape coaching conversations, making them about more than just the immediate challenge, turning them into lessons in professional growth that enable the teacher to improve when the coach isn't there.

Let's start with the overarching way that teachers with adaptive expertise see their role: with an adaptive mindset.

Adaptive mindset: 'continuous improvement is necessary'

Those with adaptive expertise have an *adaptive mindset:* they see themselves as lifelong learners, knowing that growth is essential to their success. An adaptive mindset is the belief that expertise is a process of continuous learning and adaptation because the work itself is always changing.[41] But what is a mindset? Mindsets can be viewed as a set of mental models,[42] so which mental models contribute to an adaptive mindset? In short, they are mental models of *how teaching works* - the complexity of the system teachers are working in. Let's go into more depth.

Teachers need to form an understanding of the complexity in which they work. After all, this is the reason why continuous learning is necessary. In simple systems, we can master operations pretty easily with the right experience and training. But complexity, characterised by unpredictability and change, demands ongoing learning.

Complexity and the need to continuously improve should be self-evident to teachers, since they experience change (of students, curricula, pedagogy, novel misconceptions etc.) all the time. Plus, if it wasn't true, many teachers would be masters of their craft, getting consistently perfect results with their classes, and this just isn't the case. Yet the need for an adaptive mindset isn't self-evident at all. Why?

Teachers know teaching is hard, yes. But many don't organically adopt an adaptive mindset. We suspect this is because they are led to believe in silver bullets such as:

- Research will tell you what to do.
- Simply learn a set of techniques and you will be a great teacher.
- Follow this lesson structure and all students will learn.

This quick-fix fantasy can't thrive in complex environments - it needs sunshine where complexity casts shadows.[43]

More specifically, to support teachers to develop an adaptive mindset (that they must continue to learn to keep improving), school leaders need to be honest about what it takes to improve and remember that everything they say and do communicates messages to their teachers that affect this mindset. What school leaders do and say should help teachers develop an understanding of the complexity that exists.

Schools should:

- Encourage teachers to engage with research and teach them important principles from the research, so they can contextualise the key ideas to their students.
- Deliver professional development that focuses both on techniques as well as their purpose and when to adapt them, i.e., how to turn techniques into strategies to meet powerful goals.
- Support teachers to develop their mental models to gradually cope with ever more useful complexity, so they can make better decisions.
- Remove judgement from professional development. If teachers are to embrace the need to continuously learn, they can't do so under the threat of constant evaluation. Schools must remove the fear factor[44] and make professional development formative.

These activities and actions lay the groundwork for coaching that reveals *how teaching works*. Improvement is not straightforward, research can't be transplanted, techniques aren't magic wands, it isn't possible (and is likely to be damaging) to judge the quality of teaching from watching a lesson. In reality, there is exciting, deeply professional work to be done in the shadows - where causes are unclear and effects hard to predict - to carefully craft mental models that can cope, and then thrive, in this environment.

A coach's role in fostering an adaptive mindset is to understand that they aren't just training a teacher *to* teach but also to learn *about* the complexity of teaching. They are training the teacher to expect unpredictability and change - to expect they'll need to keep learning.[45] To do this, coaches must help teachers build mental models that capture useful complexity and make the reason for, and process of doing so, explicit to the teacher. Teachers will then learn to expect and seek out increasing complexity, and also be equipped to navigate it. As Goodrich writes, 'we're committed to treating teachers as skilled professionals and communicating that teaching is a complex and challenging field that requires specialised expertise.'[46]

However, the adaptive mindset shouldn't feel exhausting. It must be supported by a school culture that values and resources professional development. When schools and coaches create these conditions, an adaptive mindset isn't just a belief, it's an honest and sustainable way to grow.

To operationalise the adaptive mindset, i.e., achieve continuous development, teachers must form particular habits of mind. We suggest then, that teachers with adaptive expertise also *think differently* about how to improve. This we call adaptive metacognition.

Adaptive metacognition: 'I know how to improve'

With an adaptive mindset, teachers understand the need to continuously improve. In the journey metaphor earlier, we said this was their reason for going. Complementing this, adaptive metacognition is the awareness and monitoring of thinking so that they can actually improve – the vehicle to get them to their destination. Teachers must be supported to get under the hood of teaching and understand how it works and therefore how to improve. This is crucial since much of their improvement happens outside of the coaching conversation. It's the teacher that understands how to improve who is likely to take more from their experiences[47] and get better even when the coach is not around.

To improve, teachers need to be aware of, and have the tools to avoid, two 'gaps' that threaten to thwart their improvement efforts. Let's see what these are and how we can train teachers to develop the mental machinery that enables them to keep improving.

1. Avoiding the knowing-doing gap

To get better, teachers know they have to make changes to their practice. But, they need to know that behaviour change is devilishly difficult, in part, because they are trying to change their habits. Habits are actions or sequences of actions cued by the environment.[48] They are made up of procedural knowledge (knowledge of 'how' to do something) that has been practised enough times to run relatively *automatically*.[49] It is the automatic cueing of behaviours that make them so hard to change because we aren't in conscious control. Habits are a double-edged sword for teachers:[50] on the one hand, habits allow teachers to operate efficiently and have the cognitive capacity to notice important cues, but on the other, habits can be ruts that prevent them from improving.[51] To illustrate the difficulty of long-term behaviour change, one study found that less than half of those who set New Year's resolutions maintained them beyond month three.[52] This chasm between knowing what we need to do and actually doing it has been dubbed the 'knowing-doing gap.'[53] For example, a teacher may know they should check students' understanding but avoid it due to, say, time constraints or feeling unsure as to how best to do it. Even more likely is a teacher who knows they need to do something but the busyness of lessons means they never remember at the right time.

What does this tell us as coaches? It means that it's safer for us to assume coaching *won't* change teachers' practice . . . unless both coach and teacher make a concerted, evidence-informed effort to bridge the knowing-doing gap. This demands that teachers have a particular way of thinking about their development: 'I must employ strategies to avoid falling into the knowing-doing gap and so that I can actually improve my practice.' As coaches, what should we teach them to do to avoid this gap?

We can help teachers understand the *mechanisms* we are using during coaching to support their behaviour change and reinforce their usage of these mechanisms outside of the coaching conversation.

Research suggests there are fourteen mechanisms that may catalyse teachers' behaviour change.[54] Here are a few examples of mechanisms highly pertinent to coaching:

- **Manage cognitive load**: focus together on small, concrete steps tailored to the teacher's needs.
- **Set and agree on goals**: align on clear goals to boost motivation and support student learning.
- **Model the technique**: provide strong models of how techniques look and sound and analyse them using clear success criteria.
- **Rehearse the technique**: make time to rehearse techniques outside of lessons and give specific, actionable feedback to improve the rehearsal.
- **Prompt action planning**: make specific plans for applying the new technique.
- **Self-monitoring:** support the teacher to understand how to see whether their practice is or is not having the positive impact on student learning they are aiming for and how to refine their practice if not. This encourages them to pay attention to their actions and the effects of them.[55]
- **Prompt context-specific repetition:** support the teacher to remember to practise the technique in their planning or lessons.

The final two mechanisms in particular are ones where the teacher will need to ensure they do them outside of the coaching conversation. Since teachers with adaptive expertise know how to improve, they are deliberate about using these mechanisms to develop their practice. Coaches must explicitly point out, model, and reinforce their usage so that teachers become familiar with them and use them when the coach is not around.

2. Avoiding the knowing-deciding-doing gap

As well as the knowing-doing gap, we think there also exists a knowing-*deciding*-doing gap. This often manifests as a teacher using a technique bluntly at the wrong moment and not fully internalising its purpose. Why does this gap exist? Well, the knowing-doing gap represents the challenge of behaviour change, but there's another key challenge too: doing the right thing at the right time for the right reasons. This challenge comes about because of the unpredictability inherent in complex systems: teachers can't be sure how their actions will affect student learning and as a result, they often need to adapt their practice in the moment.

This knowing-deciding-doing gap is even more pernicious when we remember that the cognitive structures we think underpin decision-making (mental models) are tacit, i.e., hidden from us. This makes them difficult to surface, represent and examine in order to isolate issues and develop better decision-making. What can teachers do to avoid this gap?

Teachers will need to understand the purposes that techniques serve, e.g., understanding that teachers break down processes into steps (technique) to scaffold it for their students (purpose). This means it's not always necessary to do this if students no longer require the scaffold. They also need to know how to develop their decision-making. We've said that this means developing their mental models by ensuring they are fuelled with useful knowledge and are sufficiently situation-sensitive.[56] How do teachers need to manage their thinking to do this?

We think they can adopt a process of improvement that incorporates these habits of mind:

- **Surfacing and examining:** the mental models underpinning decision-making are tacit and so need to be surfaced.[57] To improve decision-making, examining the teacher's mental models is likely to be useful.[58] Coaches can support teachers to expose their tacit mental models of situations and examine them. This is the first step to understanding issues with their current thinking. Coaching that incorporates this surfacing and examining, and draws the teacher's attention to doing so, models the importance of this as a tool for improvement.
- **Hypothesising:** there's evidence that expert teachers hypothesise and predict more so than novices[59] and spend more time understanding the problem, compared with novices who move quickly to solutions.[60] Coaches can model to teachers how to turn their hunches (guesses based on intuition) about problems in their lessons into hypotheses (explanations based on limited evidence) by testing them against the data to establish a sense of the problem and its causes. These hypotheses can be tested further to see if they bear out. They should generally be held lightly because it's difficult to establish cause and effect with certainty in a complex system.[61] For example, a coach may share that when observing the teacher, they formed a hunch that there was an issue with students' behaviour and attention during the lesson. Following the evidence, they formed a hypothesis that students were losing focus at certain points in the lesson because there wasn't a clear routine for moving between activities. They held this hypothesis

lightly, looking for evidence to support and contradict it until they felt fairly sure. This models to teachers the tentative thinking appropriate to improving in a complex system.

- **Testing and monitoring:** coaches can help the teacher see their implementation of a new approach as a test with proxies of success they should look out for to monitor its effectiveness.
- **Iterating and evaluating:** coaches can help teachers decide when and how to iterate an approach to better meet the needs of their students in different contexts.

Overall, we call this way of thinking *intelligent experimentation*. 'Intelligent' denotes the need to work from best practice principles often available in research evidence or longstanding wisdom from the profession; 'experimentation' sums up the belief that to improve in complex systems we need to hold our ideas lightly and engage in the cycle of hypothesising, testing, monitoring, iterating, and evaluating approaches. This isn't always necessary: sometimes the causes of problems are clearer than at others and so might potential solutions be. In which case, the adaptive mindset is about embracing efficiency - doing what works - and appreciating that no approach can work all the time in the same way.

We believe teachers will need to adopt these ways of thinking about improving their practice to avoid both the knowing-doing and knowing-deciding-doing gaps and continue to improve. To achieve this, they need coaches who can expose the invisible work of improvement and teach them how to achieve it.

The Adaptive Expertise Framework

Now we know the four elements that underpin adaptive expertise (knowledge, action, decision-making, and mindset and metacognition), we can turn these elements into a framework coaches can use. We'll call this the *Adaptive Expertise Framework*.

Coaches must support teachers to:

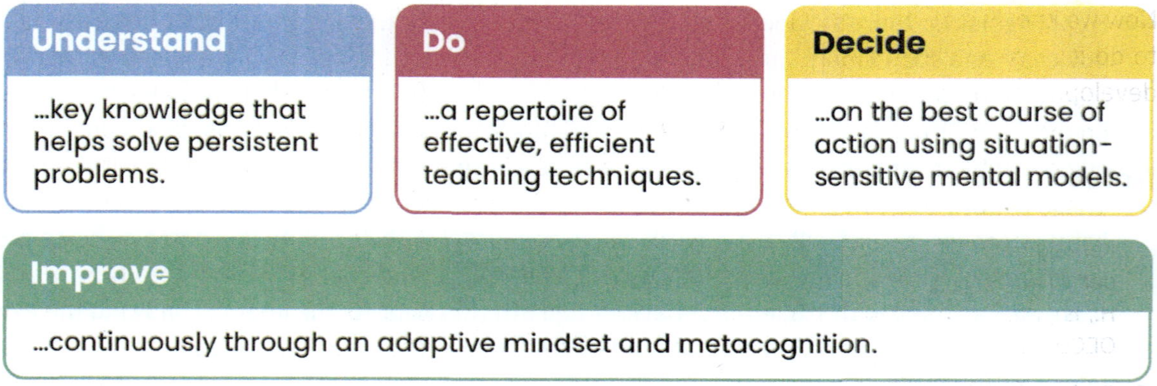

As a quick test of this framework, we can look at what happens if any area is missing:

Understand	Do	Decide	Improve	What's wrong?
✓				The teacher knows what to do but not how to do it, i.e., the knowing-doing gap exists.
	✓			The teacher knows techniques but they often use them at the wrong time for the wrong reasons.
✓	✓			The teacher knows what to do, how and why but not when. They struggle to adapt their practice, i.e., the knowing-deciding-doing gap exists.
✓	✓	✓		The teacher knows what to do, how, why and when (in many situations), but they don't see the need to continually improve and don't know how to do so without help.
✓	✓	✓	✓	The teacher knows what to do, how, when and why. They also know they need to continually work at their practice to keep improving and they know how to do so.

To sum up . . .

Adaptive expertise needn't be a woolly concept. By looking at what underpins adaptive expertise, we can get a sense of what we need to develop. We think adaptive expertise is underpinned by a teacher's ability to understand, do, decide, and improve. These four areas form the Adaptive Expertise Framework, which we will refer to throughout this book.

Now we know what we are trying to develop in the teachers we coach, we need to understand how to do it. We start by taking what we've learned and pinning down what the coach's role is in the development of teacher adaptive expertise.

Notes

1 Kennedy, M. (2016) 'Parsing the practice of teaching,' *Journal of Teacher Education*, 67(1), pp. 6-17; Schneider, M. and Stern, E. (2010) 'The cognitive perspective on learning: Ten cornerstone findings.' In: Dumont, H., Istance, D., and Benavides, F. (Eds), *The nature of learning: Using research to inspire practice*. Paris: OECD Publishing, pp. 69-90.

2 Carbonell, K. B., Stalmeijer, R. E., Könings, K. D., Segers, M., and van Merriënboer, J. J. (2014) 'How experts deal with novel situations: A review of adaptive expertise,' *Educational Research Review*, 12, pp. 14-29; Timperley, H. (2013) *Learning to practise: A paper for discussion*. Wellington: Ministry of Education.

3 Kavanagh, S. S., Metz, M., Hauser, M., Fogo, B., Taylor, M. W., and Carlson, J. (2020) 'Practicing responsiveness: Using approximations of teaching to develop teachers' responsiveness to students' ideas,' *Journal of Teacher Education*, 71(1), pp. 94–107.

4 Kua, J., Teo, W., and Lim, W.S. (2022) 'Learning experiences of adaptive experts: A reflexive thematic analysis', *Advances in Health Sciences Education*, 27(5), pp. 1345–1359; Lin, X., Schwartz, D.L., and Hatano, G. (2018) 'Toward teachers' adaptive metacognition.' In: *Computers as metacognitive tools for enhancing learning*. Abingdon: Routledge, pp. 245–255.

5 When we talk about 'knowledge', we don't just mean lists of facts. We take a broad view of knowledge as being facts and also conceptual understanding. We treat procedural knowledge as separate and discuss that in the next section of the framework: 'action.'

6 Borko, H. and Livingston, C. (1989) 'Cognition and improvisation: Differences in mathematics instruction by expert and novice teachers,' *American Educational Research Journal*, 26(4), pp. 473-498.

7 Hatano, G. (1988) 'Bases for mathematical understanding.' In: G. B. Saxe and M. Gearhart (Eds), *Children's mathematics*. San Francisco, CA: Jossey-Bass, pp. 55–70.

8 Carbonell, K. B., Stalmeijer, R. E., Könings, K. D., Segers, M. and van Merriënboer, J. J. (2014) 'How experts deal with novel situations: A review of adaptive expertise,' *Educational Research Review*, 12, pp. 14–29; Hatano, G. and Inagaki, K. (1984) 'Two courses of expertise,' *Annual Report of the Centre for Clinical Developmental Psychology*, 6, pp. 27–36.

9 Carbonell, K. B., Stalmeijer, R. E., Könings, K. D., Segers, M. and van Merriënboer, J. J. (2014) 'How experts deal with novel situations: A review of adaptive expertise', *Educational Research Review*, 12, pp. 14–29.

10 Ausubel, D.P. (2012) *The acquisition and retention of knowledge: A cognitive view*. Dordrecht: Springer Science & Business Media.

11 Kennedy, M. (2016) 'Parsing the practice of teaching,' *Journal of Teacher Education*, 67(1), pp. 6–17.

12 Bereiter, C. and Scardamalia, M., 1993. *Surpassing ourselves: An inquiry into the nature and implications of expertise. Chicago: Open Court.*

13 Nevertheless, some schools may decide to rebrand 'persistent problems' 'persistent *challenges*' to side-step this issue.

14 Bereiter, C. and Scardamalia, M. (1993) *Surpassing ourselves: An inquiry into the nature and implications of expertise*. Chicago: Open Court; Joyce, B. R. and Showers, B. (1981) 'Transfer of training: The contribution of "coaching,"' *Journal of Education*, 163(2), pp. 163–172.

15 Goodrich, J. (2024) *Responsive coaching: Evidence-informed instructional coaching that works for every teacher in your school*. Woodbridge: John Catt.

16 'Cold calling' is a technique where the teacher asks a question, pauses so all students have time to think and then chooses a student to answer. Students do not know who will be chosen so everyone becomes accountable for thinking about their answer. See Lemov, D. (2021) *Teach like a champion 3.0: 63 techniques that put students on the path to college*. Hoboken, NJ: John Wiley & Sons.

17 Schwartz, D. L., Bransford, J. D., and Sears, D. (2005) 'Efficiency and innovation in transfer.' In Mestre, J. P. (Ed.), *Transfer of learning from a modern multidisciplinary perspective*. Greenwich, CT: Information Age Publishing, pp. 1–51.

18 Kavanagh, S. S., Metz, M., Hauser, M., Fogo, B., Taylor, M. W., and Carlson, J. (2020) 'Practicing responsiveness: Using approximations of teaching to develop teachers' responsiveness to students' ideas,' *Journal*

of Teacher Education, 71(1), pp. 94–107; Witherspoon, E. B., Ferrer, N. B., Correnti, R. R., Stein, M. K. and Schunn, C. D. (2021) 'Coaching that supports teachers' learning to enact ambitious instruction,' *Instructional Science*, 49(6), pp. 877–898.

19 The reader should note that the use of the term 'mental models' differs across research domains. We have attempted to synthesise commonalities in its usage.

20 Sieck, W. R., Klein, G., Peluso, D. A., Smith, J. L., Harris-Thompson, D., and Gade, P. A. (2007) *FOCUS: A model of sensemaking*. Fairborn, OH: Klein Associates.

21 Meadows, D. H. (2008) *Thinking in systems: A primer*. Edited by D. Wright. White River Junction, VT: Chelsea Green Publishing.

22 Parrish, S. (n.d.) 'Mental models: The best way to make intelligent decisions (~100 models explained)', *Farnam Street Blog* [Blog]. Available at: https://fs.blog/mental-models/ (Accessed: 30 July 2024).

23 Khemlani, S. S., Barbey, A. K., and Johnson-Laird, P. N. (2014) 'Causal reasoning with mental models,' *Frontiers in Human Neuroscience*, 8, p. 849.

24 Jones, N. A., Ross, H., Lynam, T., Perez, P., and Leitch, A. (2011) 'Mental models: An interdisciplinary synthesis of theory and methods,' *Ecology and Society*, 16(1).

25 Berliner, D. C. (1987) 'Ways of thinking about students and classrooms by more and less experienced teachers.' In J. Calderhead (Ed.), *Exploring teachers' thinking*. London: Cassell Education, pp. 60–83.

26 Johnson-Laird, P. N. (1989) *Mental models*. Cambridge: Cambridge University Press.

27 Klein, G. A. (2017) *Sources of power: How people make decisions*. Cambridge, MA: MIT Press.

28 Lagnado, D. A. (2021) *Explaining the evidence: How the mind investigates the world*. Cambridge: Cambridge University Press.

29 Emirbayer, M. and Mische, A. (1998) 'What is agency?' *American Journal of Sociology*, 103(4), p. 971.

30 We are indebted to school leader, Chris Passey, for this important analogy.

31 This study is a nice example of how knowledge fuels the way we interpret situations: Medin, D.L., Lynch, E. B., Coley, J. D. and Atran, S. (1997) 'Categorization and reasoning among tree experts: Do all roads lead to Rome?' *Cognitive Psychology*, 32(1), pp. 49–96.

32 Correnti, R., Matsumura, L. C., Walsh, M., Zook-Howell, D., Bickel, D. D., and Yu, B. (2021) 'Effects of online content-focused coaching on discussion quality and reading achievement: Building theory for how coaching develops teachers' adaptive expertise,' *Reading Research Quarterly*, 56(3), pp. 519–558.

33 Hugo, W. (2025) 'Probabilistic professional judgement in teaching,' *Journal of Education (University of KwaZulu-Natal)*, (99), pp. 3–27.

34 Hu, Y. (2024) 'Reconceptualizing teacher adaptability: The teacher adaptive-cognition theory,' Doctoral dissertation. Michigan State University.

35 Witherspoon, E. B., Ferrer, N. B., Correnti, R. R., Stein, M. K. and Schunn, C. D. (2021) 'Coaching that supports teachers' learning to enact ambitious instruction.' *Instructional Science*, 49(6), pp. 877–898.

36 Ford, D. N. and Sterman, J. D. (1998) 'Expert knowledge elicitation to improve formal and mental models,' *System Dynamics Review: The Journal of the System Dynamics Society*, 14(4), pp. 309–340.

37 Walsh, M. E. and Schunn, C. D. (2025) 'Reconceptualizing framing theory for adaptive teaching expertise: the role of strategic and expansive framing,' *Educational Psychologist*, 61(1), pp. 1–18.

38 Maule, A. J., Hodgkinson, G. P., and Bown, N.J. (2003) 'Cognitive mapping of causal reasoning in strategic decision making.' In: *Thinking: Psychological perspectives on reasoning, judgment and decision making*, pp. 251–272.

39 Lemov, D., Woolway, E., and Yezzi, K. (2012) *Practice perfect: 42 rules for getting better at getting better*. Hoboken, NJ: John Wiley & Sons.

40 Hu, Y. (2024) 'Reconceptualizing teacher adaptability: The teacher adaptive-cognition theory,' Doctoral dissertation. Michigan State University.

41 Ward, P., Gore, J., Hutton, R., Conway, G., and Robert, H. (2018) 'Adaptive skill as the *conditio sine qua non* of expertise,' *Journal of Applied Research in Memory and Cognition*, 7(1), pp. 35–50.

42 Petrie, D. A., Lindstrom, R. R. and Campbell, S. G. (2024) 'The impact of cognitive biases, mental models, and mindsets on leadership and change in the health system,' *Healthcare Management Forum*, 37(3), pp. 121–127.

43 Klein, G. A. (2011) *Streetlights and shadows: Searching for the keys to adaptive decision making*. Cambridge, MA: MIT Press.

44 Ania Townsend Director of Communities at Steplab (in conversation).

45 We are grateful for feedback from Margaret Mullholland and Amelie Thompson, which informed this framing.

46 Goodrich, J. (2024) *Responsive coaching: Evidence-informed instructional coaching that works for every teacher in your school*. London: John Catt, p. 234.

47 Crawford, V. M., Schlager, M., Toyama, Y., Riel, M., and Vahey, P. (2005, April) *Characterizing adaptive expertise in science teaching*. Paper presented at the Annual Meeting of the American Educational Research Association, Montreal, Quebec, Canada, pp. 1–26.

48 Robbins, T. W. and Costa, R.M. (2017) 'Habits,' *Current Biology*, 27(22), pp. R1200–R1206.

49 Hobbiss, M., Sims, S., and Allen, R. (2021) 'Habit formation limits growth in teacher effectiveness: A review of converging evidence from neuroscience and social science,' *Review of Education*, 9(1), pp. 3–23.

50 Feldon, D. F. (2007) 'Cognitive load and classroom teaching: The double-edged sword of automaticity,' *Educational Psychologist*, 42(3), pp. 123–137.

51 Hobbiss, M., Sims, S., and Allen, R. (2021) 'Habit formation limits growth in teacher effectiveness: A review of converging evidence from neuroscience and social science,' *Review of Education*, 9(1), pp. 3–23.

52 Norcross, J. C. and Vangarelli, D. J. (1988) 'The resolution solution: Longitudinal examination of New Year's change attempts,' *Journal of Substance Abuse*, 1(2), pp. 127–134.

53 Pfeffer, J. and Sutton, R. I. (2000) *The knowing-doing gap: How smart companies turn knowledge into action*. Boston, MA: Harvard Business Press.

54 Sims, S., Fletcher-Wood, H., O'Mara-Eves, A., Cottingham, S., Stansfield, C., Goodrich, J., Van Herwegen, J., and Anders, J. (2025) 'Effective teacher professional development: New theory and a meta-analytic test,' *Review of Educational Research*, 95(2), pp. 213–254.

55 Sims, S., Fletcher-Wood, H., O'Mara-Eves, A., Cottingham, S., Stansfield, C., Goodrich, J., Van Herwegen, J., and Anders, J. (2025) 'Effective teacher professional development: New theory and a meta-analytic test,' *Review of Educational Research*, 95(2), pp. 213–254.

56 Petrie, D. A., Lindstrom, R. R. and Campbell, S. G. (2024) 'The impact of cognitive biases, mental models, and mindsets on leadership and change in the health system,' *Healthcare Management Forum*, 37(3), pp. 121–127.

57 Lagnado, D. A. (2021) *Explaining the evidence: How the mind investigates the world*. Cambridge: Cambridge University Press, p. 22.

58 Dreyfus, H. and Dreyfus, S. E. (1986) *Mind over machine*. New York: Simon and Schuster.

59 Berliner, D. C. (1988) *The development of expertise in pedagogy*. Washington, DC: AACTE Publications.

60 Pretz, J. E., Naples, A. J. and Sternberg, R. J. (2003) 'Recognizing, defining, and representing problems,' *The Psychology of Problem Solving*, 30(3), pp. 3–30.

61 Crawford, V. M., Schlager, M., Toyama, Y., Riel, M., and Vahey, P. (2005, April) *Characterizing adaptive expertise in science teaching*. Paper presented at the Annual Meeting of the American Educational Research Association, Montreal, Quebec, Canada, pp. 1–26.

3 The coach's role

We've argued that the coach's role is to develop teachers' adaptive expertise, which involves developing them in the four areas of the Adaptive Expertise Framework:

Understand

...key knowledge that helps solve persistent problems.

Do

...a repertoire of effective, efficient teaching techniques.

Decide

...on the best course of action using situation-sensitive mental models.

Improve

...continuously through an adaptive mindset and metacognition.

In this chapter, we'll outline broadly how coaches need to see their role in order to support teachers to develop adaptive expertise.

Select the significant situation

A large part of a coach's role is to select the right situations to coach on. Doing this is just as important as the coaching conversation itself.[1] It's like planning curricula for students: teach the wrong stuff and it doesn't matter how well you do it. So, see it as your role, first and foremost, to observe the lesson carefully and select the most significant situation where improvement to teaching may better support student learning. We show you how to do this in our upcoming chapter, Stage 0 Prepare for coaching by diagnosing need.

The coach is really well placed to identify significant situations. Why? Well, to understand this, we need to remember how mental models work. Mental models shape how teachers interpret what's happening in the classroom. But every person's mental model is at least somewhat different because it's shaped by their experience and knowledge. Coaches and teachers will always have a different

DOI: 10.4324/9781003465850-5

perspective on lessons. In contrast to the teacher, coaches have a wider, less detailed perspective to offer: wider in that they see more; less detailed in that they (usually) don't have as much knowledge of the students, their current knowledge, lesson dynamics, and sometimes, the subject being taught. A decent analogy can be made to football: the teacher is the referee on the pitch, responding to every nuance in the game. They understand the dynamics of the game, and they are interacting with the players. The referee understands how the game is likely to go and how to respond to the players. The coach is like the Video Assistant Referee (VAR) watching from above: they are detached from the action and can make less meaning of the interactions on the pitch, but they are able to spot patterns or issues that aren't visible from ground level. That doesn't mean the coach understands everything better, but it does mean they see things the teacher might not.

This broader view is one of the coach's biggest assets. Coaches aren't managing 30 students: their cognitive load is lighter. As a coach, your role is to use that mental capacity to spot moments that might be worth digging into then bring those to the teacher. There's no getting around it though, to do this the coach needs strong mental models of how learning happens and how teaching can support learning. Schools must train coaches to develop these mental models.

So what does that mean in practice? It means the coach should feel responsible for *choosing significant situations* to focus on, i.e., a situation when student learning seemed to be well supported (to praise during coaching) and could be better supported (to problem solve during coaching). In terms of the latter, the coach doesn't need to have the solution (although often they will prepare one) but it is definitely their role to bring a hypothesis to explore.

Coach using your expertise

Coaches aren't just there to ask questions - they are there to support the teacher to tangibly and sustainably develop. That means drawing on their own expertise, not hiding it.

But, what makes the coach think they have expertise worth sharing? First, as we've just said, coaches are well placed to select the significant situation due to their different perspective on the lesson - unburdened by the task of actually teaching students, they can spot problems the teacher can't. To suggest coaches shouldn't share their expertise is to deny one of the main benefits there is to having a coach.

Secondly, coaches deserve to be well trained. Being a great teacher is valuable when coaching but it's not all there is. In fact, being a great teacher often means your teaching practice is fluid and automated - it's probably been a long time since you broke it down into steps. This is why coaches need ongoing, high-quality training to ensure they coach well. Indeed, the difference between the most and least effective coaches is broadly the same as the average effect of coaching.[2] If trained well, coaches should be knowledgeable about how learning happens, have a repertoire of teaching techniques they can decompose and analyse, and know how to help teachers close the knowing-doing and knowing-deciding-doing gaps. This being the case, they are very well placed to share their expertise with the teachers they coach when appropriate.

But timing and tact matter. Great coaches don't play 'guess what's in my head'; they seesaw between seeking the teacher's expertise and sharing their own depending on the weight of the teacher's expertise in that moment. For example, a great coach asks a teacher to explain when it might be appropriate to use a particular technique. If they are unsure, the coach might scaffold their question by providing a brief scenario or simply share their expertise. If the teacher still can't answer after the coach has scaffolded the question, the coach always shares their expertise. Seek, scaffold, share. This seesawing of support gets the teacher thinking as hard as they can but prevents them becoming frustrated.

Coach meaningfully

We wouldn't teach students something without trying to build from what they know, and we shouldn't with teachers either. To coach meaningfully, coaches need to build on the teacher's current understanding so they can connect new ideas with their existing practice.[3]

What does this mean? First off, it means asking questions to surface and map a teacher's decision-making process. This represents the teacher's starting point - their current mental model of the situation. We can support them to develop from there, meeting them where they are.

But, is there tension here? We've said the coach needs to share their expertise *and* coach meaningfully by working from their teacher's starting point. On the face of it, this might be considered contradictory. But this tension only exists if we focus on surface features of coaching. What we mean by this is that some people think a coach is withholding their expertise if they ask a lot of questions. But asking questions is not a coaching technique in and of itself. It's the *purpose* of those questions that matters.

The coach should start by surfacing a teacher's mental model of a situation so they can understand their starting point. You surface a teacher's mental model by asking specific questions. It's only when you know the teacher's starting point that you will be able to build meaningfully from there. We will show you how to do this in an upcoming chapter, Stage 2 Study the problem.

Coach for learning

The coach's role is not to pass judgement on their teacher, but to diagnose the most important issue affecting student learning and support the teacher to improve it. This diagnosis must be anchored in student learning, not personal preference or the coach will erode trust in the process. It's natural for coaches to form quick opinions about what a teacher is doing wrong, especially when something doesn't align with their own teaching style. But coaching for learning demands more than instinct or hunch. A good coach slows down, gathers non-judgemental evidence, and tests a hypothesis about what's causing a problem. This helps them move from 'I didn't like that' to being prepared to support the teacher to see what they noticed and why it matters. This makes them a credible coach because they can 'show their working out'[4] and it all comes back to what is best for student learning. You'll see examples of this approach from coaches throughout the book and how it is likely to cultivate the same thinking in the teachers they work with.

Coach for alignment

As we know, no two people's mental models of a situation will be exactly the same. The coach (with a broader, less detailed perspective) will have a different mental model of the situation they bring to the teacher than the teacher themselves. As we know, mental models affect what we notice and interpret. This means coach and teacher will both have 'versions' of events and interpretations of what those events signify. Before any change can happen then, after the coach has surfaced the teacher's mental model, they must work together to align their mental models of the situation. In other words, the teacher and coach must broadly agree on what happened, what is significant about it and what the problem is that they are going to work to solve together.

Sometimes, the coach will adjust their mental model when they realise the teacher's version is more plausible. This is more likely to happen when coaching more experienced teachers or when coaching someone outside of your subject or phase specialism. Usually it is because, when you hear their reasons for their actions, they make sense in a way you couldn't have predicted using your current mental model. However, more often than not we find that the coach's version of the situation contains useful information and places significance on things the teacher didn't appreciate in the moment, causing the teacher to update their mental model of the situation. This happens with our approach (coaching for adaptive expertise) because the coach prepares for coaching using a systematic, non-judgemental method to form and test their hypotheses - we explain this in depth in Stage 0 Prepare for coaching by diagnosing need.

For now it's enough to understand that when the coach keeps their observation of the teacher grounded in what is best for student learning, forms a lightly held hypothesis and collects concrete evidence, their version of the situation is likely to be valuable to the teacher.

Coach for change

Coaching fails if it doesn't help teachers improve their practice. This involves two types of change: behaviour (by which we mean changes in actions) and decision-making. By focusing on both, coaches help teachers squeeze every drop of learning out of their experience.

Coaching for behaviour change

The 'knowing-doing gap' occurs when teachers know what to do but don't do it.[5] We've looked at this in relation to how teachers need to think about improving their practice (in reference to 'adaptive metacognition'). Coaches need to harness methods to support behaviour change and be explicit about what they are doing so that teachers can adopt these methods when the coach is not around. Here's a reminder of some of the most pertinent ones to the coaching session itself:[6]

- **Manage cognitive load**: focus on small, concrete steps tailored to the teacher's experience level.
- **Set and agree on goals**: align on clear goals to boost motivation and support student learning.
- **Model the technique**: provide a model of how the technique looks and sounds, along with clear success criteria.
- **Rehearse the technique**: allow practice outside the lesson context to build confidence.
- **Prompt action planning**: help teachers make specific plans for applying the new technique.

As with everything though, it's both what you do *and* the way that you do it.[7] In this book we show high-quality implementation of these mechanisms in coaching practice.

But coaches should not see their role as kick-starting the change of discrete teaching behaviours. Just like student learning, teacher learning shouldn't bounce around from one area of practice to another. The coach's role is best seen as supporting the teacher to develop their practice incrementally in a wider area, e.g. developing their ability to secure attention through various methods appropriate to different situations.[8] This will build a toolkit of techniques teachers can be supported to use strategically to meet powerful goals related to student learning.

Changing teacher practice is vital. But for teachers to develop adaptive expertise, they must also develop ever more situation-sensitive mental models to improve their decision-making. How do coaches support this?

Coach to develop decision-making

Developing actions and decision-making (and the mental models that underpin them) are interconnected. Banks et al. (2024) found that teachers developed the ability to use teaching techniques adaptively through models and rehearsal in various decomposed/recomposed chunks. Thus, mechanisms for behavior change – like modelling and rehearsal – can also be harnessed to develop more situation-sensitive mental models. In this book, we also look at how to develop decision-making through every stage of the coaching process.

But the issue we have with developing decision-making is that the mental models underpinning it are tacit, hidden even from their owner (in this case, the teacher). Examining and developing or abandoning a current mental model is probably not something teachers can do without high-quality support.[9]

If we break this down, we actually have two issues:[10]

1. How do we surface the teacher's tacit mental model?
2. How do we represent it so we can examine it with them?

To address these issues we need to make the construct of a 'mental model' more concrete by stating the components that make up a mental model. This enables us as coaches to surface these components by asking teachers questions about them. We have also developed a simple method coaches can use to represent mental models that we call *mapping*. Let's start by looking at the four components of a mental model and then how to map them.

What do we map?

We need to think of mapping mental models as mapping paths. When we think about a situation (entering a restaurant, speaking to a friend, holding a class discussion), we can map it as a path, for example:[11]

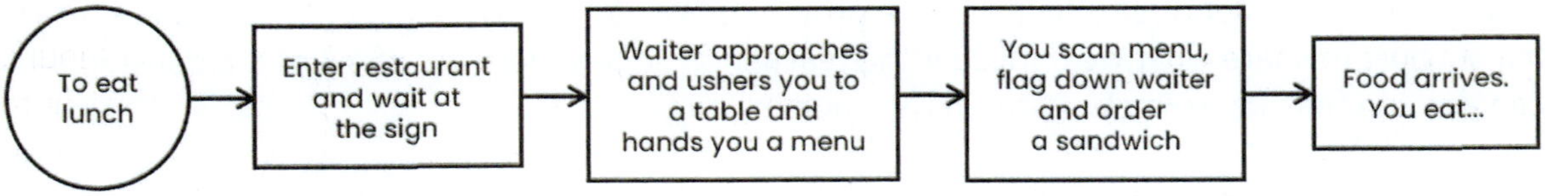

This path contains certain components:[12]

- **Goals**: What was your objective in this situation? In this case, to eat lunch.
- **Actions and events**: What actions were taken? What events occurred? In this case, you enter the restaurant and wait to be seated (actions), the waiter approaches (event), etc.
- **Cause and effect**: What led to what? In this case, the arrows show one action and event leading to the next.

We can also add in reasons for actions, which we call *decision drivers*:

- **Decision drivers**: What were the reasons for each action? In this case for example, your reason for entering the restaurant was hunger and the fact you wanted to eat the food in this restaurant.

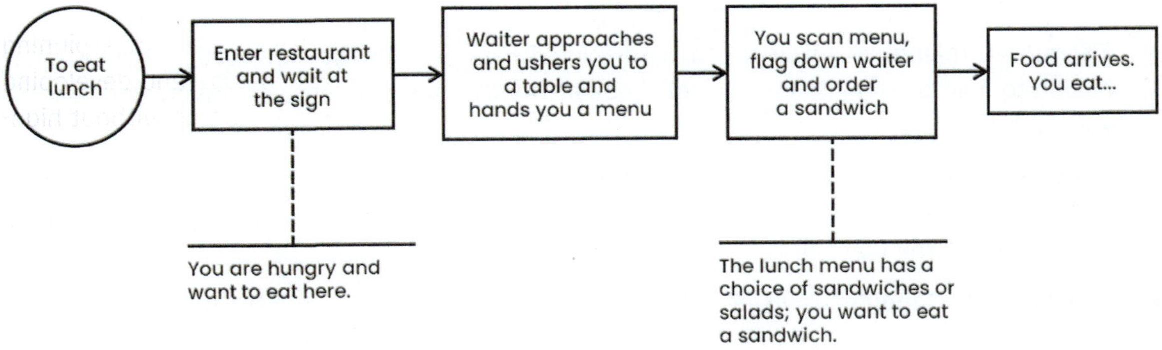

Generically then, mental models could be said to contain these components:

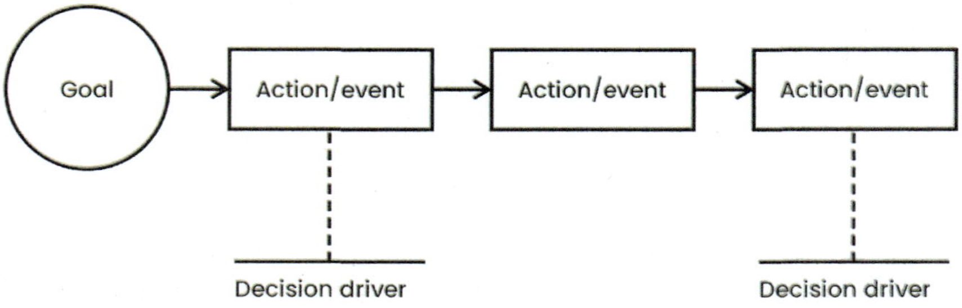

Now we know the components, we can coach to surface our teacher's mental models of the significant situation we identified when we were observing. We do this by asking questions and seesawing support to share what we noticed if the teacher struggles. Here are some of the questions we can ask and that we exemplify later in the book:

- Let's zoom in on the paired discussion/modelling/explanation of . . ./retrieval task. What was your goal in that situation? (Goal).
- Tell me what you did and what happened. (Actions/events – often this also surfaces cause and effect too).
- What did you notice about the effect on students when you . . .? (Cause and effect).
- What was your reason for doing that? (Decision driver).

These questions help us to address the first issue of surfacing the teacher's mental model. We address the second issue around representing the teacher's mental model by visually drawing each component as we surface it as a map like the ones you've just seen.

How is mapping useful for developing decision-making?

The coach can target their questions at the components of the teacher's mental model and visually represent them by mapping. Mapping then allows coach and teacher to:

- **Examine thinking**: by surfacing and capturing mental models, we can discuss them without having to hold them in mind, e.g. 'Let's look at whether your actions are driving you towards your goal.'
- **Depersonalise feedback**: by creating a 'third' entity in the conversation[13] (the map), we shift focus from improving 'the teacher' to improving 'the mental model.' This depersonalises the experience for the teacher.
- **Clarify understanding**: by visually displaying what happened and what the teacher was thinking, we can begin to align our mental models (our versions of events).

- **Coach meaningfully**: by identifying a clear starting point for improvement, the coach and teacher know where they are building from.
- **Develop adaptive metacognition**: by visibly mapping the teacher's mental model, the coach is modelling to the teacher a tool they can then use to improve when the coach is not around.[14]
- **Spot problems**: visual maps make issues with decision-making easier to recognise.

This final benefit, 'spot problems,' is a good one to expand upon because it often worries coaches: 'how do I get the teacher to understand the problem I saw?' Here's an example of how mapping can help:

> A coach asks questions to surface all the components of a teacher's mental model of a situation. The teacher says their goal is to get students' attention. The teacher remembers some of the actions and events and the coach helps out. The teacher explains their decision drivers. They map it like this:

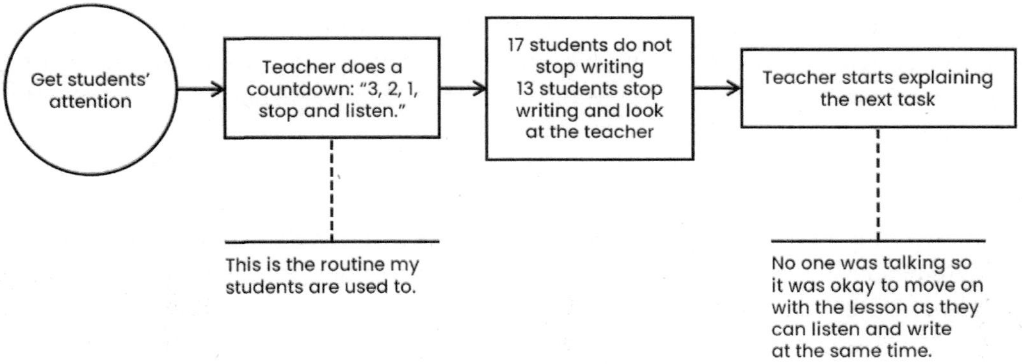

With the map, they can isolate the problem: the teacher didn't hold all students accountable for paying attention and moved on without everyone's visible attention. The coach can help the teacher see that they can adopt a more powerful goal: secure *all* students' visible attention. And, the coach can see the teacher needs to develop a better understanding of how students learn: even if they aren't talking, if they are writing, they can't be fully paying attention. In this book we will show you how to use mapping to spot problems and coach meaningfully from the teacher's starting point.

Note that you won't always need to map. Sometimes just asking a teacher about a particular situation triggers an insight about the problem. Other times, mapping is an important tool for engineering insight.

But how we support a teacher to change their practice and decision-making depends on their level of expertise in the area we are working on. This leads us on to our final point - it is possible and beneficial for everyone to have a good coach.

Coach everyone

Coaching benefits teachers at all levels of expertise by helping them develop ever more situation-sensitive mental models and break less-effective habits. Because no lesson unfolds exactly as planned (due to complexity) even experienced teachers can gain from coaching that is focused on developing ever more situation-sensitive mental models and practice. Let's look at what it means to coach teachers who are, broadly speaking, in three categories: new to the profession, growing their expertise, and who have a lot of expertise. You can also imagine the seesaw of support we mentioned earlier is weighted in favour of the coach sharing their expertise with new teachers and moves gradually to seeking expertise more often than not with those teachers with a lot of expertise. Although, this should be judged in the moment, avoiding blanket assumptions.

Coaching new teachers

It's difficult to categorise teachers as 'novice,' 'intermediate,' or 'expert.' This is because expertise appears to confine itself to particular domains, e.g. I may be relatively expert at teaching Macbeth but not Hamlet, or even relatively expert at teaching Macbeth to older students but not to younger students. Indeed, expertise doesn't seem to transfer easily even across very similar areas.[15] However, when a new teacher is just starting out, we can usually say they are novice in most teaching domains as their experience teaching a whole class of students is usually limited. Let's start with these teachers.

New teachers do have mental models of teaching despite never having been teachers themselves. Where do they come from? Their mental models are formed from watching their own teachers when they were students.[16] These overly simplistic mental models of how teaching 'works' can be unhelpful. For example, they may be fuelled by poor knowledge about how students learn, and a naive conception of the teacher's role (e.g. to be liked by their students). For example, this may be a mental model of a new teacher when it comes to transitioning their children from the carpet to their tables:

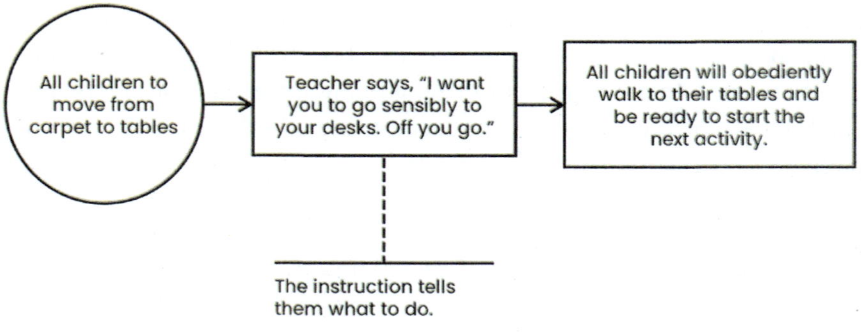

But this sense of cause and effect (prediction) is naive. Any experienced teacher can predict the actual outcome of this instruction:

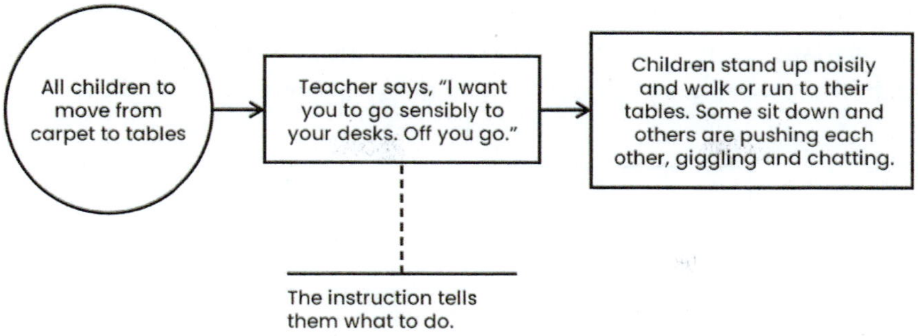

To avoid this, new teachers need to develop a mental model with a better goal, effective teaching techniques (breaking down instructions, narrating the positive, scanning), an understanding of their likely effects and more powerful decision drivers. This might be the standard mental model for transitions they need to learn:

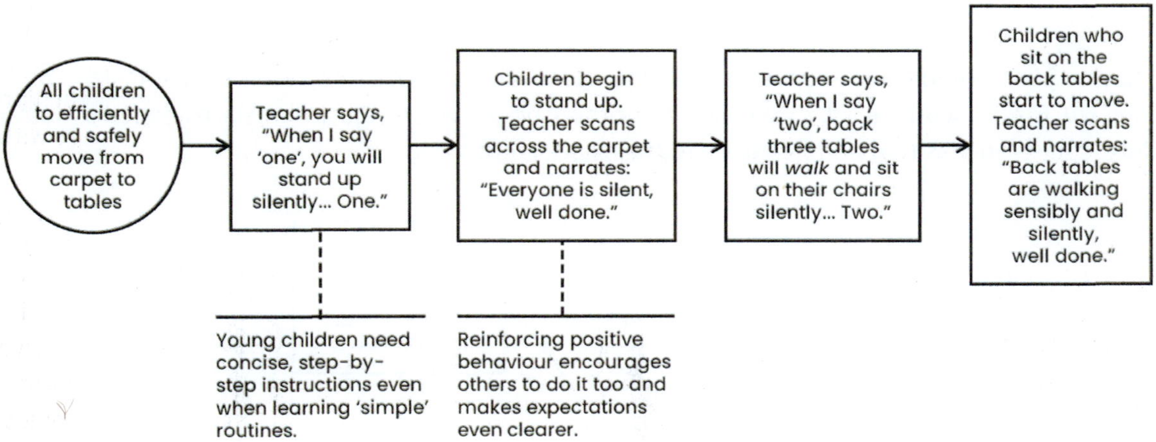

Having this standard mental model for transitions will support the teacher to do it well every time and they can free up cognitive capacity to notice cues that mean they may need to adapt it slightly.

So, to establish these standard paths, coaches coaching new teachers need to surface these naive mental models and explain how to think and act to achieve powerful goals in common situations. New teachers will need lots of support to develop their repertoire of efficient techniques so that 'what is tactically desirable is technically possible.'[17] But what about teachers with growing expertise?

Coaching teachers with growing expertise

With experience and expertise, coaching shifts to refining these standard paths, making them more efficient and effective (increasing student participation or getting better outcomes, e.g. more students grasping a key idea). This may include helping the teacher deviate appropriately from the standard path.[18] The standard path is helpful but sometimes it's a straitjacket. For example, a teacher has this mental model for giving instructions:

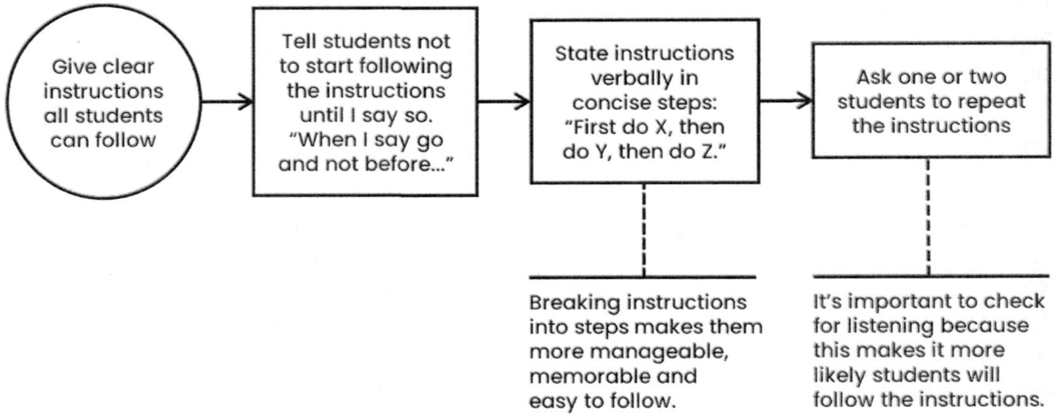

They employ it rigidly and even when they are giving long, complicated, or unfamiliar instructions, they still list them off verbally. Coaching helps them notice when adjustments are needed by introducing 'if' branches that add flexibility to their decision-making:

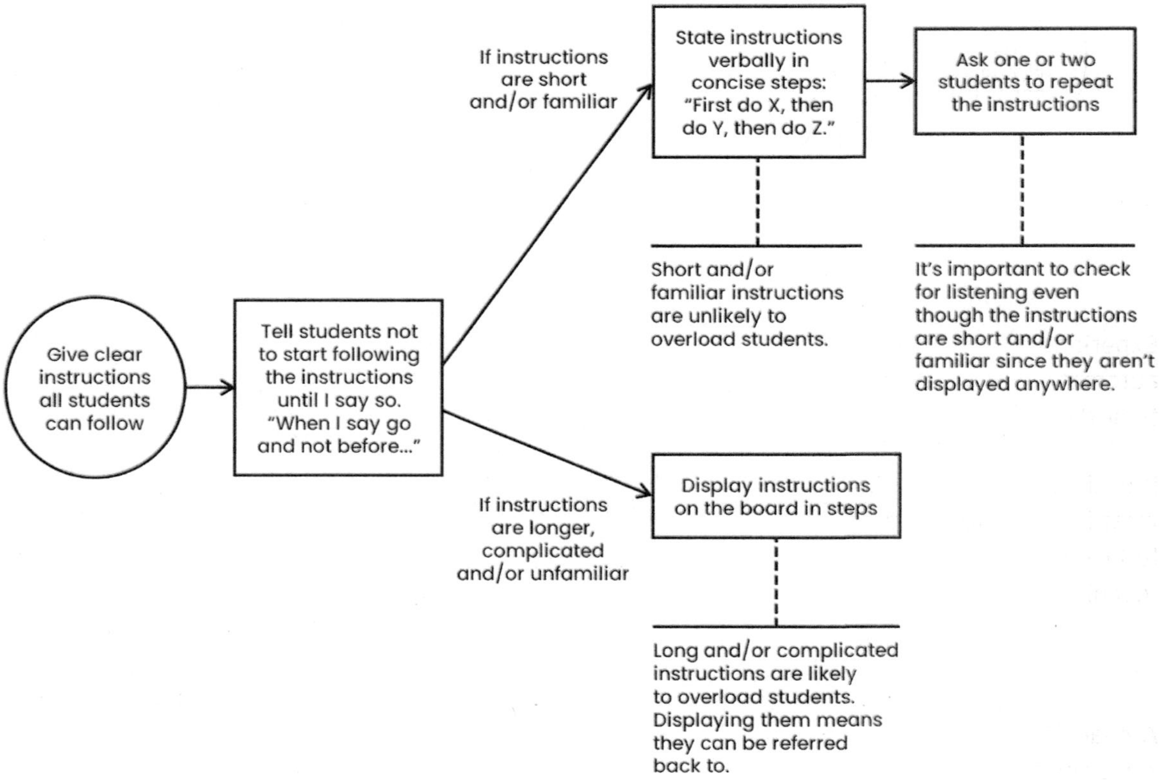

You can see here that the teacher's mental model is becoming gradually more complex and situation-sensitive.

So, this means coaching more experienced teachers often means developing more situation-sensitive mental models by adding complexity. This involves more 'if' branches and the thoughtful deployment of efficient techniques. Essentially, these teachers have more appropriate strategies to reach powerful goals.

What about those teachers with lots of expertise?

Coaching teachers with expertise

As expertise grows further, teachers move beyond standard paths to solving more nuanced or novel problems. They may need to refine strategies for uncommon situations or innovate entirely new approaches when the usual methods don't work optimally. More branches or new paths are devised and adopted so their mental models are more situation-sensitive.

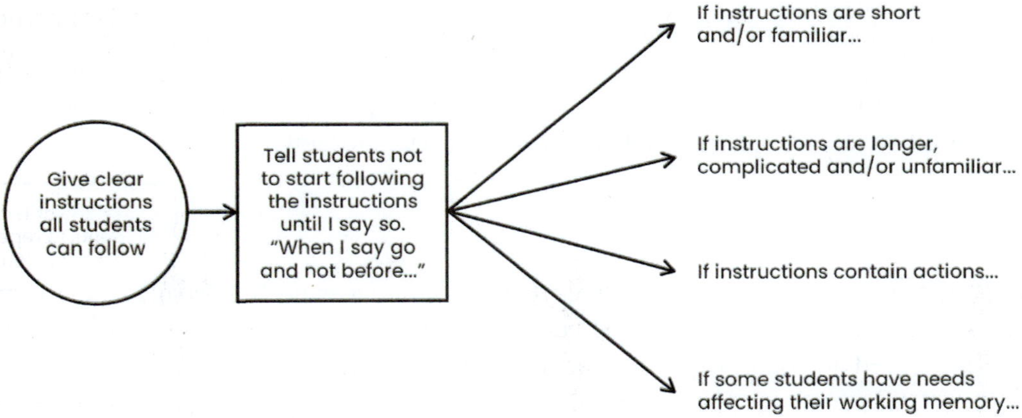

Experienced teachers may also need help breaking particularly stubborn habits. Since habits are automatic, unconscious behaviours, teachers can be blind to them and blind to misalignments in their decision-making. Mapping their mental models makes these mismatches visible.

It is clear then that the adaptive expertise perspective on coaching gives us a concrete sense of what it means to coach a teacher of any level of expertise in a domain. Teachers can always stand to break unhelpful habits and become more situation-sensitive in their thinking. This is because teaching keeps changing and 'an expert' teacher cannot exist.

To sum up . . .

A coach's role is to identify significant situations to coach on, which they are well placed to do since they have a different lens on the lesson. Because the coach and teacher are likely to have different mental models (versions) of these situations, part of the coach's role is to align these mental models by surfacing the teacher's mental model and comparing it with their own.

Well-trained coaches should feel empowered to share their expertise at the appropriate times and usually once they have sought the teacher's expertise and the teacher has shown that they need support. While coaches should share their expertise, they must first understand the teacher's mental model to ensure coaching builds from the teacher's current thinking; this makes coaching meaningful.

To ensure coaching is credible, coaches must root their observation, diagnosis, and comments in what is best for student learning. They must be prepared to show their working out so the teacher knows the standards they are applying: optimising teaching to support learning.

Coaching must lead to behaviour change, using mechanisms such as modelling and rehearsal and coaches should also help teachers develop their mental models so they make better decisions. Mapping is a key tool for developing decision-making, as it makes goals, actions and events, cause-and-effect relationships, and decision drivers explicit. This helps both coach and teacher identify issues in decision-making while depersonalising feedback and supporting the teacher to be metacognitive.

Coaching is beneficial for all teachers, regardless of experience. New teachers need to establish standard paths, i.e., how typical situations work, while more experienced teachers often need to refine and start adapting their approaches. As expertise grows, teachers need more complex, situation-sensitive models with additional branches or paths forged.

On to Part 2 . . .

Now we have a sense of the coach's role in developing adaptive expertise, we move on to part 2 of the book where we take a forensic look at each stage of coaching. Broadly speaking, to close the knowing-deciding-doing gaps, we think coaching should involve these stages:

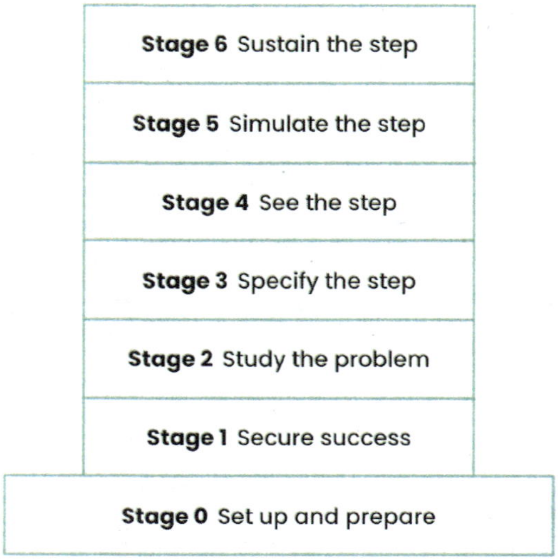

We aren't calling this a coaching model for a reason. We don't want schools or coaches to chuck out their current model and try to learn a whole new one – indeed, most schools will be using a version of these stages in their model already. Instead, see how you can improve your current model or coaching practice within each stage. With this in mind, how should you read part 2?

Read part 2 from start to finish if you'd like to, although you may want to read it in chunks to focus on developing one stage of your coaching practice (or the coaching practice of the coaches you train) at a time.

The structure of each chapter is similar:

- **Purposes:** we outline the purpose of this stage of coaching so you know what you're aiming for.
- **Pitfalls:** we outline common things that can undermine the development of your teacher's adaptive expertise in this stage. This is not to cast judgement on the way coaching is done in some contexts, but to help you avoid some of the pitfalls we have made along the way. We tackle the pitfalls first so you know where the land mines are before plotting your route!
- **Coaching techniques:** we codify concrete, practical ways to coach that we think will help to develop teachers' adaptive expertise. These operationalise the theory in part 1. Some are fundamental to coaching well in that stage and others can be used more flexibly to meet certain purposes.
- **Examples:** we show you coaching excerpts that are annotated to illustrate the techniques at work.
- **Coaching commentary:** we explain how the coaches in our examples are likely to be helping teachers develop their adaptive expertise as per the Adaptive Expertise Framework.
- **Do this in your coaching:** in this final section of each chapter, we help you use these techniques straight away by giving you a sequence and sentence stems.

So, let's get going with part 2. First up, how does a coach set up coaching?

Notes

1 Eraut, M. (2000) 'Non-formal learning and tacit knowledge in professional work,' *British Journal of Educational Psychology*, 70(1), pp. 113–136.

2 Kraft, M. A. and Blazar, D. (2018) 'Taking teacher coaching to scale: Can personalized training become standard practice?' *Education Next*, 18(4).

3 Ausubel, D. P. (2012) *The acquisition and retention of knowledge: A cognitive view*. Dordrecht: Springer Science & Business Media.

4 This phrase for this idea came from a conversation with Dr Neil Gilbride (2025).

5 Pfeffer, J. and Sutton, R.I. (2000) *The knowing-doing gap: How smart companies turn knowledge into action*. Boston, MA: Harvard Business Press.

6 Sims, S., Fletcher-Wood, H., O'Mara-Eves, A., Cottingham, S., Stansfield, C., Goodrich, J., Van Herwegen, J., and Anders, J. (2025) 'Effective teacher professional development: New theory and a meta-analytic test,' *Review of Educational Research*, 95(2), pp. 213–254.

7 Dr Stuart Kime as cited in Scutt, C. and Harrison, S. (2019) *Teacher CPD: International trends, opportunities and challenges*. London: Chartered College of Teaching. Available at: https://my.chartered.college/teacher-cpd-international-trends-opportunities-and-challenges/

8 Kochmanski, N. and Cobb, P. (2023) 'Identifying productive one-on-one coaching practices,' *Teaching and Teacher Education*, 131, p. 104188.

9 Walsh, M. E. and Schunn, C. D. (2025) 'Reconceptualizing framing theory for adaptive teaching expertise: the role of strategic and expansive framing.' *Educational Psychologist*, 61(1), pp. 1–18.

10 Eraut, M. (2000) 'Non-formal learning and tacit knowledge in professional work,' *British Journal of Educational Psychology*, 70(1), pp. 113–136.

11 This is drawn from the seminal work on scripts: Schank, R. C. and Abelson, R. P. (1977) *Scripts, plans, goals and understanding: An inquiry into human knowledge structures*. Hillsdale, NJ: Lawrence Erlbaum Associates.

12 These four components are our way of making the vague idea of mental models more concrete and useful. Mental models aren't directly observable, but this framework helps us treat them as something we can actually develop.

13 Caviglioli, O. (2019) *Dual coding with teachers*. London: Hachette UK.

14 These authors discuss the need for tools to develop adaptive expertise of which we think mapping is one: Hammerness, K., Darling-Hammond, L., Bransford, J., Berliner, D. C., Cochran-Smith, M., McDonald, M., and Zeichner, K. (2005) 'How teachers learn and develop.' In: L. Darling-Hammond, J. Bransford, P. LePage, K. Hammerness, and H. Duffy (Eds), *Preparing teachers for a changing world: What teachers should learn and be able to do*. San Francisco: Jossey-Bass, pp. 358–389.

15 Eisenstadt, M. and Kareev, Y. (1975) 'Aspects of human problem solving: The use of internal representations.' In: P. J. Feltovich, M. J. Prietula, and K. A. Ericsson (Eds), (2006) *The Cambridge handbook of expertise and expert performance*. Cambridge: Cambridge University Press, pp. 41–67.

16 Darling-Hammond, L., Schachner, A. C., Wojcikiewicz, S. K., and Flook, L. (2024) 'Educating teachers to enact the science of learning and development,' *Applied Developmental Science*, 28(1), pp. 1–21.

17 Launder, A. G. and Piltz, W. (2013) *Play practice: Engaging and developing skilled players from beginner to elite*. Champaign, IL: Human Kinetics, p. 59.

18 This rule-following behaviour and inability to contextualise is characteristic of early stages of expertise: Dreyfus, S. E. (2004) 'The five-stage model of adult skill acquisition,' *Bulletin of Science, Technology & Society*, 24(3), pp. 177–181; Persky, A. M. and Robinson, J. D. (2017) 'Moving from novice to expertise and its implications for instruction,' *American Journal of Pharmaceutical Education*, 81(9), p. 6065.

PART 2
Delivering coaching for adaptive expertise

Stage 0

Set up coaching by contracting

The effectiveness of coaching is significantly influenced by the quality of the coaching relationship, which is built on trust, clarity, and shared expectations. 'Contracting' is the process of establishing clear agreements between coaches and teachers. It helps kickstart a shared mental model of how coaching works, which prevents misunderstandings. It ensures that coaching relationships are productive, professional, and goal-oriented.

We suggest that schools take a centralised approach to explaining why coaching is a powerful vehicle for their professional development, ensuring staff all hear the same message. This enables coaches to pick up on those messages during 1:1 contracting conversations.

Before we dive in, let's examine the purposes of the contracting stage.

Purposes

This is what we want teachers to feel and know after this stage.

Get the goal: 'I understand that coaching will be focused on student learning.'
We need to make sure the teacher understands that the coaching conversations will be focused on student learning. The coach commits to observing with student learning in mind and the teacher and coach commit to making sure their diagnosis and discussion are focused on improving student learning.

Feel safe: 'I feel psychologically safe to discuss the challenges in my lessons.'
Psychological safety is essential in coaching relationships.[1] Contracting allows teachers to understand that coaching is a supportive, not punitive, process. This could help reduce anxiety and foster openness. This is also emphasised by Schein's concept of humble inquiry, which argues that effective coaching involves mutual respect and genuine curiosity.[2]

Know what to expect: 'I know how coaching will run.'
The coach and the teacher must have a shared understanding of what coaching entails. Contracting should define expectations for both parties, such as the frequency and structure of coaching sessions, communication norms, and how feedback will be given and received.

DOI: 10.4324/9781003465850-7

Pitfalls

Pitfalls are typical ways we can undermine this coaching stage. We need to know them so we can avoid them.

Fear factor: if there is no psychological safety[3] then teachers may be scared to take risks, ask questions and admit mistakes in their coaching sessions. Mistakes should be seen as opportunities for learning rather than failures, since this makes teachers more likely to engage in reflective practice and seek feedback. If psychological safety is absent, teachers may hide their mistakes from their coaches and resist change, or even feel defensive about feedback. This will stunt the development of adaptive expertise because being adaptive means holding things lightly and feeling empowered to intelligently experiment with new approaches to tackling novel problems.[4]

Unaccountable thinking: coaching needs to be focused on student learning. When teachers and coaches are discussing teaching, there may be moments when their thinking strays into the territory of personal preference or ideas that are not accountable to how students best learn. To avoid this, it is important that both coach and teacher commit to holding their thinking accountable to what is best for student learning. That is not to say that a coach cannot discuss other things with their teacher, but time in schools to coach is precious. Therefore, the sessions need to be kept on track with this focus.

A commitment by the coach to hold their thinking accountable to student learning also feeds into psychological safety. It means that teachers understand the standards their teaching should drive towards rather than being held to arbitrary goals linked to their coach's personal preference.

Job done: a teacher's learning does not end after a coaching session. This is just the beginning. Teachers need to understand how to improve through closing the knowing-doing and knowing-deciding-doing gaps. This involves the teacher committing to what Joyce and Showers term 'a second stage of learning'[5] after the coaching session. This is where they work to make the practice part of their repertoire. This expectation needs to be made explicit during the contracting stage.

Coaching techniques

Use these coaching techniques to help you set up coaching through **contracting**.

Some techniques are foundational, i.e., we should always use them, and some are flexible, i.e., we should use them when appropriate, depending on the level of the teacher's expertise in the moment.

Foundational or flexible	Technique	What it is	Examples	Non examples
Foundational	Define the purpose and process	Define the purpose and scope of coaching by discussing – **Why** What's the goal of coaching for the teacher and the school? **What** What is coaching and how will it work?	"The goal of coaching for our school is to support teachers, and coaches, to implement evidence-informed strategies at the right time for the right reasons by making great decisions. What are your immediate goals for your practice? Take some time to think and write if you need to." "You have been introduced to the coaching process we use at this school but let's go over what will happen from start to finish so you are clear and can ask any questions."	**Vague purpose:** "We will meet when we can to talk about your teaching."
Foundational	Check for concerns	Check how the teacher feels about coaching and if there is anything they need clarification on. Make the question as open as possible to invite any and all concerns.	"What concerns do you currently have about coaching?" "When I first started coaching, I had some worries about the process. Perhaps you're the same, is there anything you're concerned about?"	**Assuming everything is fine:** "Now you know how it will run, we can get going."
Foundational	Roles and responsibilities	Establish roles and responsibilities. Clarify what the coach will and will not do and discuss what the teacher is responsible for.	"I will observe your lesson once a week with a previously agreed focus and provide some feedback. You will need to commit to adjusting your teaching based on the feedback and practising between coaching sessions."	**Woolly roles:** "I will observe when I can and we will have a chat about what I observed. You will discuss this with me."
Foundational	Lock in logistics	Everyone is busy. Lock in the times you will observe and meet for the coaching conversation. Get into a routine (e.g. coaching every 2 weeks) where possible. You may need to communicate about coaching in between conversations. Agree (where necessary) how to communicate (email, face-to-face, video conferencing), who is responsible for rescheduling and how feedback will be delivered.	"You said that you are more comfortable with face-to-face coaching. If a session needs to be rescheduled, are you happy to do this after school? You also said you would like verbal and written feedback."	**Lack of a plan:** "Sorry I had to cancel the session, let's catch up when we get a chance."

Foundational or flexible	Technique	What it is	Examples	Non examples
Foundational	Link to learning 	Be explicit that coaching is about supporting student learning and model this throughout the contracting conversation.	"As a coach, I commit to observing your lessons and providing feedback which is centred on student learning. You need to be committed to planning, teaching and reflecting with student learning in mind." "That's a great goal for your teaching practice. Tell me about the effect you want this change to have on your students?"	**Unaccountable thinking:** "I will come in and watch you teach. I'll focus on the teaching techniques you use."
Foundational	Psychological safety 	From the outset, coaches need to reaffirm that coaching is non-evaluative and designed to support professional growth. Doing this in the contracting is an ideal time. Confidentiality could also be discussed here: what will and won't be shared with school leaders?	"Where possible, what we discuss here is confidential. We are learning from mistakes and discussing our challenges openly." "Leaders will know that we've met and what step you are working on but not the details of our work together."	**Fear factor:** "Coaching will feed into your performance management and be used as evidence for your pay progression."
Flexible	Adapting and responding 	Coaching is also a dynamic process and the coaching process may need to be adjusted at times by revisiting the contracting stage. Therefore open dialogue and regular check-ins should also be encouraged at this stage and beyond, so that processes can be re-evaluated and adapted over time.	"How are things going for you? Are you finding watching and discussing the video models helpful?"	**Assuming everything is fine:** "We started off well so I'm sure everything has remained fine."

Example 1 Foundational techniques

Let's see an example of a coach using the foundational techniques.

Context

Coach Andy has been asked to coach teacher Claire. Coaching has been embedded in the school for many years and they have a school-wide coaching model and expectations of staff.

Andy is a senior leader and Claire has been a teacher for a number of years. Claire has experienced coaching at the school for a while now. Andy and Claire haven't worked closely before though and so they need to establish trust. Andy wants to ensure Claire knows the purpose and process of the coaching, their roles and responsibilities, as well as how their communication will work. This creates psychological safety – another foundational technique.

Watch how coach Andy uses the foundational techniques for this stage: define the purpose and process, check for concerns, roles and responsibilities, lock in logistics, link to learning, and psychological safety.

Coaching Excerpt

Coach Andy: Thanks for making time to meet, Claire. I want to start by acknowledging that you've been here a long time and I'm very aware I'm new. I really respect the work and experience you bring, and I'm looking forward to learning from you as much as supporting you.

Teacher Claire: Thanks, Andy. I'm a little unsure why the school is changing their coaching approach.

Coach Andy: Totally understandable. That's why I wanted this first conversation to be really open, just to talk through what coaching is for, what coaching is (and isn't), and how we might work together.

Define the purpose and process: coach recaps the school's goals and asks the teacher about their goals

I wanted to start by recapping the school's goals for coaching, which have changed a bit over the years as research on coaching has developed. As we heard in the briefing the other week, we'll all be involved in coaching now (either coaching, being coached or both) with the aim being to develop our teaching techniques even further and our decision-making too in order to best meet the needs of our students. We'd focused more on techniques before but not decision-making, so we'll be working on that too now.

So, just to be clear: the purpose of coaching here isn't about performance management or checking up on anyone. It's still about professional growth - supporting your goals, in your context. The focus will always be on student learning.

Psychological safety: coach is clear that coaching is not about performance management but professional growth

Tell me more about your goals for your practice.

Teacher Claire: I'm hoping to work with you on developing my routines so they are slick. I've been a teacher for a while now and relied on the students doing what I say but I want to pull together with the rest of the school and get on board with the routines they are putting in place.

Coach Andy: Brilliant. When we schedule the first observation, I can come in when you're trying out a routine and look at how it's going. What impact on students are you hoping to see?

Link to learning: coach ensures the teacher links the goal for their teaching to the impact they want to see

Teacher Claire: I think routines will save learning time. I can then repurpose that time to focus on the content of the lesson and thinking hard.

Coach Andy: So important. Thank you for outlining that.

Define the purpose and process: coach recaps the school's coaching process so they are both clear on what will happen

As there have been some changes to the coaching too, I think it would be useful for me to share the stages we might go through and why they are there. The ultimate aim is to develop your adaptive expertise and this means focusing on unpacking your decision-making and practice. I'll come and observe focusing not just on your actions but decision-making too. During our coaching conversation, we'll make sure you own your success so you can keep doing what seems to be working. We will then identify the problem to focus on and what issues might be causing this problem. Once we have diagnosed the problem and come up with a suggested solution (in the form of a granular action step), I'll show a model of how it might look and support you to rehearse it. Rehearsal, as we know, makes it more likely you'll be able to do it in the busy lesson environment or in your planning. There are also effective methods you can use to improve outside of coaching too.

Roles and responsibilities: coach outlines the main roles and responsibilities and checks the teacher has been able to execute these before

Teacher Claire: Okay, that's helpful to recap and broadly similar to what I'm used to.

Link to learning: coach makes sure the teacher knows they are holding their thinking accountable to what is best for student learning

Coach Andy: Great. So as part of that, we can define our roles and responsibilities. My role is to observe and be that extra pair of eyes and ears in the lesson. Because I'm not teaching, I can actually focus on the effects of your teaching on student learning. I'll make notes focused on cause and effect and not on judgement of your practice. It's my role to reinforce what's working well in your teaching and find a situation to examine where changes to your practice may better support student learning. That's my primary role.

For you to get the most out of coaching, I ask that you are open to owning your success and examining your decision-making and actions in the situations I bring to our coaching conversations. Engaging as much as possible in all the stages of the coaching conversation will be critical for building the tracks to changing your practice. But ultimately, your responsibility is to enact the practice in your teaching and planning. This is where the change happens. How have you found this when you've been coached before?

Teacher Claire: Generally good. I've made changes to my practice when it comes to getting students' attention with a clear signal. I've found adopting the whole-school approaches have been game-changing for my students. It does take a lot of work after the coaching session like you say, but I've seen the value so I get that it can work.

Check for concerns: coach models a concern and asks the teacher about their worries

Coach Andy: That's great to hear. There may be parts of the process that can feel tricky to master though, even if we know they are important. For me, it's running the rehearsal so it's really useful for you. I'm keen to work on this together. Is there anything about the process you're unsure or worried about?

Teacher Claire: Yes, we can definitely do that - I've found rehearsal really useful when we spend time planning for it beforehand, so we can ensure that happens. For me, I find that point where we pivot from praise to looking at a problem a bit awkward sometimes. I don't mind being given developmental feedback but sometimes the coach tiptoes around it. I'd rather you just be open.

Coach Andy: Noted! Thank you. That's really helpful to know. I'll zoom us in on a specific situation and ask you what happened. If you struggle to recall or didn't see what I saw, I'll respectfully share what I noticed. What else?

Check for concerns: coach invites the teacher to express all her concerns by asking an open question ('what else?' instead of 'anything else?')

Teacher Claire: I'm really busy, as we all are, so I want to make sure we schedule things in advance. Sometimes with previous coaches, it's been a little haphazard.

Coach Andy: Yes. Let's lock in the logistics of our coaching then. The school has freed me up for a two week cycle where I observe one week and feedback the next. I don't want feedback to feel too far (time-wise) from the observation so I think I'll observe towards the end of week 1 and we'll make the coaching conversation towards the beginning of week 2. I've looked at your timetable and I'm thinking we could meet on a Monday 1.30–2.15 in your classroom. Does that sound like the kind of rhythm and time that could work for you?

Lock in logistics and communication: coach ensures they know when they will meet and how they will communicate

Teacher Claire:
Yes, that's great and every couple of weeks feels manageable. So, the first observation is next week and feedback on the Monday 1.30–2.15.

[Claire writes it down]

If you can come and see 8b period 5 on the Thursday before then, I'm trying out the whole-school transition routine.

Coach Andy: I'll double check and email you to let you know for sure. Is email the best way to communicate?

Teacher Claire: Yes definitely.

Coach Andy: And I know things come up sometimes. If we need to reschedule, I'll be responsible for finding another time as I have oversight of both our timetables and mine is quite changeable.

Teacher Claire: Sounds great, thank you.

Coach Andy: Great. And I wanted to finish by emphasising: you're aware that senior leaders check coaching is happening and what targets we are working on but they aren't using that to judge your teaching. They use it to inform the content of our whole-school professional development as well as coach training for me and the coaching team. Anything we talk about is between us unless you specifically want to share something wider.

Psychological safety: coach is clear on what is shared and what is between them only

Teacher Claire: That's great to hear. I could see that from previous cycles: things we were all working on got extra attention in whole-school sessions.

Coach Andy: That's exactly what I'm aiming for. If you're happy, I'll jot down some notes from this conversation so we can look back and remind ourselves of what we discussed and are committing to.

Teacher Claire: Sounds great, thanks Andy.

Example 2 Flexible technique

Let's see an example of a coach using a flexible technique.

Context

It is a term later and coach Andy has been working with teacher Claire. They have been focusing on her entrance and exit routines as some of her classes seem unsettled after break and lunch times and it appears to be wasting valuable teaching time.

The coaching has mostly been going well but Andy has noticed that Claire has been a bit quiet and more reluctant to discuss why she is using strategies. He questions Claire to adapt and respond to her needs.

Watch how coach Andy uses the flexible technique for this stage: adapting and responding.

Coaching Excerpt

Coach Andy: Hi Claire, good to see you. Before we jump into today's focus, I just wanted to check in. I've noticed you've seemed a little quieter than usual the past couple of sessions. I just want to make sure the process still feels useful for you, or if anything's changed?

Adapting and responding: coach checks in with the teacher to see what might be wrong and how it can be addressed

Teacher Claire: Hmm, yeah... I suppose I've just felt a bit unsure lately. I've been trying the entrance routine we planned, but I'm not sure it's making much of a difference with Year 9. Also, I guess I don't always feel confident explaining why I'm using certain techniques in my practice. It's hard to put into words.

Coach Andy: Thanks for being honest, that's really helpful. It's fine not to have all the answers. The aim of coaching isn't to "perform" your reasoning, it's to think it through together. It sounds like we might need to pause and reflect a bit more on what's working and what's not.

Teacher Claire: Maybe. I do want it to work, but sometimes it feels like I'm just doing the moves without being sure why.

Adapting and responding: coach suggests a way they could change their approach to better support the teacher's needs

Coach Andy: That's such a valuable insight. What if we shifted the focus a little? Maybe we take a step back and explore what you're noticing in those first five minutes of the lesson - what the students are doing, how you're feeling, what's different on the days it works. Would that feel more helpful than sticking rigidly to the routine itself?

Teacher Claire: That actually feels like it could be a big relief for me. I think I've been putting pressure on myself to make it "look right" rather than figuring out what's really happening.

Coach Andy: Exactly and coaching should be about what you need in the moment, not just sticking to a plan for the sake of it. How about we use the next session to video the start of a lesson, and then review together what we both notice? We can look at where the entry routine we rehearsed is working and where it might need tweaking.

Teacher Claire: I'd like that.

Example 3 Foundational techniques

Let's see an example of a coach focusing on one foundational technique.

Context

Coach Helen is coaching new teacher Mike as part of her role as his mentor. This puts her in a different position to many coaches: she observes Mike to help him improve and what she notes down can be used as evidence of formal progress towards his teaching qualification. This means there is a higher-stakes element to the coaching than in many other coaching relationships. Before coaching starts, coach Helen begins by contracting with Mike. Her aim is to allay his fears and ensure he understands that the priority is his development.

Watch in particular how coach Helen uses a foundational technique for this stage: psychological safety.

Coaching Excerpt

Mentor Helen: Mike, I'm really looking forward to working with you this year in your first year of teaching! Before we get started on coaching next week, I want to spend a bit of time on how the coaching process will work and what you can expect from me – that's what this conversation is about. But first, you said the other day that you were nervous about coaching. Tell me more.

Check for concerns: mentor starts by openly inviting the teacher to express their concerns so she can allay his fears

Teacher Mike: Well, it feels very high stakes you coming in to see me teach. I'm concerned you won't see me teaching very well - especially with some classes I've met this week.

Psychological safety: mentor clarifies that coaching is focused on development

Mentor Helen: I appreciate you saying it. Starting out as a teacher is a big step, and it can feel daunting. So first things first, our coaching is here to help you improve your teaching so that students learn more. This is not about catching you out or giving you a grade. I'm here to help you make progress, whatever your starting point.

Teacher Mike: That's reassuring to hear. I've heard horror stories from some friends about being observed and how high stakes it all feels.

Mentor Helen: That won't happen here. Let me be specific. Yes, as your mentor I do need to gather evidence that will be used to support your teaching qualification. But coaching is developmental. When we're in coaching mode, we're focused on one step at a time, i.e., something small, specific, and doable that you can practise to improve your teaching and impact on student learning. You will need to commit to putting your all into the coaching sessions and implementing what we work on in your practice. Shall I tell you more about how it will run? I think that might make you feel a little more relaxed about it.

Roles and responsibilities: mentor distinguishes between her mentor and coaching roles and sets expectations

Teacher Mike: Yes please.

Define the purpose and process: mentor explains the goal of their coaching and how coaching will run

Mentor Helen: The goal of our coaching is to accelerate your progress so you get better and better at supporting student learning. I'll come in to observe you teach every week for the first term. You'll always know in advance what I'm focusing on when I come in because mostly it will be the last small step we set together and I'll stick within that teaching area.

After the lesson, we'll meet to reinforce what is working, unpick what happened that could go better, agree a really granular next step, which I will model to you, and we will rehearse it together so you feel confident. It's my responsibility to make sure feedback supports you to get better. I'll be working hard to make sure it supports you to improve your practice. Part of that is only setting small steps you can manage. As I said, it's your role to commit to developing by being focused and open in our coaching sessions and dedicated to implementing the action step afterwards.

Teacher Mike: small steps sound good. I can definitely hold up my end by implementing the steps. I can already see where my gaps are! So, you'll help me teach like some of the more experienced teachers in the department?

Mentor Helen: Perhaps your teaching will closely resemble their teaching and certainly you'll learn some of the same techniques. But most importantly, I'll support you to teach in the best way to support your students' learning. This involves you developing a repertoire of teaching techniques and learning to make decisions about when to use them and how. This will be based on what is best for your students when you plan lessons and in the moment. You can be sure I'll be focused on that and not my personal preference or trying to mould you into another teacher. Plus, you and I are helped along by the theory that underpins our work together. You're completing a course as part of your initial teacher training with the university. I've got access to that

Link to learning: mentor emphasises that the focus is on improving teaching for the purpose of supporting student learning content too and we'll use that to drive our thinking around your practice too.

Teacher Mike: OK, that makes sense. And, if I have a terrible observation, does this get shared with other staff?

Mentor Helen: You're learning and will inevitably have challenging lessons. I'm interested in your commitment and progress over time. I will share that progress with the other support roles you have, but the details of our day-to-day coaching conversations (the trial and error, the challenges, the tweaks) stay between us. This is your space to take risks and grow.

Psychological safety: mentor is transparent about the stakes while framing coaching as a supported path to progress

Teacher Mike: That makes sense. When do we get started?

Mentor Helen: I've looked at our timetables and I'll observe on Tuesday mornings and we'll meet Wednesday after school each week in your classroom. If anything needs changing, just let me know and we'll adapt. The best way to make changes to this routine is probably over email so we have a record of the change to go back to.

Lock in logistics: mentor comes prepared with the days they can observe and feedback to lock in a routine and what to do if someone needs to reschedule

Teacher Mike: Great, I can do that. I do want to get better at behaviour management to begin with and that's the focus of my self-study modules for university too. I've found that really tough in the first week.

Mentor Helen: That's a great place to start. I'll focus on that. As I say, we'll focus on making small changes you can manage and that will add up to tangible progress.

Coaching commentary

This is where we get meta and analyse the quality of the coaching in the examples above.

Below we explain how the coaches' use of techniques supports their teachers to understand, do, decide and improve, i.e., to develop their adaptive expertise. As coaching has not yet begun during the first contracting meeting, contracting is setting the groundwork for developing the teacher's adaptive expertise.

Understand	Do	Decide
...key knowledge that helps solve persistent problems.	...a repertoire of effective, efficient teaching techniques.	...on the best course of action using situation-sensitive mental models.

Improve
...continuously through an adaptive mindset and metacognition.

Understand

Teachers need to feel that coaching will develop their ability to understand key ideas that will enable them to teach better. By using the technique **link to learning**, coach Andy makes it clear to Claire that he is there to do what's best for student learning and not to arbitrarily judge her teaching. Mentor Helen does the same. Her teacher, Mike, is new to the profession and concerned that coaching will be high stakes. He also has the misconception that Helen will be training him to teach like others in the department. Helen supports him to understand that she is training him to do what is best for student learning and not attempting to mould him into someone else.

Do

It's important that coaches are clear on how coaching will run. By sharing the process in detail, the teacher can begin to understand how they will learn new teaching techniques so they can build their repertoire. Coach Andy uses the technique **define purpose and process** to ensure Claire understands that mechanisms like modelling and rehearsal will help her develop these techniques. Mentor Helen uses the same coaching technique to help Mike see that coaching is focused on his incremental development and not on high-stakes accountability.

Decide

During contracting, coaches can explain that part of the purpose and process of coaching is to improve their decision-making (a key facet of adaptive expertise). Coach Andy does this by clearly **defining the purpose and process** with Claire so she can see that coaching won't just be about developing her repertoire of techniques but her decision-making too. Mentor Helen also emphasises to Mike that she won't be trying to mould him into other teachers but instead help him develop teaching techniques and great decision-making to use them appropriately to best support student learning.

Improve

Much of the contracting process is helping the teacher understand how coaching will help them to improve. This involves establishing **psychological safety** by being transparent about confidentiality and ensuring teachers know that coaching is not about catching them out or forming lasting judgements about their teaching. It is also about being clear on both people's **roles and responsibilities**. Coach Andy commits to observing with integrity by holding himself accountable to student learning, and he explains teacher Claire's role and commitment to continuously learning beyond the coaching. This supports Claire to understand, in a broad sense, what she needs to do to improve. She can learn this more specifically when the coaching starts.

In a different situation, mentor Helen works hard to establish **psychological safety**. She carefully explains her **roles and responsibilities** focusing on her dual role as coach and mentor. She ensures Mike understands that she shoulders a lot of the responsibility for his progress and his responsibility is to commit to coaching and the work that happens after in his planning and lessons. She reassures him on more than one occasion that coaching is focused on his progress despite the fact that evidence from his lessons can be used towards his teaching qualification.

Part of developing **psychological safety** is providing the space for the teacher to express – and the coach to address – any concerns by doing a **check for concerns**. Coach Andy checks Claire's concerns after he explains the coaching purpose and process. This allows Claire to express concerns from a place of understanding. By contrast, mentor Helen asks about teacher Mike's concerns upfront as she has heard that he is worried. She recognises that he will struggle to take in the rest of the conversation if she does not first allay his fears.

Coaches need to get teachers into the habit of improvement. This can't happen unless they **lock in logistics** to ensure coaching actually happens. Both coaches ensure they've come prepared with when coaching will happen and preempt how to communicate about any changes. This greases the wheels for coaching and confronts the reality of busy schools.

The contracting stage is not over once the initial contracting conversation has been completed. Coach Andy uses the technique **adapting and responding** to address changes he has noticed in Claire's willingness to engage in coaching. This 're-contracting' is important for ensuring the coaching relationship continues to be productive, and it can happen periodically (perhaps at the start of each half term to check in on the process) as well as to address any particular challenges.

Do this in your coaching

Let's look at how we can use these coaching techniques at the right time for the right reasons in our coaching.

Get started with these foundational techniques

When you're trying something new in your coaching, you need some foundational techniques to adopt. Try these techniques using one of the suggested sentence stems.

Define the purpose and process:

- The purpose of our coaching partnership is to support your professional growth by . . .
- The aim of our coaching work together is to enhance student learning by focusing on . . .
- What are your goals for coaching?
- Let's talk through the coaching process so we both know how it will run . . .

Check for concerns:

- I've not always found the coaching process easy, although I see the point of every stage. What concerns do you have?
- Tell me more about your concern.

Roles and responsibilities:

- As your coach, my role is to see positive effects you're having on student learning and situations where small changes could make a big difference.
- Your role is to commit to the coaching process and the evidence-led aspects of it, whilst being open about what is and isn't feeling comfortable or working so I can better support you.
- In this coaching relationship, I'll work alongside you to explore strategies and practice, and you'll spend time practising putting the feedback into action between sessions.

Lock in logistics:

- We'll meet once a fortnight at 1.30 in your classroom?
- Are you happy to meet after school if we have to rearrange a session?
- What's the best way to contact each other? Shall we agree that whoever needs to reschedule does the rescheduling?

Link to learning:

- My observations and feedback will always be accountable to student learning and not personal preference.
- If you realise your goal, how will it impact student learning?

Psychological safety:

- This process is not tied to any high-stakes monitoring. It is about your professional growth.

- What we discuss is confidential. The only thing that is shared is that coaching has happened and which action step you are working on.

Adapt your coaching appropriately using this flexible technique

Adapting and responding:

- Tell me about how you found the coaching process last half term.
- I've noticed you seem less keen to rehearse the step recently. Is this fair? Tell me more.
- What do you need from me to . . .?

Notes

1 Costa, A. L., Garmston, R. J. (2002) *Cognitive coaching: A foundation for Renaissance schools*. Boston: Christopher-Gordon Publishers Inc.

2 Schein, E.H. (2013) *Humble inquiry: The gentle art of asking instead of telling*. New York: Berrett-Koehler Publishers.

3 Edmondson, A. (1999) 'Psychological safety and learning behavior in teams,' *Administrative Science Quarterly*, 44, pp. 250–282.

4 Hatano, G. and Inagaki, K. (1986) 'Two courses of expertise.' In: H. Stevenson, H. Azuma, and K. Hakuta (Eds), *Children development and education in Japan* (pp. 262–272). New York: Freeman.

5 Joyce, B. and Showers, B. (1982) 'The coaching of teaching,' *Educational Leadership*, 40(1), p. 4.

References

Costa, A. L., Garmston, R. J. (2002) *Cognitive coaching: A foundation for Renaissance schools*. Boston: Christopher-Gordon Publishers Inc.

Edmondson, A. (1999) 'Psychological safety and learning behavior in teams,' *Administrative Science Quarterly*, 44, pp. 250–282.

Hatano, G. and Inagaki, K. (1986) 'Two courses of expertise.' In: H. Stevenson, H. Azuma, and K. Hakuta (Eds), *Children development and education in Japan* (pp. 262–272). New York: Freeman.

Schein, E. H. (2013) *Humble inquiry: The gentle art of asking instead of telling*. New York: Berrett-Koehler Publishers.

Stage 0

Prepare for coaching by diagnosing need

Before coaching can take place, coaches need to prepare. Some of this preparation takes place as they observe the teacher's lesson while other aspects take place after. The preparation work you do as a coach is vitally important. As we've said in previous chapters, selecting the right situation to coach on, i.e., the right moment that reveals a problem and an opportunity for the teacher to change their practice for the better, is *as important* as the discussion itself.[1]

But we have a problem. It's a natural tendency to jump to judgement when we watch someone teach. Our brain wants to take shortcuts and find a problem quickly. If we allow this to happen, we may pick a problem that isn't the most important. Even if we do manage to pick an important problem, we won't be able to explain it properly to our teacher, which means that if they disagree with us, we won't have specific, non-judgemental evidence to analyse together. Coaching for adaptive expertise is fundamentally about being able to develop your teacher's mental model. You can only do this if you can credibly answer this question from your teacher: 'How did you come to that hypothesis about my teaching?' In other words, you need to be able to *show your working out*.

This chapter gives you a clear, five-step process to slow down and streamline your diagnosis so you avoid jumping to judgement and diagnose need in a credible way. This will support you to bring your teacher along with you and develop their mental model of the problem at play. By engaging in this process, you will also develop your own mental model of teaching situations. You will see lesson events through the lens of dynamic teacher development rather than static evaluation.

Let's start by looking at the purposes of diagnosing need when preparing for coaching.

Purposes

This is what we want coaches to know after this stage.

Find the issue: 'I've found an important issue in the teacher's lesson that seems to be leading to a problem.'

DOI: 10.4324/9781003465850-8

Coaches need to make sure that they have found an important issue to focus on in the coaching session and are holding it lightly at this stage. This means that when they are watching lessons, they need to use a strong mental model of how learning happens to identify an issue that seems to be impacting student learning: this is the situation to coach on.

Show my working out: 'I've not just gone with my first hunch. I've actively gathered evidence to test my hypothesis.'

Coaches must be able to explain why they've focused on a certain situation. This means being able to relay the evidence of a problem and their hypothesis about the issues that may have caused it. This can only happen if the coach gathers non-judgemental evidence to test their hypothesis when they are observing the lesson.

A plan for development: 'I have a sense of what the teacher's current mental model is and how we might need to develop it to better support student learning.'

Coaches prepare well for coaching when they have a sense of what they are trying to develop in the teacher, although they must hold it lightly at this stage. Coaches can infer the teacher's current mental model (situation model) and what a better mental model would be (solution mental model) so they know how they might need to help them develop.

Pitfalls

Pitfalls are typical ways we can undermine this coaching stage. We need to know them so we can avoid them.

Everything and nothing: when we're watching a teacher teach, there is a lot going on. It can be tempting to think you can work on multiple aspects of the teacher's practice at once and this might develop their practice quicker. Avoid this. We know that the classroom is an incredibly complex environment and so teachers will find it difficult to consciously change their practice. We can ease this challenge somewhat by making sure that we ask them to think hard about changing *one small aspect* of it at a time, even if this means that we have to wait a while to see the cumulative effect on students. We can share this rationale with the teacher so they remain motivated.

Grab and go: with so much going on in school and long to-do lists, it can be tempting to observe your teacher and grab the first problem you see. Avoid doing this because it is important that coaches think upstream when they observe lessons. They need to find the thing that will make the biggest difference to student learning. Goodrich suggests a hierarchy of five teaching problems for coaches to focus on: secure attention, optimise communication, drive thought, gather and give feedback, and ensure consolidation.[2] We must prioritise problems further upstream in most cases, e.g., there is little value in working on how a teacher communicates a concept to the class if they have not first secured attention.

Often (not always), we also want to prioritise something related to the same problem the teacher is currently working on. This helps to develop their practice meaningfully in one area rather than jumping from one thing to the next. So, avoid assuming the first thing you see is the thing to work on and decide based on the teacher's current target, what is upstream and, of course, the evidence of impact on student learning.

Preparing to forget: often, coaches try to capture as much as possible about what is going on in the lessons because they know that they are likely to forget some or even most of it later.[3] This is absolutely the right concern to have but the way that these notes are organised is of underestimated importance. Capturing lesson events in a long list of notes does mean that you will capture more of what happens but it doesn't mean that you will capture the *significance*. For example, we know cause and effect are the building blocks of our mental models. Listing notes of what happened makes it difficult for us to later remember how events linked together.

Instead, we show you a five-step process for organising your notes as you go so you can form and test a clear hypothesis about a problem as you observe. You'll still capture what you see specifically, but you'll do it more meaningfully, better supporting you to have the coaching conversation.

Preference over problem: coaches are teachers as well and all teachers have their own personal preferences about how to teach. It is natural when watching another teacher to notice when they have done something that you don't personally like to do. However, this presents a potential issue if you assume that this action will lead to a problem. When observing a teacher, it is important to suspend your own personal preferences about the actions they take and instead focus on the evidence about the effect of that action: has it contributed to a problem? We must keep our diagnosis accountable to student learning if our coaching is going to be credible and impactful. For example, imagine a coach who does not like to use cold calling in their own practice because they feel it puts students on the spot and can make them feel uncomfortable. If they were to observe another teacher using cold call, they may assume that the students feel uncomfortable and prepare to coach on that rather than look for evidence that cold calling is leading to a problem. Suspend personal preferences and go with the evidence.

Jumping to judgement: imagine you are watching a teacher modelling and at three points during the modelling, they turn to the class and say, 'OK, so everyone understands?' and they nod and put their thumbs up indicating that they want the same response back from the class. You know that this is likely to be a poor proxy for whether or not students actually do understand and so there is a temptation to make a judgement such as, 'this teacher does not know how to check for understanding.' What's wrong with this natural tendency to jump to judgement?

First, jumping to judgement commits the sin of ignoring the complexity the teacher is experiencing. We can't fully understand the merits or otherwise of what the teacher did until we also surface their mental model of the situation during coaching. Of course, it may be true that the teacher does not have the knowledge about how to check for understanding reliably, but it could also have been that they were using this as an opportunity to refocus the attention of the class. If 100% of the class nod and put their thumbs up, their attention is likely on the teacher at that moment. They might plan a proper check for understanding afterwards when we had to leave the observation. We don't know about their decision-making until we ask.

Secondly, your role is not to judge but to develop the teacher's adaptive expertise. Jumping to judgement is natural because it's your brain taking short cuts (especially easy to do if you're busy or stressed).[4] But it's not helpful for your teacher. Think of jumping to judgement as akin to students who skip showing their working out in maths lessons. Even if they get the right answer, we can't learn anything about their thought process. We also can't trace back their mistakes. So, what should coaches do instead?

Coaches need to put in place safeguards against this natural tendency to jump to judgement.[5] Do this by forming good habits through the five-step process we show you below. This involves forming a hypothesis about the issue you see and then recording evidence to test it. If evidence bears this out, there is more weight to their hypothesis. If not, they look for something else. Preparing this way allows the coach to show their working out when the time comes - this makes coaching credible.

Making the teacher the problem: when you get to the point of settling on what you think the issues impacting student learning are, it is easy to frame this as an issue with the teacher. For example, a coach is observing a teacher delivering an explanation and they are doing so in a highly performative way that the coach feels detracts from the main point of the explanation. The coach phrases the problem as: *The teacher is being too performative in an effort to keep students interested*. This phrasing communicates a lot of assumptions that we simply can't make before we have spoken to the teacher. Better phrasing would be: *The salient points of the explanation are not highlighted and so students do not appear to be sure what to focus their attention on*. (And of course, they'll only have come to that conclusion after testing their hypothesis against evidence from the lesson).

The preparation process

First, we prepare for coaching by identifying something that is going well and recording specifically what happened so we can share and reinforce this with our teacher. This is often linked to the previous target they are working on since they are likely to have made progress here and we want to reinforce that. Plus, our teacher is likely to value praise on this. We will look at how to communicate this praise in the chapter Stage 1 Secure success.

However, in this chapter, we will focus on the second way we prepare for coaching: identifying the significant situation where a problem might be at play. To avoid the pitfalls above and efficiently capture what you need when observing your teacher, follow the five-step GRIPS process.

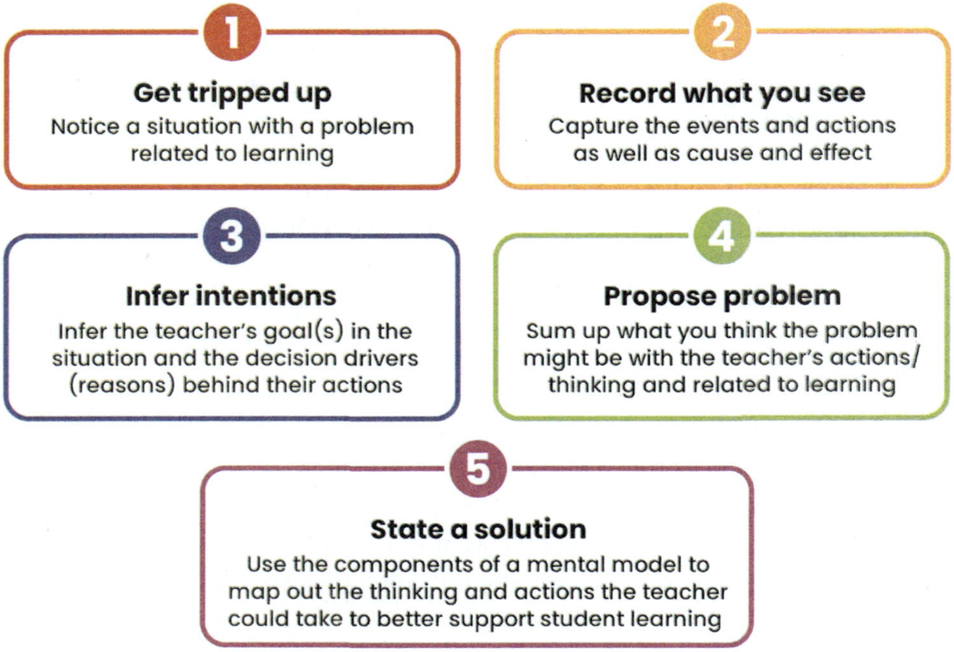

A big part of this process is recording what you see by mapping the teacher's situation mental model. Previously, we said mental models contain these components:

- Goal: the goal(s) a person has in a situation e.g., 'Get all students' attention.'
- Actions and events: what the teacher does and the events that occur.
- Cause and effect: arrows linking teacher actions to effects (usually on students).
- Decision drivers: reasons for the teacher's actions.

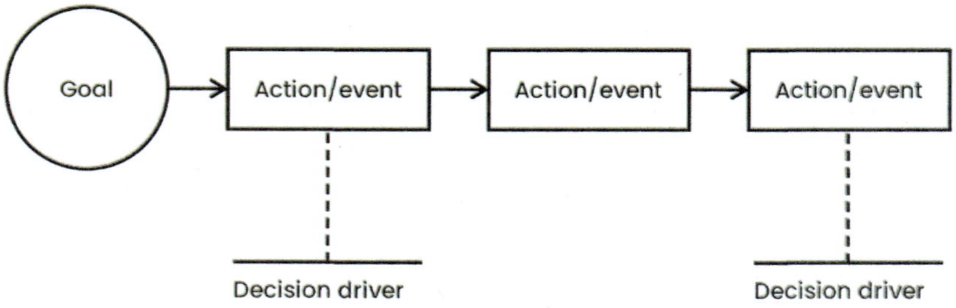

Here's more detail about each step of the GRIPS process followed by examples.

Step of the process	What it is	How to do it
Get tripped up	Notice something that happens that does not align with your mental model of how learning happens best. At this point you have either – A hunch (instinct) that there is a problem: 'There's something wrong with that explanation'. Or a more developed hypothesis (a testable idea): 'I think that explanation contained too many challenging words to be understood by students.'	**Hunch to hypothesis:** Notice your instinct that something is jarring with your mental model of how student learning best occurs. Form a hypothesis about what this might be. **Prioritise particular problems:** Check that you are focusing on an upstream area. For example, if it's a problem with their check for understanding, is there also a problem with ensuring attention? Choose that instead since it's upstream. You may also want to consider sticking in the broader problem you are currently working on with the teacher to develop their understanding further.
Record what you see	Record the events that unfold and how they relate to each other (cause and effect).	**Gather evidence to test the hypothesis:** Write down specifically what is happening using quotations for speech and attempting to record the number of students doing things as well as timings where appropriate. Capture this in a neutral, non-judgemental way as if you are a court stenographer (not judge or jury). **Map the situation model:** When you gather this evidence, visually map the actions/inactions of the teacher followed by the effects you can see on the students. Map these actions/events in boxes connected by cause-and-effect arrows (see this chapter's examples for details). **Hold your hypothesis lightly:** If the evidence doesn't suggest there's a problem at play, scrap your initial hypothesis and get tripped up by something else. You must hold your diagnosis accountable to student learning.
Infer intentions	Infer the teacher's goal in that situation and the decision drivers (reasons) for their actions.	**Your best guess:** It seems strange to try to infer the teacher's goals and decision drivers but it's important because it helps you with the next step of the GRIPS process – proposing the problem. You want to be able to understand both the problem with the teacher's actions and their decision-making, so you need to prepare by inferring their intentions. Do your best, given the evidence, to infer the teacher's goal in that situation (this is not the lesson or task learning goal – it's their goal at that particular time) and decision drivers. **Map the situation mental model:** Add to the mapping of actions and events and cause and effect by inserting the goal you've inferred and the decision drivers (see this chapter's examples for details).

Step of the process	What it is	How to do it
Propose problem	Do this in two parts: **1. Learning problem:** Describe the problem in relation to student learning. For example: *Learning problem: students are answering the questions quickly and easily without much thought. This is unlikely to deepen their understanding.* **2. Teaching problem:** a. Relate this to the most fundamental of Goodrich's teaching problems: • Securing attention • Optimising communication • Driving thought • Gathering and giving feedback • Ensure consolidation b. Specifically state the actions and decision-making that may have caused the learning problem. *Teaching problem: the teaching problem appears to relate to 'driving thought' because the teacher's questions are very simple (actions). This may be because she doesn't believe she can ask more from these students (decision-making).*	**Think 'cause and effect':** Propose the problem in two ways: First, propose the learning problem, i.e., the effect you saw on student learning. Second, the teaching problem, i.e., the likely causes of the learning problem – both in terms of the teacher's actions and their decisions (we have inferred their decision drivers in the step before this). **Tread tentatively:** Even though the evidence suggested your hypothesis might be correct, you still can't be sure. This is because you've inferred intentions on behalf of the teacher. You'll need to surface their mental model to know for sure. Phrase your problem statements concisely but tentatively to reflect this.
State a solution	Map out what you *think* a solution mental model would be in this situation to better support student learning. Then, write a specific action step that might be a good solution to the problem you've proposed. Use the format 'when, what and why' to construct the action step.	**Your best bet:** To prepare well for coaching we need a sense of what might improve the teacher's actions and decision-making. You've only inferred the teacher's decision-making so hold the potential solution lightly at this stage but do prepare one. **Map a solution mental model:** Using all the components of the situation mental model (goal, actions and events, cause and effect, decision drivers - see this chapter's examples), map out what a teacher would think and do to better support student learning here. This gives you a sense of the end goal for your coaching conversation should your diagnosis be correct. **Granular action:** The action step should solve the proposed problem and be incremental enough to be adopted by the teacher without overloading them.

Example 1 Straightforward diagnosis

Context

Coach Nimrat has gone into teacher Percy's lesson as part of the school's usual coaching cycle. Coach Nimrat and teacher Percy have been working on teacher Percy standing in a visible position in the room when giving instructions to ensure that attention can be on him. In the example, coach Nimrat goes into the start of the lesson.

Coaching Excerpt

Coach Nimrat comes into the lesson at the start and watches the first part where teacher Percy gives a set of instructions from a position in the room where he is visible to all students. Every student has their eyes on him during this point of the lesson. This all goes well and so coach Nimrat records specifically what she sees teacher Percy do that she feels is particularly effective so that she can discuss this with teacher Percy in the coaching session.

Teacher Percy then decides it is time to bring the class back together and he does this in the following way:

Teacher Percy: OK, 3,2,1 eyes on me

Coach Nimrat feels immediately tripped up by the possibility that this may not get students' attention. She noticed that teacher Percy did his countdown really quickly and that in full, it took about 2 seconds. She hypothesises that from the start point of every child speaking, it is unlikely that such a quick countdown is going to be successful at getting them to stop.

Get tripped up

Record what you see

Getting tripped up is coach Nimrat's cue to record what she sees.

"3, 2, 1, eyes on me."

She carefully watches and records teacher Percy's actions that follow this point.

It's important that coach Nimrat continues to map actions and events linked by arrows that signify cause and effect in order to test her hypothesis that there are actions or events causing a learning problem. Coach Nimrat sees that, immediately after finishing his countdown, teacher Percy follows up with:

Teacher Percy: Jack, Shhh please.... Naomi, that's enough now.

Coach Nimrat scans the room and she sees most students now attending to teacher Percy but she notices 9 students looking around the room, evidently not paying attention to teacher Percy. As she keeps watching, teacher Percy continues with his teaching. Coach Nimrat continues to record what she sees by mapping actions and events linked by cause-and-effect arrows:

Record what you see

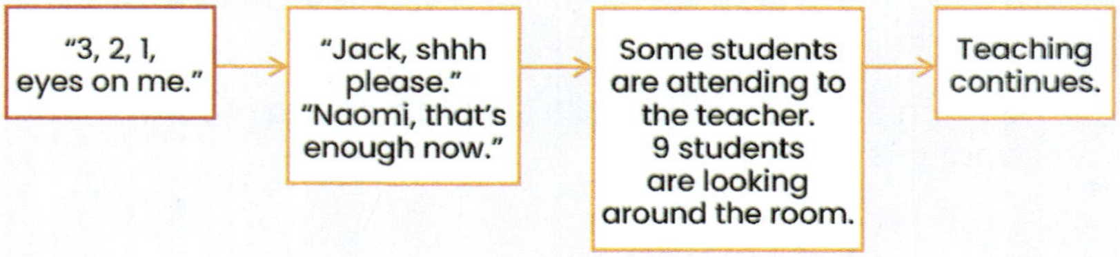

Infer intentions: goal

Coach Nimrat then considers what she thinks teacher Percy's goal might have been in this situation. She saw him use a countdown and so she infers that his goal was to secure students' attention. She maps this as follows:

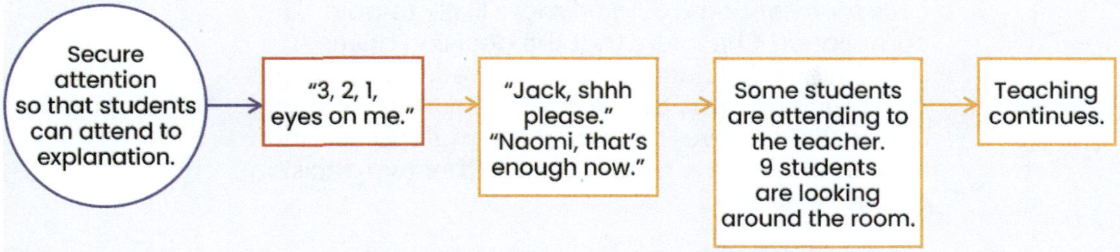

Coach Nimrat then considers what may have driven teacher Percy's decision to do the initial countdown as he did. She thinks teacher Percy's decision driver for using a countdown (3,2,1) is because it is a whole school approach. She suspects that the speed of the countdown could have been due to a feeling of urgency around getting on with the lesson.

Infer intentions: decision drivers

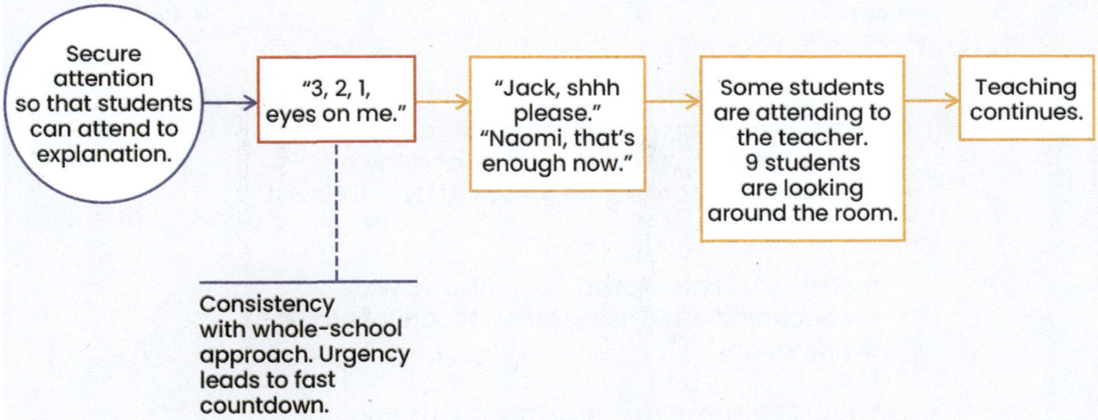

Coach Nimrat then makes the same consideration about the other two actions. She thinks that the decision driver behind Percy saying "*Jack, Shhh please*" and "*Naomi, that's enough now*" was that Percy did not believe the whole-class call for attention would be effective (this is further reinforced by the fact that teacher Percy didn't wait at all to see if it would work) and that individual calls for attention would be more likely to gain compliance. She infers that the decision driver behind the third action she's mapped (continuing with teaching) was that Percy felt the need to move on in order to cover the rest of the material planned for that lesson. She maps these further two decision drivers on too:

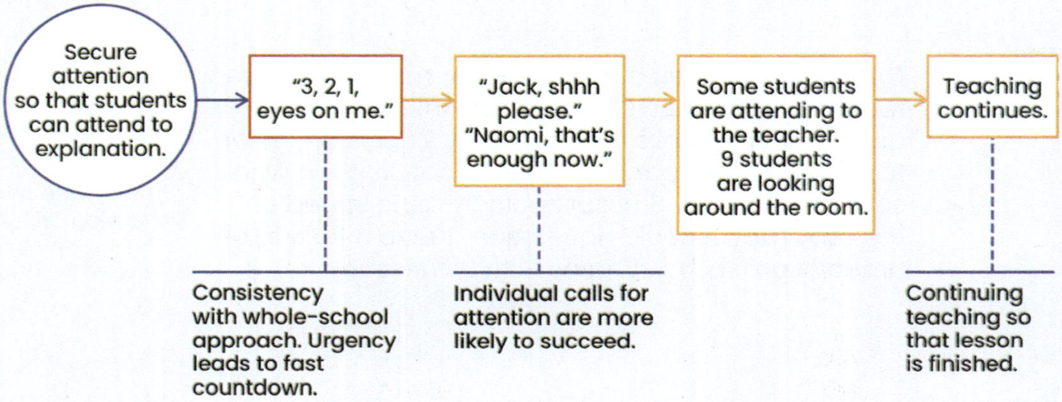

Coach Nimrat then spends some time mapping other evidence that might confirm or deny her hypothesis. She notices the following over the next five minutes:

- 4 other students picked up pens and were preoccupied with these during teacher Percy's explanation.
- When she spoke to 7 students about what they understood following the explanation, they were not able to explain this.
- The quick "*3,2,1*" call for attention occurred again a further three times in the lesson and each time, it was followed by individual corrections. In each case, not all students attended to the subsequent teaching.

This evidence adds weight to her hypothesis, leading coach Nimrat to be confident that she has found the right situation to coach on.

Overall, coach Nimrat has mapped what is called a situation mental model. That is, Nimrat's sense of Percy's mental model of that situation.

Coach Nimrat immediately proposes the problem in writing.

Propose problem

She proposes the problem in two ways:

Learning problem: describe the problem in relation to student learning.

Teaching problem: relate this to one of Goodrich's teaching problems. Also state the actions and decisions that may have caused the learning problem.

Learning problem: *not all students appeared to pay attention and learning time seemed to be wasted trying to get it. Some students did not then attend to the teacher's explanation and so cannot have learned from it.*

Teaching problem *(causes of the learning problem): this appears to be a problem related to 'ensuring attention'. The very brief countdown and individual reminders did not seem to hold students accountable for paying attention. The teacher seemed to lack confidence that the routine would work and appeared to be in a hurry to move on.*

Coach Nimrat is aware that she has made inferences about the teacher's mental model (particularly the goal and decision drivers). This means the proposed problems are also hypotheses she holds lightly. This is good preparation for the coaching conversation because she has an idea of what to coach on, she has a hypothesis to test with teacher Percy but she's not wedded to it.

Coach Nimrat can now prepare for the solution. She does this by asking herself, '*What mental model would the teacher need to adopt to better support student learning in a similar situation?*' Coach Nimrat maps this out in what is called a solution mental model (recall that the previous mapping of the issue was called a situation mental model).

State a solution: solution mental model

Solution mental models have all the same components of situation mental models, so coach Nimrat starts by thinking about the goal.

She thinks the goal needs to be improved slightly by adding that the expectation of silence applies to all students (earlier she inferred that teacher Percy's goal was looser than this).

She then turns her attention to the teacher's actions and the events as well as linking them with arrows to show cause and effect. Coach Nimrat thinks that breaking down the '*3,2,1 countdown*' with instructions after each number and inserting deliberate scanning and narrating of the positive responses is likely to achieve that powerful new goal of getting the attention of all students. She maps out her proposed solution model like this:

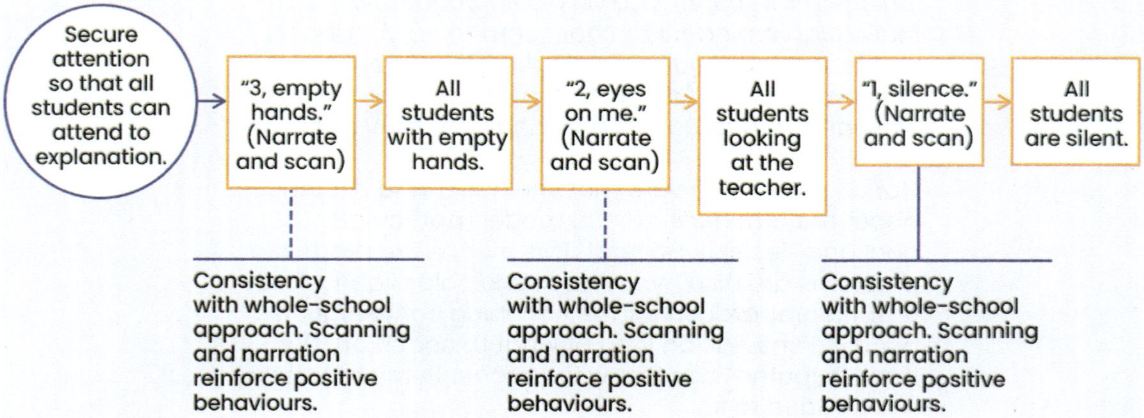

Coach Nimrat knows that this solution mental model could change depending on what teacher Percy says in the coaching session but based on the information she has so far, she thinks this solution mental model is likely to be helpful.

State a solution: action step

She writes the action step that she thinks she will work on with teacher Percy. The format she uses is 'when what why':

When calling for student attention following paired discussion, use a countdown routine with scanning and positive narration in between each stage to secure attention efficiently.

Example 2 More complex diagnosis

Context

Coach Jake has gone into teacher Lorna's lesson as part of the school's usual coaching cycle. Coach Jake and teacher Lorna have been working on the clarity of her explanations. In the example, coach Jake enters in the middle of the lesson.

Coaching Excerpt

Coach Jake enters the maths lesson when students are doing some independent practice. The students are working on solving a problem in their books. The problem is also displayed on the board and it says:

Yemi and Toni are cycling around a track at the same speed. Yemi started earlier and so has completed 4 laps by the time Toni has completed 2. How many laps will Toni have completed when Yemi has completed 16?

Get tripped up

Coach Jake spots two students gazing out of the window. They are not talking or causing a disturbance but do not appear to be working out the problem. Coach Jake gets tripped up by this. He thinks this could be suggestive of a problem. He immediately records what he sees.

Record what you see

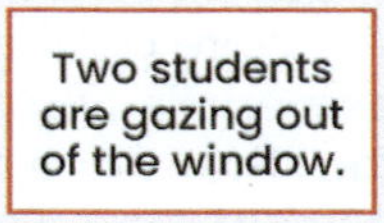

Record what you see

He sees teacher Lorna circulating the room and stopping to give a student some feedback. She doesn't seem to notice the students who are gazing out of the window. Coach Jake records the two events but one is not causing the other so he doesn't draw the cause and effect arrow:

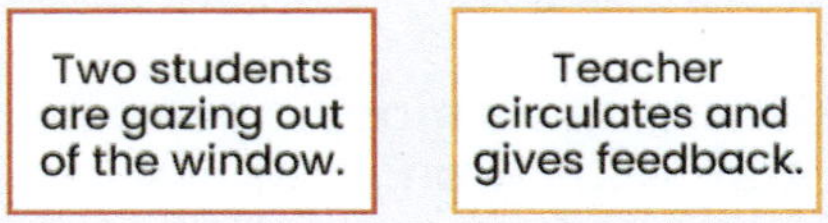

Coach Jake sees the two students continuing to look out of the window. He maps this :

Record what you see

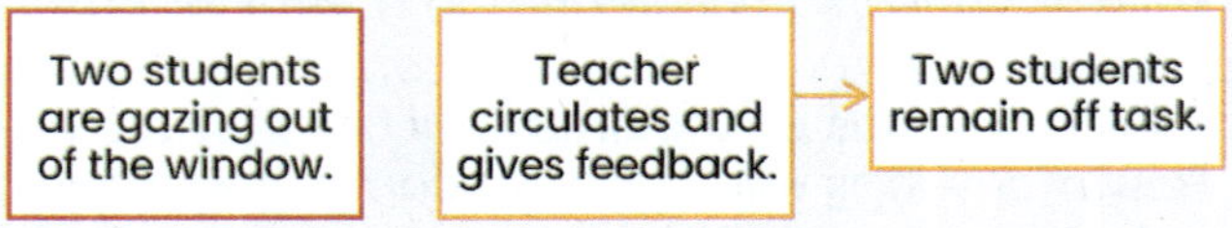

Coach Jake hypothesises that teacher Lorna's focus on the other students has led to the continued off-task behaviour and therefore a problem around attention. He knows he needs to test his hypothesis to check that the issue really is that teacher Lorna has not spotted the off-task behaviour and it has led to a continued lack of attention. And he's glad he did because as he keeps watching he notices that the two students who were gazing out of the window have picked up their pencils and are working. He goes over to see what they have done and they have drawn the following model and solution:

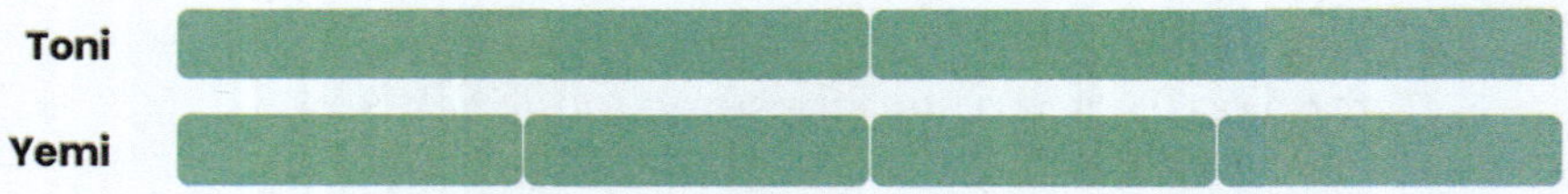

Yemi: 4 + 12 = 16

Toni: 2 + 12 = 14

When Yemi has done 16 laps, Toni will have done 14 because both are cycling at the same speed.

Coach Jake looks at his mapping and thinks that he may have picked the wrong moment to be tripped up because the students have both worked out the problem's solution: they have identified that at the point of Yemi having done 4 laps, Toni has done 2 and they then continue cycling at the same speed, meaning that Yemi will have done his 4 laps plus another 12 and Toni will have done his 2 laps plus another 12. This makes him think perhaps they weren't off task but actually thinking hard about the problem.

Gazing out of the window doesn't appear to have led to a learning problem. It seems they were probably just trying to work out the solution in their heads. So, coach Jake decides to abandon that hypothesis and keep watching the lesson.

Get tripped up

Coach Jake notices teacher Lorna is circulating to a lot of students to support them. There seems to be quite a few misconceptions. This trips coach Jake up again. He starts recording what he sees by mapping it out again:

Record what you see

Lots of misconceptions in student answers.

Coach Jake decides to check the work of a sample of students. He checks 6 students and in all 6 cases, students had initially written:

Yemi: 4 x 4 = 16
Toni: 2 x 4 = 8

When Yemi has done 16 laps, Toni will have done 8 because 4 is double 2 and 16 is double 8.

Record what you see

Following teacher Lorna's feedback, all 6 had then corrected their work and had the correct solution.

Coach Jake maps what he sees:

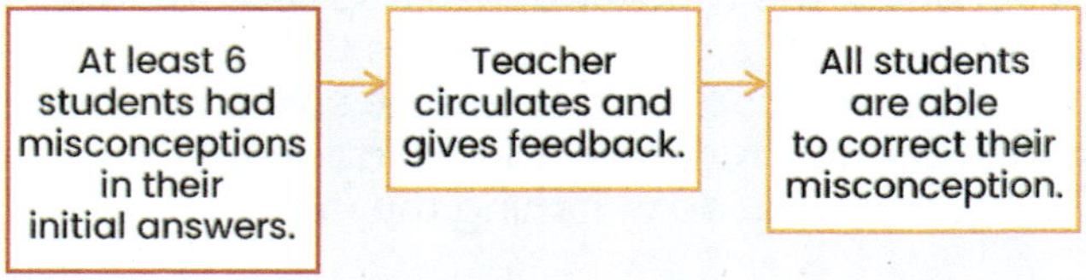

Coach Jake initially hypothesises that this signifies a problem related to 'gathering and giving feedback'. Addressing each student one-by-one appears to be taking a long time and students are sitting with the misconception rather than practising an effective method.

However, coach Jake takes a moment to consider that the problem for him to focus on might be upstream of 'gathering and giving feedback'. It might be with the way teacher Lorna explained the method for working out the problem in the first place - this might be why she's discovering misconceptions she needs to feed back on. It therefore might be a problem with 'optimising communication'.

Coach Jake looks for evidence to test his hypothesis. He looks on the teacher's whiteboard and in students' books and can't see evidence of the teacher providing and explaining a model to students. He thinks this might be why so many students have misconceptions and why the two students he saw appeared so deep in thought trying to work it out without much help. He assumes teacher Lorna did an explanation but didn't show a model (an assumption he can check in their coaching conversation).

He adds the lack of a model before the independent practice to his map:

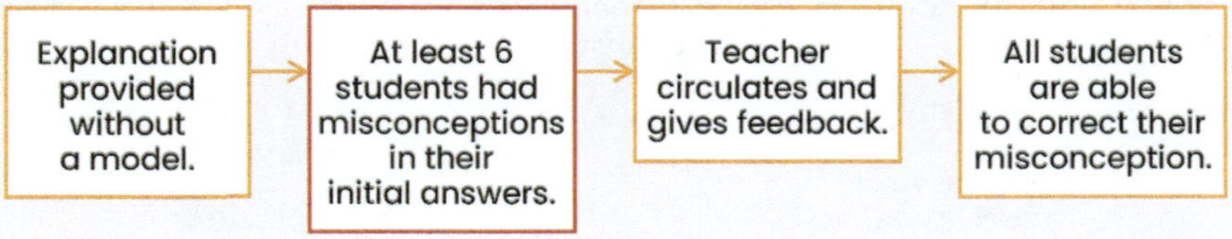

Coach Jake is now in a position to infer the teacher's goal in the situation he has seen. He thinks he can safely infer that it was 'To enable independent practice so that students have the opportunity to apply new learning'. This is why she set them off on the task and is now circulating to support. He maps this too:

Infer intentions: goal

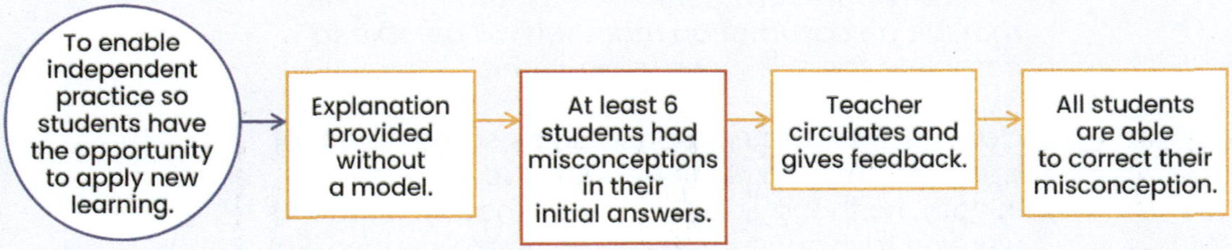

Infer intentions: decision drivers

He then infers teacher Lorna's reasons for her decisions (decision drivers). He thinks she doesn't model because she assumes the class doesn't need it and she corrects misconceptions one-by-one because she doesn't realise the same one is so prevalent until she has supported quite a few students. He maps these decision drivers:

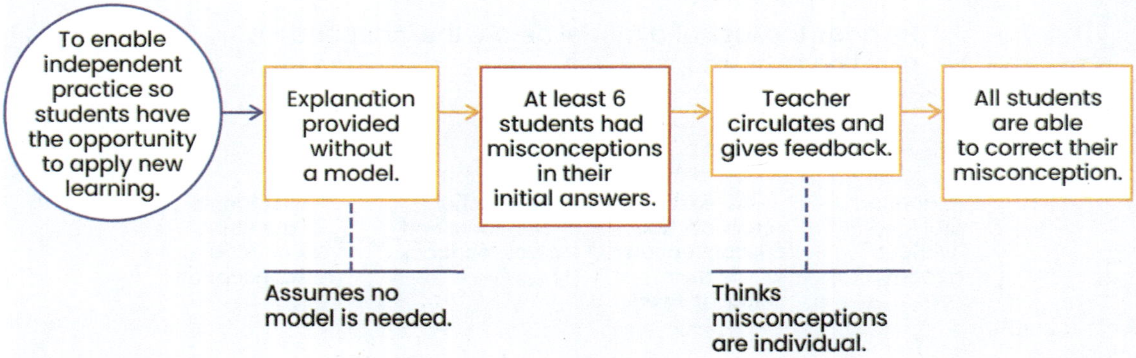

Now coach Jake feels ready to propose the problem.

Propose problem

Learning problem: *many students were not ready for independent practice and practised the wrong method, embedding misconceptions.*

Teaching problem *(causes of the learning problem): this appears to be a problem related to 'optimising communication'. There doesn't seem to be a model communicated to students. There may be an assumption that they will be able to complete the questions without one.*

Coach Jake was first tripped up by something that appeared to be a problem with student attention. Initially, he thought the issue was that two students were off task and teacher Lorna hadn't noticed. But by following the evidence, coach Jake changed his mind. The two seemingly off-task students seemed to actually be deep in thought. Instead, there was a pretty widespread misconception in other students' work that teacher Lorna was trying to tackle for each individual. For a moment he thought this might be a problem to do with gathering and giving feedback but then he thought to check upstream, hypothesising that the issue could lie in how the teacher taught the problem. He noticed that there didn't appear to be any modelling of the process for solving problems of this type. His new hypothesis therefore had some weight. This experience reminds him that sometimes the cause of a problem he sees when he observes is actually something that happened before he entered the room.

Coach Jake is now ready to map a solution mental model. He does this by asking himself, '*What mental model would the teacher need to adopt to better support student learning in a similar situation?*'

State a solution: solution mental model

Coach Jake thinks the original goal he inferred is a good one but if teacher Lorna shows a model she can expect more from students, so the goal should not just be that students can apply their learning, but also that they avoid common misconceptions. Coach Jake maps this:

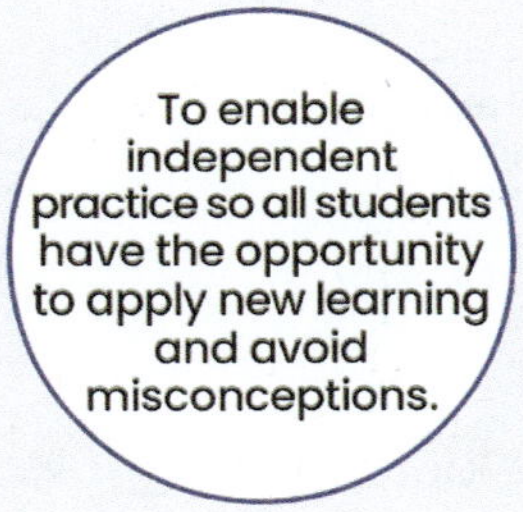

Then, coach Jake maps on the actions and events linked by cause and effect. He thinks teacher Lorna should model how to solve a similar problem, narrating her thought process. She should tackle the common misconception students had head on during her modelling by also modelling a non-example too and then reinforcing the correct process again:

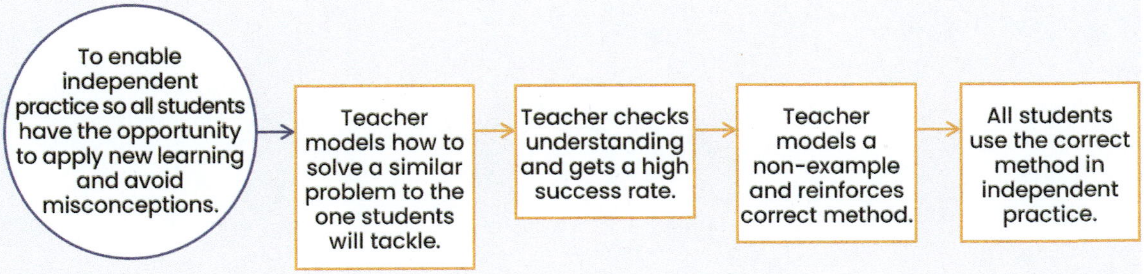

Coach Jake also maps on the decision drivers he wants Lorna to have so she is doing things for the right reasons. He finishes by adding these:

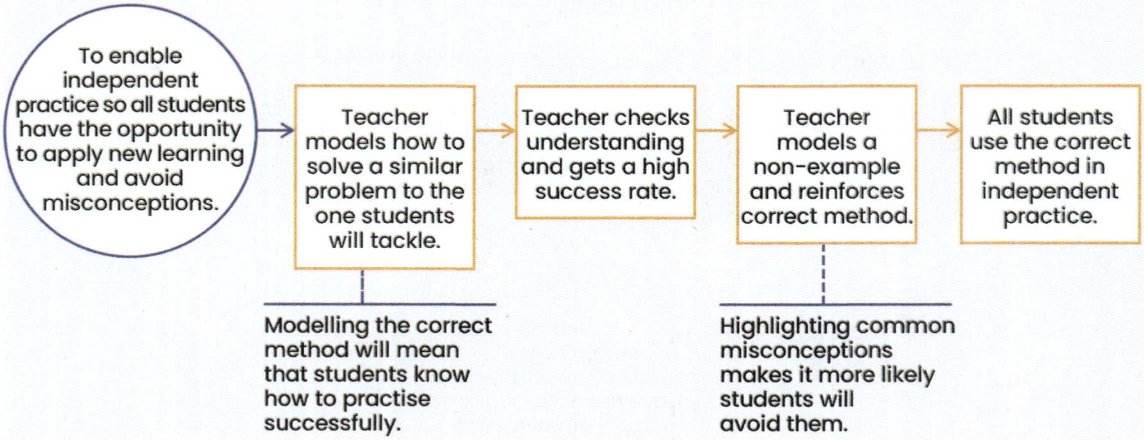

He then plans the action step, making sure it states when, what and why:

When preparing students for independent practice, provide a model and a non-example so that students can follow the correct process and avoid common misconceptions.

State a solution: action step

Coaching commentary

This is where we get meta and analyse the quality of the coaching in the examples above.

Below we explain how the coaches' use of the GRIPS process will support their teachers to understand, do, decide, and improve, i.e., to develop their adaptive expertise.

Understand

...key knowledge that helps solve persistent problems.

Do

...a repertoire of effective, efficient teaching techniques.

Decide

...on the best course of action using situation-sensitive mental models.

Improve

...continuously through an adaptive mindset and metacognition.

Understand

Developing your teacher's understanding of how learning best occurs in their context is critical if they are to develop their adaptive expertise. Coaches need to have an eye to this even as they prepare for coaching. By following the GRIPS process, your diagnosis will be fully accountable to learning and you will show your working (how you got to your diagnosis) by explaining the effects of actions on student learning. This is so you can help to develop your teacher's understanding of how learning occurs and how their teaching affects it.

First off, the coach **gets tripped up**. This means something in the lesson jars with their mental model of how learning happens. This is why it's so important that coach mental models of how learning works are evidence-informed and well-organised (we think around persistent problems). You won't **get tripped up** by the most important things without a really good understanding of how learning happens.

Getting tripped up is a sign to pay attention. It tunes you into a particular situation you may decide to coach on and begins the process of zooming in on a teacher's actions and thinking. Coach Nimrat **gets tripped up** on teacher Percy's countdown. But it's possible to **get tripped up** by the wrong thing: something rooted in personal preference or something that doesn't lead to a learning problem. This is why the coach must immediately then **record what they see**, following the evidence and testing their hypothesis to work out the effect on student learning. It's possible this will lead the coach to change what trips them up based on the evidence, which is what happened when coach Jake saw evidence to suggest two students he thought were off task in fact were probably deep in thought and actually the problem is manifesting elsewhere.

Propose the problem (the penultimate stage of GRIPS) ensures the coach states the learning problem tentatively and proposes the problem that may have caused it. For example, coach Nimrat writes:

> Learning problem: not all students paid attention and learning time was wasted trying to get it. Some students did not then attend to the teacher's explanation and so cannot have learned from it.
>
> Teaching problem (causes of the learning problem): this appears to be a problem related to 'ensuring attention.' The very brief countdown and individual reminders did not seem to hold students accountable for paying attention. The teacher seemed to lack confidence that the routine would work and appeared to be in a hurry to move on.

Ensuring you do this keeps your thinking accountable to student learning and supports you to develop this understanding in your teacher.

Do

Preparing for coaching involves diagnosing what a potential issue might be with the teacher's current actions (based on the impact on student learning) and then what a potential solution could be too in the GRIPS stage **state a solution**. Preparing to develop the teacher's repertoire of efficient teaching techniques therefore means identifying a technique the teacher could have used to better serve student learning. This is where the solution mental model and action step come in.

Coach Nimrat plans for what she *thinks* the solution mental model is for teacher Percy in this situation and decides on the action step. This helps her know exactly where she *might* take the coaching session. In this instance the action she will coach on is likely to be a countdown that is broken down with instructions in between the numbers as well as scanning and narrating the positive. So, preparing for coaching through diagnosing need also involves preparing the action to coach on and holding this lightly.

Decide

We need to prepare not just for how to support the teacher to change their actions but also how to develop their *decision-making* by altering their mental model. This is why it's important for the coach to infer the teacher's goal and decision drivers. This is what we're preparing to do in the **infer intentions** stage of GRIPS. Inferring the teacher's situation goal and the decision drivers for their actions gives us a starting point from which to test our assumptions by surfacing their actual mental model and, if we are right, we know their starting point to develop from there. Because the reasons for decisions are often subconscious, preparing for coaching by mapping what we infer the teacher's decisions to be supports us during the conversation to analyse their decision-making together.[6] Look how coach Nimrat has done this in this situation mental model:

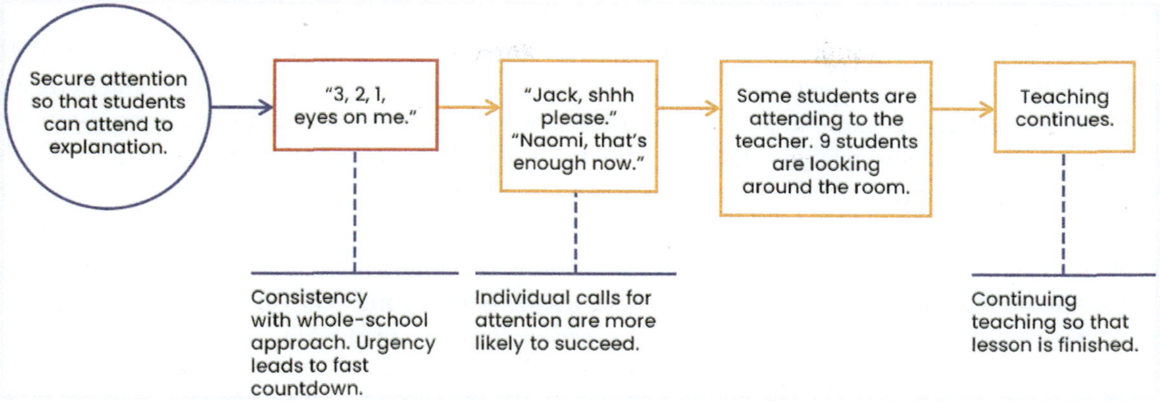

Coach Jake ends up altering his situation mental model based on the evidence he sees. He infers that teacher Lorna is assuming too much knowledge on the part of her students. He's aware he does not know her decision drivers for certain and will have to surface her mental model to find out. This will help him to develop her mental model from where she currently is.

In the final stage of GRIPS, **state a solution**, coaches propose a solution mental model which involves how the teacher's actions *and decision-making* would need to change to better support student learning. This is crucial preparation to help the coach support the teacher to develop a better mental model. A situation mental model is where (the coach thinks) the teacher is and a solution mental model is where their decision-making may need to be.

For example, coach Nimrat alters the goal, actions, and decision drivers like so:

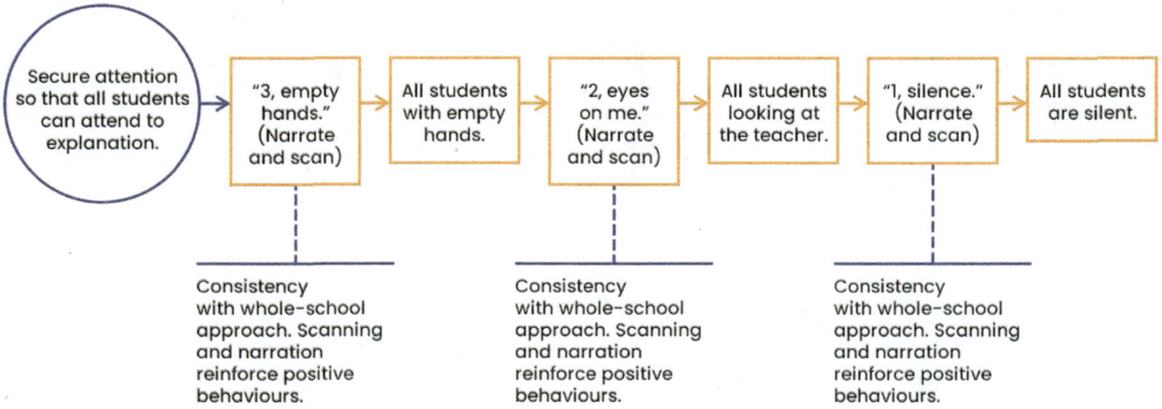

Improve

Supporting your teacher to understand how to improve themselves is a meta aim of coaching, since you are only rarely there to help! The GRIPS process is you modelling how they need to think in order to identify an issue in their practice. The way you spot potential issues (by **getting**

tripped up) and follow the evidence to test your hypothesis (**record what you see**) is how you want your teacher to diagnose problems in their own practice: they should notice something that trips them up, hold their hunch lightly, test their hypothesis by following the evidence and ensure their thinking is accountable to student learning (and not teaching fads or personal preference). You can imagine coach Jake explaining to teacher Lorna how he got tripped up initially by students looking out of the window but then when he followed the evidence, he saw that the impact on student learning appeared to be the misconceptions other students had; this led him to infer that there was an issue with a lack of modelling. This communicates to teacher Lorna that she too should follow the evidence of the effect on student learning and avoid jumping to conclusions. In future chapters, we show how coaches can expose their meta-thinking to model this to their teachers.

Do this in your coaching preparation

Of course, there are always times when one or more of the stages of the GRIPS framework are difficult to apply to the process of preparing for coaching. Happily, the framework is adaptive and so you can still use it when the situation demands a slightly different approach.

Get tripped up

How it often happens . . .

Getting tripped up happens when you see something that jars with your mental model of how learning happens. You might find yourself thinking things like:

> *Ah, that looks like an issue that might lead to a problem . . .*
>
> *This looks like it isn't going as the teacher would have wanted it to . . .*
>
> *Something feels like it's not quite right there . . .*

Sometimes you will be tripped up by an action a teacher takes (doing a countdown too quickly) and other times by the effects of those actions (students being off task following an explanation). Getting tripped up is your cue to record the specific actions and events linked by cause and effect arrows where appropriate.

But, sometimes it's more complex . . .

Sometimes, something trips you up that turns out *not* to lead to a learning problem. Holding your hypothesis lightly is the sign of a great coach (a coach with adaptive expertise in fact!). When this happens, don't hesitate to discard or change your current hypothesis in light of the evidence. Re-map when you get tripped up a second time.

On the flip side, sometimes you might see a learning problem at play but you can't work out the issues that caused it. This happens because teaching is complex and cause and effect are not always easy to infer. If this occurs, record what you see as specifically as you can and be ready to work out possible causes with the teacher during the coaching conversation.

Record what you see

How it often happens . . .

You can't record everything in a lesson in the detail you need for coaching. Getting tripped up is the trigger for recording in detail what you see. Often, what you need to record will be contained to the situation you are observing and any events that happen after. For example, you watch a teacher's explanation, get tripped up and record cause and effect from there. This is a neatly contained map where you don't feel you need to have seen actions/events from earlier in the lesson.

But, sometimes it's more complex . . .

Sometimes you will get tripped up, record what you see and realise that some of the causes of the problem are likely to have happened before you went into the lesson. In which case, you'll need to infer these actions/events too by looking at students' work from earlier in the lesson or if you have it, the teacher's lesson plan/resources. This means you'll want to ask your teacher questions about what happened before you came into the room (or in their planning or previous lessons) as part of surfacing their mental model during the coaching conversation.

Sometimes, there will be so much going on that the coach can't capture all the actions and events as specifically as they want to. Do your best. If you need to just scribble down what you see and organise it into the map when the lesson is over, do this. The best way to get mapping off the ground is to commit the components (goal, actions/events, cause and effect, and decision drivers) and their corresponding shapes to memory so recalling these imposes almost no cognitive load when you are observing.

Infer intentions

How it often happens . . .

Sometimes, a teacher's goal in a situation and their decision drivers for their actions are reasonably clear. For example, when a teacher is doing a countdown in the middle of a lesson, their goal is likely to be to secure the attention of the class so that they can move on to the next part of the lesson and a teacher doing a countdown at the end of the lesson may be securing attention to set up their exit routine. Make sure you are mapping the teacher's goal in that situation and not the learning goal they have for the students (although the two may be similar sometimes). For example, when a teacher is explaining something to their class, you would phrase their goal as, 'Students to pay attention and grasp the meaning of the word "persuade." You wouldn't phrase their goal as, 'Students to be able to write persuasively using a variety of techniques' (as might be the lesson learning goal) because this isn't the teacher's goal *in that situation*.

The actions they take may be driven by reasonably easy-to-infer drivers: they do a countdown because it is their consistent cue for attention; they don't scan the class to check for compliance because they aren't in the habit of doing so (which appears to lead to a problem around ensuring attention).

But, sometimes it's more complex . . .

Sometimes the teacher's goal and decision drivers are not obvious. In this case, it is important to remember that the goal of coaching is not for you to be *right*. Once we remember this, then there really is no problem with proposing what you think is a plausible goal and what are plausible decision drivers and holding these lightly (they are inferences after all). In fact, it can open up a really interesting dialogue about where those inferences came from and can help the teacher to reflect on the extent to which their actions really did serve their goal and how their decision drivers contributed to this.

Propose the problem

How it often happens . . .

When you have mapped the teacher's situation mental model, you are ready to propose the problem you think is at play. When proposing a problem, think of it in two parts:

1. **Learning problem:** describe the problem in relation to student learning.

   For example, students didn't seem to grasp the teacher's explanation of covalent bonding – no student accurately stated the definition to their partner.

2. **Teaching problem:** a) relate this to the most fundamental of Goodrich's teaching problems and b) specifically state the actions and decision-making that may have caused the learning problem.

   For example, this appears to be a problem with optimising communication. The teacher's explanation was quick (took under 2 minutes) and not accompanied by any diagrams or words to prevent it being transient. I've inferred that the teacher did this because they decided students would easily grasp the explanation because students appear to be familiar with some of the key terms like 'electrons,' 'outer shell,' etc.

But, sometimes it's more complex . . .

Sometimes, there might not be an obvious learning problem. Perhaps you've formed some hunches but your hypotheses are not substantiated by much evidence about learning. This could be because you suspect something the teacher has done may impact learning in the future but you don't have evidence of it there and then. For example, a teacher may not pick up on a misconception students have, but this doesn't impact the current lesson. In this instance, it's fine to map what you think the effect might be in future lessons and propose the problem you think may occur. You'll hold this especially lightly, but it's a plausible hypothesis rooted in how learning happens.

If you cannot find any problems, it's fine to ask the teacher to share one with you that they are experiencing but you weren't there to witness. As long as the problem is one that shows their understanding of how learning happens, it makes sense to go with this. For example, the teacher might say they find students are often unfocused during independent work (this feels like a worthy problem to dig into).

State the solution

How it often happens . . .

When you are clear on the problems you have observed, move to proposing a potential solution mental model - how the teacher might decide and act differently in future to solve the problem. This may be a small tweak or a larger change. It may involve changing what they do and the decision drivers behind their actions or it may also involve supporting them to adopt a more powerful goal for the situation. As well as a solution mental model, draft a potential action step as this prepares you with a suggestion if coaching goes the way you predict.

But, sometimes it's more complex . . .

Sometimes you will find you cannot think of a potential solution. This happens more often when coaching a more experienced teacher or when you are coaching outside of your specialism. Remember, it is your role to select a situation where there appears to be a problem. It is not your role to have all the answers. Sharing your working out and problem solving together is, in this circumstance, the honest and credible way to coach.

Notes

1 Eraut, M. (2000) 'Non-formal learning and tacit knowledge in professional work', *British Journal of Educational Psychology*, 70(1), pp. 113-136.

2 Goodrich, J. (2024) *Responsive coaching: Evidence-informed instructional coaching that works for every teacher in your school*. London: John Catt.

3 This is obviously less of a concern when using video.

4 Parrish, S. (2023) *Clear thinking: Turning ordinary moments into extraordinary results*. London: Penguin.

5 Parrish, S. (2023) *Clear thinking: Turning ordinary moments into extraordinary results*. London: Penguin.

6 Dreyfus, H. and Dreyfus, S.E. (1986) *Mind over machine*. London: Simon and Schuster.

Stage 0

Prepare for coaching by planning a model

Once you've prepared for coaching by tentatively diagnosing the problem and stating a solution as we've shown you in the previous chapter, there's one more key thing you can do to prepare: plan a model of better.

Modelling increases the chances of the teacher improving in the future as it helps teachers develop a mental image of the focal teaching practice, which supports them to put theory into practice.[1] The best models have been carefully thought out and exemplify the success criteria[2] of the technique as clearly as possible. The success criteria are the key things to do to make the action step work effectively. They contain important information about what to do, when to do it and why to do it. For example:

Action step	**Success criteria**
When you want to probe understanding, cold call students to hold everyone accountable for thinking hard.	• **Question then name**: pose the question and then name the student so all students engage in thinking. • **Pause before you name**: leave an appropriate pause after posing the question and before naming the student so all students have thinking time. • **Scan deliberately**: during the pause, scan the room deliberately to communicate an expectation that all are thinking. • **Step away**: as you name the student to answer, step away from that student so other students know the response is to everyone and the answerer has to speak up.

DOI: 10.4324/9781003465850-9

In this chapter, you will see how to plan two different types of models: performance models and planning models.

- **Performance models:** necessary when modelling action steps that involve in-lesson teaching techniques, e.g., action steps about delivering explanations, questions, responding to students' answers, managing behaviour, etc.
- **Planning models**: necessary when modelling action steps that involve developing a thought process when planning, e.g., action steps about planning lesson-learning goals, retrieval questions, hinge questions, planning to increase challenge, etc.

Let's look in more detail at what makes them different.

In a performance model, the coach stands up and takes on the role of the teacher in the lesson, even though no students are present. They also keep their delivery as close as possible to the authentic delivery they want the teacher to aim for. For example, this could mean pausing for a full five seconds if this is what they are wanting the teacher to do during the rehearsal and in the real lesson environment.

In a planning model, the coach is seated and verbalises their thought process as they plan so that the teacher can grasp it. The coach uses real materials and a real upcoming lesson to model the planning so that it is as realistic as possible.

But, we have said throughout this book that it is important for coaches to hold their ideas lightly and we have deliberately used the word 'thinks' instead of 'knows' to describe the coach's work in preparing for coaching. Why then is it so important to plan a model in advance? Does this not risk wasted preparation?

Just as teachers prepare for the most likely course of events when teaching their students, coaches should do the same. In most cases, the coach's wider lens of awareness will enable them to identify an important problem worth coaching on. It's likely then that they will end up coaching on the problem they diagnosed. But even if the coaching conversation changes their mind, having a clear initial plan enables the coach to evaluate the merits of an alternative route to improvement. Plus, the model will no doubt come in handy at another point in time.

Purposes

This is what we want coaches to feel and know after this stage.

Know what to show: 'I have a clear plan of what to model.'

We need to ensure that we are really clear on what the model will look like so that it can be delivered cleanly during coaching. This involves knowing the technique well and the upcoming situation in which you will model it so you are not having to think on the spot.

Know what to stress: 'I know that my model focuses the teacher's attention on the success criteria.'

We need to be sure that the success criteria are not just included but are *unmissable*. This can mean stripping back extraneous detail so that there are no distractions from what counts – keeping the model *clean*. It also means thinking about the teacher in front of you: which success criteria do they really need to focus on in the model? This might be because it's something subtle or because it's a success criterion they're likely to struggle with.

Pitfalls

Pitfalls are typical ways we can undermine this coaching stage. We need to know them so we can avoid them.

Messy models: we know that everyone sees situations differently through their own unique mental models. It's likely then that the teacher won't naturally 'see' all the success criteria at play in your model. To make sure they do, coaches need to precisely exemplify the success criteria. Messy models clutter things for the teacher so they can't focus on how to put the success criteria into practice. An example of a messy model would be a coach modelling how to plan a retrieval task by emphasising elements that aren't in the success criteria such as how to word specific questions – this detracts from the key ingredients we want the teacher to see and therefore the thought process we want them to develop. Instead, stay tight to the success criteria and emphasise them throughout.

Over-modelling: teachers need to be able to focus on the success criteria of the model and they have limited cognitive resources with which to do this. Therefore, model only the practice that you want the teacher to focus on. Avoid adding extra bits to your model. For example, if you are modelling an explanation, go straight in with that, don't model how you would get the class's attention first. Likewise, stop the model at the end of the explanation. Don't go on to show how you would then check for understanding following your explanation. Over-modelling can quickly cloud the focus.

Clean but not close: part of the rationale for modelling and rehearsing techniques during coaching is that it happens in a 'quiet' environment where the teacher can focus on the technique without distractions. In this sense, the model is usually stripped back and in some senses unrealistic (e.g. we might model it in full then in parts). We describe this as making the model *clean*. This is beneficial as long as the model is in many ways realistic. We describe this as *close*, i.e., close to reality. For performance action steps (which you'll recall are about the teacher's practice in the lesson), if a coach just talks through what they would do instead of showing the teacher how to do it, the model is unlikely to be useful: the model isn't *close* enough to reality. So, when modelling a performance action step, make sure you stand up and model as if students are in front of you. This keeps the model close to reality and helps the teacher begin to imagine themselves in the situation.

Keeping it close to reality in this way may be particularly important when modelling in a different subject or phase to the teacher. For example, if you are an English teacher and you're modelling to a geography teacher, you may struggle to do so in their subject and so stick to yours. This can work just fine for many techniques (and may even be less distracting sometimes) but it does mean you need to ensure everything else is as close to reality as possible. If the model is outside of their subject or phase and doesn't look like real teaching, it won't be close enough to be useful.

Subtle success criteria: not knowing the success criteria means teachers could invest time and energy watching and thinking about details of your model that aren't important. Success criteria mustn't be subtle; they must be unmissable. Stamp your success criteria onto your model by first planning what you want the success criteria to be, then planning the model to exemplify those success criteria and finally, planning which specific success criteria to ask your teacher about. After that, practise your model so that you can be certain that you are exemplifying the success criteria.

Unaccountable thinking: teachers don't just need to know how to do a model but also why they should do it. It's easy for coaches to accidentally give the impression that the teacher must adopt their model wholesale, but this is rarely what we want, and we certainly wouldn't want them to do it blindly. In fact, this would go against the development of the teacher's adaptive expertise because they wouldn't be developing a mental model of how to use the technique flexibly depending on context. It would also give the false impression that to improve, the teacher should just do what the coach shows them exactly as it's shown. We know that improving in a complex system requires much more than this.

This is why it's important for the coach to plan not just what they will model but also how they will explain (or ask the teacher to explain) why each success criterion of the step is important for supporting student learning. This extends to the coach being able to explain why a success criterion requires precision (should be done in a certain way) or a decision (a choice based upon particular factors).

Coaching techniques

Use these coaching techniques to help you **plan a model**.

Some techniques are foundational, i.e., we should always use them, and some are flexible, i.e., we should use them when appropriate, depending on the level of the teacher's expertise in the moment.

Foundational or flexible	Technique	What it is	Examples	Non examples
Foundational	Clean but close 	Although you won't have students present, plan for your model to be as close to the real act of teaching as possible. If modelling a planning action step, make it about real materials and upcoming lessons rather than a hypothetical situation.	"I need to make sure that I am stood up for the model, and I also need to make sure that we have a room that is big enough for me to step back noticeably because that's something I really need the teacher to see in my model."	**Clean but not close:** "I'm pretty sure the teacher will get it without me actually standing up as if I'm teaching. We'll probably both be more comfortable from a seated position anyway." **Over-modelling:** "I won't just plan to model the action step. I'll model what happens after too to make it more realistic."
Foundational	Plan success criteria 	Plan the success criteria that you want the teacher to pay attention to during the model. These should be the components of the action step that are likely to make it effective for supporting student learning.	"When scripting an explanation, teachers need to: 1. Be concise 2. Link to prior knowledge 3. Plan concrete examples"	**Messy models:** "When scripting an explanation, teachers need to be clear on what to say."
Foundational	Precision and decision 	Be clear on which success criteria need to be adhered to (precision) and which can be contextualised and adapted (requiring a decision) – crucially, model how to make the decisions around these success criteria.	"For self-interrupt, (where a teacher is interrupted by a student and the teacher stops teaching mid-sentence), the success criteria: 'return to the beginning of your sentence when resuming teaching' is precise because if teaching continued from the middle of their sentence, students might not recall the first part." "For the same technique, the length of the pause between the self-interrupt and the resumption of teaching requires a decision because it depends on when the student stops the interruption and the teacher has sent a clear signal."	**Unaccountable thinking:** "I'll explain to my teacher that I like to see at least a 2 second pause."

Foundational or flexible	Technique	What it is	Examples	Non examples
Foundational	Link to learning 	Be prepared to explain why each success criteria is important for supporting student learning so you support your teacher to understand their purpose.	"When using self-interrupt, it is really important to go back to the start of the sentence after you interrupt yourself because if you were to continue from mid-sentence, following the pause, students are likely to have forgotten what you said, impacting their understanding."	**Unaccountable thinking:** "I'll just tell my teacher that each of these success criteria must be done if the action step is to work."
Foundational	Spotlight specifics 	Make sure that you plan which success criteria to ask the teacher about after the model, depending on their current practice or what they are likely to find hard about the action step.	"What did you notice me doing right after I asked the question?" "Which success criteria did I exemplify when I thought through how to structure the questions?"	**Messy models:** "I haven't got any success criteria as such, so I'll just ask my teacher what they liked about the model."
Flexible	Narrate your thought process 	For planning action steps (and therefore models), plan how you will think aloud to use each success criteria and achieve the action step.	Success criteria: 1. Clear answer format. 2. Concise question. I'll plan to say to my teacher: "I want to plan a question with **an answer format that is going to be fairly short. (success criteria 1)**. I need it to be a short answer format because I want to check the answer of every student in the lesson and I won't be able to do that with a longer answer format..."	**Subtle success criteria:** "I'll show my teacher this multiple-choice question I've planned, which is generally a good example."

Example 1 Foundational techniques: a performance model

Let's see an example of a coach using the foundational techniques for this stage to plan a performance model.

Context

Coach Annie has been to watch teacher Dan. They have previously worked on 'driving thought'[3] to ensure students have to think hard by phrasing questions carefully. In the lesson she watched, coach Annie was 'tripped up' by teacher Dan asking questions just after his explanation. He took hands up for the answer. This tripped her up because she felt it would allow students who did not want to answer to avoid participating.

Coach Annie mapped this situation model when preparing for coaching:

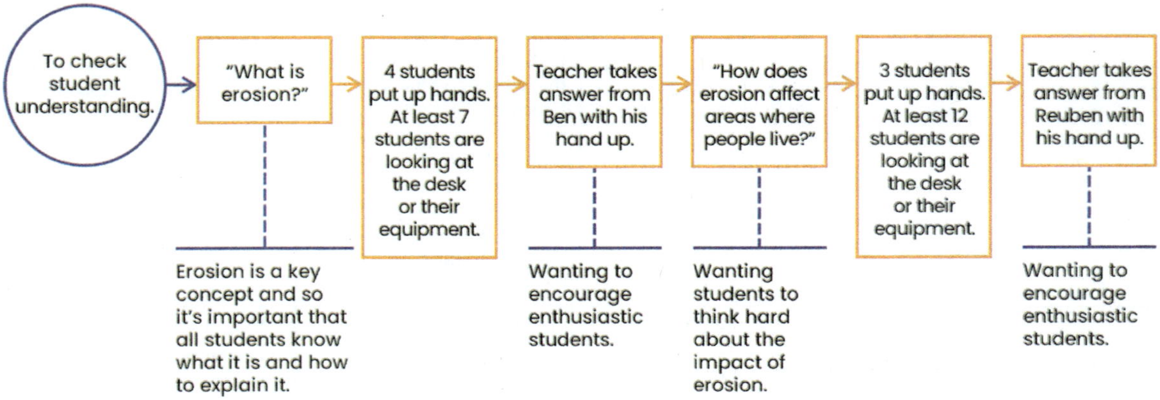

She proposed this problem:

> Learning problem: not all students are accountable for thinking and therefore are less likely to be improving their understanding.
>
> Teaching problem (causes of the learning problem): this appears to be a problem with 'driving thought' as not all students are thinking because the teacher is only taking answers from students with their hands up.

Coach Annie planned the following solution mental model and action step:

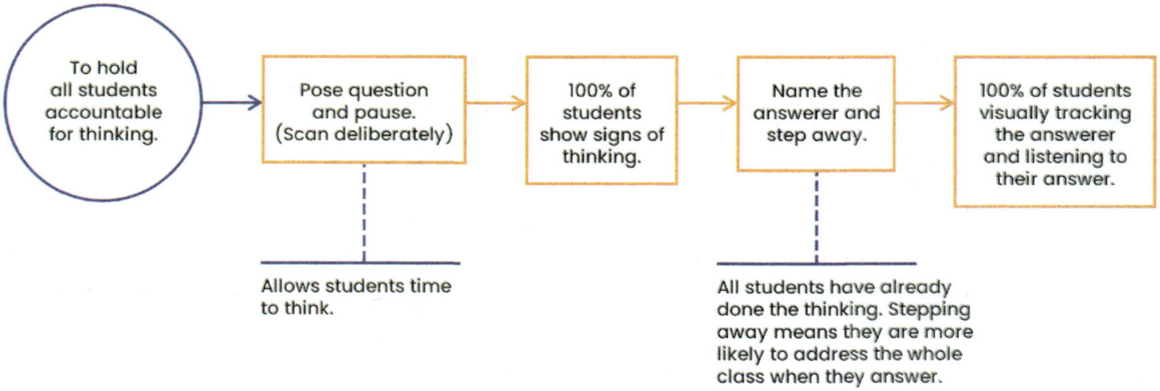

> Action step: *When you want to probe understanding, cold call students to hold everyone accountable for thinking hard.*

Watch how coach Annie uses the foundational techniques for this stage: clean but close, plan success criteria, precision and decision, link to learning, and spotlight specifics.

Coaching Excerpt

Coach Annie: *[thinking as she plans her model for Dan]* So, what do I want to emphasise when I do my model of cold calling for Dan? I'll need to be stood up for sure and look out across the room as if the students were there. I'll also need to make it clean by just focusing on the technique of cold calling and not how to deal with any losses of attention that may or may not occur. To start with, the model needs to be really clean so that teacher Dan knows exactly what to do.

Clean but close: while there won't be any students during the model, coach makes it as close to reality as possible but keeps it clean by just focusing on the technique

I need to plan the success criteria for the cold call action step so I know how exactly to exemplify the step and what to emphasise in my model:

Plan success criteria: coach makes sure they are really clear on what needs to be emphasised in the model

- **Question then name:** pose the question and then name the student so all students engage in thinking.
- **Pause before you name:** leave an appropriate pause after posing the question and before naming the student so all students have thinking time.
- **Scan deliberately:** during the pause, scan the room deliberately to communicate an expectation that all are thinking.
- **Step away:** as you name the student to answer, step away from that student so other students know the response is to everyone and the answerer has to speak up.

Before I actually get down to modelling the actions, I need to make sure that teacher Dan knows exactly what the success criteria are and which require precision (he needs to stick closely to them) and which require decisions (there's flexibility and choices to be made). I need to exemplify the importance of saying the question then name in all cases, i.e., this is a precision success criterion. Pause before you name isn't

Precision and decision: the coach is clear on which aspects of the practice require precision and which are more flexible and require decisions the same every time. It requires a decision because what the appropriate pause is depends upon how hard the question is for the class. I'll model my thought process for deciding on this.

'Scan deliberately' is a precision success criterion because it will always need to be done. I also want to make sure that teacher Dan knows that he has to step away as he names the student to answer. That's a precision one too. If he doesn't do that, it could become a one-to-one dialogue and others will tune out.

Link to learning: the coach makes sure she is clear on how each success criteria is important for ensuring the action step supports student learning

Let's just make sure I'm clear on how I'm going to explain the importance of those success criteria, i.e., how they link to learning. 'Question then name' means that everyone is more likely to be thinking because they don't know who will be called to answer - it drives thought.. If we put the name first, then it's more likely only the named person will be thinking hard. I need to pause before I name for an appropriate length of time to actually give students a chance to do their best thinking. Without this time, hard thinking can't happen.

'Scan deliberately' is that accountability piece: students need to know the teacher expects them to be thinking hard. The teacher needs to consider their students' prior knowledge when deciding this. If I don't step away, students might think that the person answering is just responding to me rather than contributing to the whole class discussion and that might make them less likely to listen to, and think about, the response. OK, now I'm clear on how the success criteria link to learning, so I can check teacher Dan is too and then fill in any gaps in knowledge that he has.

Now I can script my model of cold calling:
'OK, the next lesson I'm teaching is with year 9 tomorrow morning. I'll want to ask: What is the name of the process that turns liquids into gases? I'll ask Rubena because she is usually someone whose answers are indicative of how much the class remember. It's a question that she should know

the answer to because we've returned to it a few times now so I think I'll pause for just three seconds and scan deliberately. Then, when I say her name, I'll step away from her so that the rest of the class know that her answer is for all of them to listen to, not just for me to listen to and Rubena will have to throw her voice.

Putting all of that together, my model will go like this: "What is the name of the process that turns liquids into gases… *[pauses for 3 seconds and scans deliberately]* Rubena?" *[Steps away]*

Once I've modelled, I'll make sure teacher Dan knows what I did that made the strategy effective. I'll do this by asking him what he noticed with reference to the success criteria. That will give me a clear idea of what his mental model of the technique is.

I'll ask him: "What do you think the effect of 'question then name' is on student learning?" I'll specifically ask him this because that's one success criteria that really stands out as different to what I have seen teacher Dan do before. I'll then ask him: "What did you notice about how I 'stepped away'?" and "What impact is that designed to have on learning?" This is an important question to ask because that step away is something he may miss in the model or not fully understand the purpose of – I often find this happens with this success criterion.

Spotlight specifics: coach plans questions that direct the teacher's attention to specific success criteria the teacher is not currently doing, may miss or may not understand

Example 2 Flexible techniques – a planning model

Let's see an example of a coach using the flexible technique for this stage to plan a planning model.

Context

Coach Denise is preparing to coach teacher Aaron. They have recently been working on 'optimising communication'[4] when explaining key concepts in lessons. In the lesson coach Denise watched, she was 'tripped up' by teacher Aaron's explanation. He explained how to add two fractions together in a way that was very wordy and confused coach Denise as she watched. It also didn't seem to link to prior knowledge. This tripped her up because she thought it would lead to a lack of student understanding.

As she watched the lesson unfold, coach Denise noticed that at least 14 students were unable to answer a question that Aaron had set following the explanation. Coach Denise thinks that they should focus on planning his explanations.

Coach Denise mapped this situation mental model from the part of the lesson she observed:

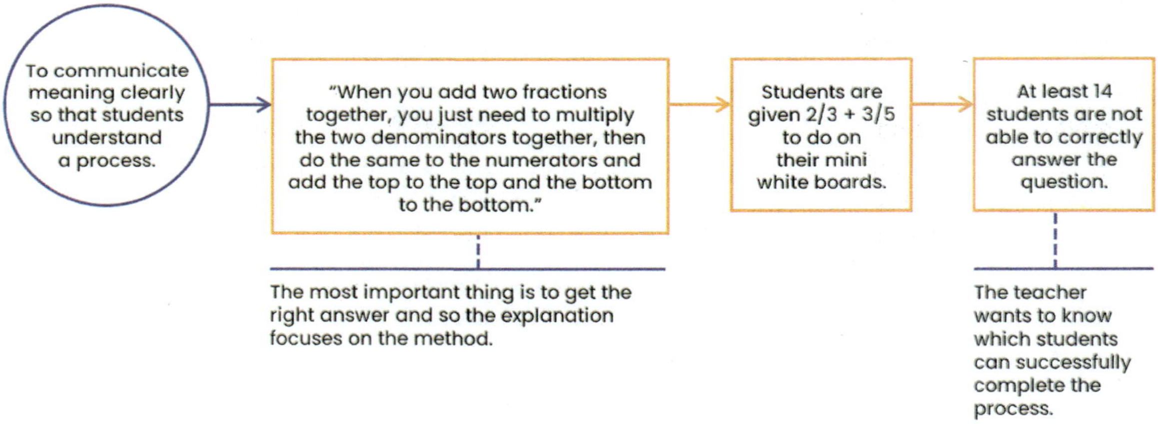

Coach Denise proposes the following problem:

> Learning problem: not all students had understood the concept well enough to answer a similar question.
>
> Teaching problem (causes of the learning problem): this appears to be a problem related to 'optimising communication' as the explanation focused on completing a process that would lead to the correct answer but it was not presented as related to the concept at all. This meant that students did not develop an understanding of the concept or an ability to apply this understanding to solve problems.

Coach Denise has also come up with the following solution mental model and action step:

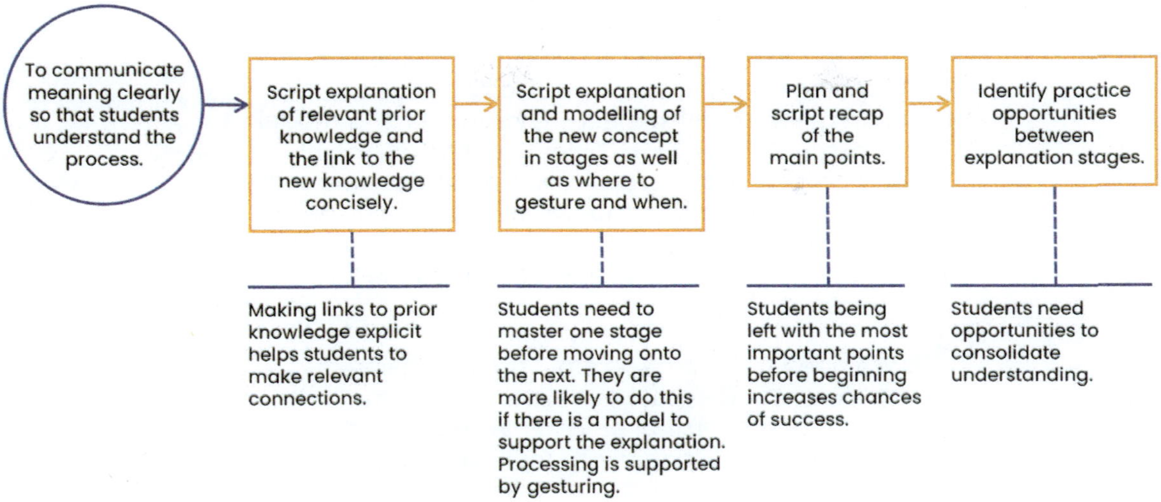

Action step: When explaining the application of a concept, plan well-structured and clear explanations to ensure student understanding is robust.

Watch how coach Denise uses the flexible technique for this stage: narrate your thought process.

Coaching Excerpt

Coach Denise: I want teacher Aaron to really be able to focus on the process of thinking about planning an explanation and so I'll model an example from my subject - English. If I try to model an example from his subject (maths), we might end up getting hung up on some details related to the subject itself and that will take the focus away from the success criteria. Plus, I'll struggle with a model outside of my subject, and it will likely be messy.

Clean: coach wants teacher to be able to focus on the success criteria so they plan a model within their own subject

I will need to make sure that I am modelling my full thought process though. I won't assume that anything is implicit or obvious because when I plan my explanations, I am really thorough and I need teacher Aaron to see the whole process I go through. Because I am planning a model from within my own subject area, I'll be able to make it as close to my reality as possible.

Close: coach wants the model to be as close to reality as possible

OK, within my model of planning an explanation, I want to draw teacher Aaron's attention to these success criteria:

- **Lean language:** keep explanations to the point and use language that will be accessible to students when learning a new concept so they can process it more effectively.
- **Link to prior knowledge:** explicitly explain how the concept links to one the students already know well so they can connect it to existing knowledge.
- **Concrete example:** give an example that the students will know so they have something familiar to anchor their understanding in.
- **Recap:** after explaining, recap the main points to increase the likelihood that students understand.
- **Gesture:** point to the different parts of the model during the recap to direct student attention.

Plan success criteria: coach pre-plans the success criteria they want to explain to teacher

When I introduce the success criteria to teacher Aaron, I'll also explain why these are so important for learning. Planning to use lean language is important because it enables students to focus clearly on the main points in the explanation

Link to learning: coach knows why each success criterion is important for learning so they can ask about or explain this and not have to work out what the important parts are. By planning to explicitly link to prior knowledge, students are more likely to understand the new concept being taught because they relate it to something that they already know, making it easier to remember. Planning to explain using a concrete example is important because it allows students to see how the abstract concept is applied. Planning how to recap is important because the final thing we want to emphasise to students are the key ingredients. Planning where to use gesturing is important because it helps students know precisely where to put their attention.

I'll then plan out my modelling for my teacher, Aaron. I'll exemplify each of those success criteria. To do this, I will need to plan how to narrate my thought process as I plan my explanation. This is what I'll model to Aaron:

Narrate your thought process: coach plans how they will think aloud so that the teacher understands how to think in order to plan effective explanations

I want to plan an explanation of what juxtaposition is. I need to keep my language lean so I am going to define it in quite simple terms to begin with. I'm going to say: *"Juxtaposition is two things being close together in a piece of writing that have contrasting effects."*

I'll then plan to link this to prior learning by saying, *"Juxtaposition builds on what we already know about contrast and how we can describe positive and negative symbols in the same piece of writing. We learned about this when we wrote that descriptive piece about the child in the emporium who noticed the doll that was sitting in front of that painting. The doll looked familiar and was a symbol of safety but the painting was of a war scene and was a symbol of suffering."*

I'll then give a concrete example of juxtaposition. I'll use: Harry has a generally kind nature but a wicked temper.

That's a good example because both 'kind' and 'wicked' are adjectives they know well.

I'll then recap the main points which are that two things - kindness and wickedness - are close together and they contrast. I'll gesture to the words at the point of saying them as well.

Spotlight specifics: coach spotlights the success criterion that is most powerful for the teacher to think about as it is clearly different to their practice

After I have then planned out my explanation exemplifying the success criteria, I'll ask Aaron to tell me what he noticed in terms of how I applied the success criterion: lean language. This will help me work out if he understands how it sounds in practice and what he should be aiming for when he plans his explanation. 'Lean language' is the right success criterion to ask about because it is the one that is most obviously different to teacher Aaron's current practice (his explanation was very wordy and unclear as a result) and so the one that he should find hardest to miss.

I'll then explain which of the success criteria require precision and which require decisions. The precise aspects need to be done in the same way all the time. For example, lean language should always be used because it is always important to make sure that students are not confused by unnecessary language. The concrete example is a success criteria that requires decision-making because sometimes this will be a familiar example while at other times, it will be an example that is new to the students but exemplifies the point that the teacher is trying to make.

Precision and decision: coach is clear on which aspects of the practice require precision and which are more flexible and require decisions

Coaching commentary

This is where we get meta and analyse the quality of the coaching in the examples above.

Below we explain how the coaches' use of techniques will support their teachers to understand, do, decide, and improve, i.e., to develop their adaptive expertise.

Understand
...key knowledge that helps solve persistent problems.

Do
...a repertoire of effective, efficient teaching techniques.

Decide
...on the best course of action using situation-sensitive mental models.

Improve
...continuously through an adaptive mindset and metacognition.

Understand

A good model helps a teacher to understand why a particular practice is likely to be successful. Coach Annie plans for what she will say to teacher Dan to explain how each of the success criteria **links to learning**. For example, she plans to communicate that 'Planning to use lean language is important because it enables students to focus clearly on the main points in the explanation and not have to work out what the important parts are.'

Do

A well-planned model is one where the coach considers how it will help the teacher to actually do the practice well. For this to happen, coaches need to be crystal clear about what they want teachers to actually do. Thus coaches must **plan success criteria** before planning the model so they are clear on what makes the technique work and they can make it unmissable in their model. When we then ask the teacher about them afterwards, we **spotlight specific** success criteria we think the teacher might miss or find challenging based on our knowledge of the technique and their current practice. For example, coach Annie plans to ask: 'What do you think the effect of "question then name" is on student learning?'

Sometimes models are for planning action steps, i.e., action steps to support the teacher with an aspect of their planning such as planning explanations, hinge questions, etc. Where this is the case, showing them what to 'do' is not a physical process but a mental one. Coach Denise plans to **narrate her thought process** to support her teacher to adopt this in his planning.

A well-planned model also minimises noise so teachers can focus on the one thing that the model is aiming to show them but it is also close enough to lesson reality to help teachers become more likely to do the practice well. Coach Annie ensures that her planned model is **clean but close** by standing up and planning to do the coaching in a classroom.

Decide

A well-planned model also prepares the teacher to make decisions about how to adapt the model. Coaches do this by being clear on which success criteria require precision (must be done in a particular way) and which require decisions. Coaches Annie and Denise use the technique **precision and decision** to plan how to explain to their coachees which success criteria are which and how to make the necessary decisions. Doing this will avoid the teacher copying and not contextualising the model and it will help the teacher develop a more sensitive mental model around the technique.

Improve

A well-planned model is important because it leaves nothing to chance. This greatly increases the chances that it will have the desired effect on teacher understanding and practice. Coaches should plan a model for their coaching sessions in order to show the teacher the importance of modelling as a mechanism to improve their practice. This helps to communicate to teachers that, to improve their practice, they should source a model and, with support, decompose it into its success criteria, ensuring they understand why each is important for student learning. To help teachers improve over time, it is important that modelling is a consistent feature of all efforts to improve their practice.

Do this in your coaching

Let's look at how we can use these coaching techniques at the right time for the right reasons in our coaching.

Get started with these foundational techniques

When you're trying something new in your coaching, you need some foundational techniques to adopt. Try these techniques using one of the suggested sentence stems in your preparatory thinking:

Clean but close:

- When modelling this performance action step, I'll make it close to reality by . . .
- When modelling this technique, I'll make it clean by . . .
- When modelling this planning action step, I need to use authentic lesson materials such as . . .

Plan success criteria:

- When using this technique, teachers need to . . .
- The most important aspects of this action step are . . .
- To be successful at this action step, teachers would need to . . .

Precision and decision:

- These success criteria are precise - they are pretty well always the same . . .
- These success criteria require decisions. I'll make sure my teacher understands the decisions are based on . . .

Spotlight specifics:

- My teacher is likely to miss/struggle with this success criteria . . .
- I'll ask my teacher this question about this success criterion . . .

Link to learning:

- Doing this success criterion is important because . . .
- The benefit of this for learning is . . .

Adapt your coaching appropriately using flexible techniques

Narrate your thought process:

- I want to . . . at . . . point, because . . .
- I'll make sure my language is really lean by saying . . .
- I have a choice at this point and I am going to choose to . . .

Notes

1 Sims, S., Fletcher-Wood, H., Godfrey-Fausset, T., and Meliss, S. (2023) *Modelling evidence-based practice in initial teacher training: causal effects on teachers' skills, knowledge and self-efficacy*. Ambition Institute. Available at: www.ambition.org.uk/modelling-evidence-based-practice-in-initial-teacher-training/ (Accessed: 4 June 2025).

2 We are indebted to Steplab for their high-quality and extensive codification of action steps and success criteria, which have supported us in our coaching work (and in writing about coaching for this book).

3 Goodrich, J. (2024) *Responsive coaching: Evidence-informed instructional coaching that works for every teacher in your school*. London: John Catt.

4 Goodrich, J. (2024) *Responsive coaching: Evidence-informed instructional coaching that works for every teacher in your school*. London: John Catt.

Stage 1

Secure success

We've called this first stage of the coaching conversation **secure success**. Why? Well, often this first stage is called 'praise,' but we don't think this captures the value this stage can have in developing teachers' adaptive expertise. 'Praise' can sound like pat-on-the-back platitudes, whereas **secure success** captures the goal: to squeeze every drop of learning out of a situation that supports student learning and help the teacher do it again at the right time for the right reasons.

Let's look at the purposes of the secure success stage.

Purposes

This is what we want teachers to feel and know after this stage.

Get why: 'I get why I was successful and how to be successful in future.'
We need to make sure the teacher understands what they did that was successful, why it seemed to be successful for student learning, and how to do it again under similar and different conditions. This involves reflecting back on what they did and projecting forward to what they will do in future lessons.[1]

Own success: 'I achieved this success through my hard work and growing expertise.'
It's motivational to believe you have control over your impact on student learning.[2] We can support the teacher to reflect on and replicate the ways they have made sure their practice improves. This may include doing things such as reinforcing their use of the technique multiple times in their practice (context-specific repetition), testing the technique in their lessons, monitoring the effect of their efforts (self-monitoring), and adjusting when necessary.

Pitfalls

Pitfalls are typical ways we can undermine this coaching stage. We need to know them so we can avoid them.

Scattergun successes: avoid naming a vast array of successful moments from across the lesson: 'I really like how you restated the norms for group work, your explanation of photosynthesis was

DOI: 10.4324/9781003465850-10

spot on, and how you supported Charlie seemed really successful.' While this may feel like you're celebrating lots of things the teacher did well, in reality it won't be clear to the teacher *why* what they did was successful. This means they won't necessarily do it in the optimal way next time.

Instead, zoom in on *one* part of the teacher's practice to secure that success. This enables you to have a rich conversation about the event and really probe and celebrate their actions, decision-making, and understanding of how to improve. Often it's clear what you should zoom in on because it is the successful implementation of their previous target.

Pat-on-the-back praise: the *secure success* stage of coaching can sometimes feel tokenistic. This often happens when we treat it as a prelude to the main event, i.e., discussing what the teacher needs to work on. A coach might use what we call pat-on-the-back praise.

Pat-on-the-back praise has one or more of these features:

1. Vague: 'You did such a good job today.'
2. Not linked to the effect on student learning: 'You did some nice questioning after the starter activity.'
3. Not even related to student learning: 'Every single book had ticks on each page.'
4. Fails to ask the teacher what they did and why: 'I thought it was really impressive how you used stretch questions. Great stuff. Now let's think about your next step . . .'

To avoid these, there are a number of safeguards you can put in place.

First, banish vague praise by keeping this in mind: the specificity of your praise shows how closely you were watching the teacher's lesson. Vague praise signals that you were distracted or didn't value being there. Highly specific praise shows you were (and are) interested and invested in your teacher's development. Compare –

> Example 1: There was a lovely atmosphere during the pair work.
>
> Example 2: Pair work was so purposeful: every single pair started talking straight away. I listened to four pairs as I circulated and I could hear the key terms being used accurately. At one point, Robert said to Dean, 'What do you think?' and paused to listen. This shows those pair-work habits you've been trying to embed seem to be taking root. What did you pick up on from circulating?

Example 1 could have been said by someone who just walked past the lesson and glanced in. Example 2 shows genuine interest and investment in the teacher's development.

Secondly, link your praise to the previous action step you and your teacher have been working on. As you've discussed this in detail in the previous coaching conversation, it's likely you'll be specific and link to learning. Plus it's likely to be something they will value hearing about.

Finally, don't feel you have to say it all yourself. Ask the teacher how the action step has been going and what effect it has had on student learning.

Personal preference: avoid implying that your personal preference is at play. It's easy (because it's natural) to say things like, 'I loved your use of show-me boards' or 'I thought it was great when you used pair work' and leave it there. This might be heard as, 'My coach is a fan of show-me boards and pair work,' which can lead to overgeneralisation: 'I'll do them whenever she comes to watch me teach.'

Avoid this issue entirely by explaining *why* you liked it – spotlight good decision-making and actions and link your analysis to student learning (or ask the teacher to explain why it was effective). You can then ask questions and provide guidance if necessary to ensure they understand when and when not to use the technique. You may even decide to ban yourself from phrases that even imply a hint of personal preference and stick to, 'I think it was effective when . . . because . . .' instead.

Changing the (success) subject: we've all been in a situation where someone has highlighted something we did well and we've felt a mix of pride and angst. Positive feedback can feel deeply uncomfortable, causing us to bat it away: 'Yes but did you see what happened next? I didn't handle that very well.' Your teacher may well do the same, answering your questions by pointing out negatives rather than focusing on what caused the success.

But it's important they sit with success if they are to learn from it. To help your teacher do this, explain to them that experts spend time examining their wins,[3] and by changing the subject, they rob themselves of opportunities to improve. If they are really struggling, have them develop a stock phrase to respond to the positive feedback such as, 'Thank you for noticing that. Let's work out what I can learn from that success.'

Sometimes coaches themselves change the success subject! They do this when they qualify successes by tagging on something to improve: 'Your example was really concrete but I think you could have used a slightly different one for greater impact.' This detracts from the power of the secure success stage by turning it into advice on how to improve. Trust the coaching process. It's important that this stage focuses on securing a success by ensuring the teacher does it at the right time for the right reasons in future.

Praise that fails to push: praise can sometimes feel like the easy part of the coaching conversation for the teacher: they sit back and are showered with positive commentary from the coach. This is not the case if we see coaching as developing adaptive expertise. *At all times* we need to be checking and developing the teacher's mental model of the situations we are working on. The situation we are praising is no exception. In fact, given that this section is about something the teacher did well, we can usually push their thinking even harder! We do this by getting them to retrieve their previous action step and success criteria from memory (to strengthen their recall of it) and checking the sensitivity of their mental model by asking them how they would decide differently if conditions were different. For example, 'What would you do if students hadn't all looked up by the end of your countdown?' This way we can see if those 'if-then' branches of the teacher's mental model are in place to support appropriate decision-making in plausible alternative situations.

Coaching techniques

Use these coaching techniques to help your teacher **secure success.**

Some techniques are foundational, i.e., we should always use them, and some are flexible, i.e., we should use them when appropriate, depending on the level of the teacher's expertise in the moment.

Foundational or flexible	Technique	What it is	Examples	Non examples
Foundational	Zoom in	Focus on *one* situation to examine. Usually this is the teacher's action step from the previous cycle.	"Let's focus on the moment where you began questioning students about the different types of triangle using wait time."	**Scattergun successes:** "You did this well… oh and it was great when you asked Bryony a stretch question and later when you…"
Foundational	Surface mental models	Between you, articulate relevant parts of the teacher's mental model: goals, actions and events, cause and effect and decision drivers.	"Tell me about your goal when you put Jamil's work under the visualiser… What effect did that have? What happened next?" "What drove your decision to choose Kirsty to answer that question?"	**Pat-on-the-back praise that fails to include the teacher:** "I thought it was great when you used the visualiser to showcase Jamil's work."
Foundational	Spotlight specifics	Between you, specify the great decisions and actions the teacher took to support student learning. Celebrate this success.	"You said, "Think back to when we spoke about devotion last lesson…" Then you paused and looked as if you too were deep in thought. Why was this a powerful moment, do you think?" "Every single student was paying attention after your countdown signal. What an incredible environment for learning."	**Pat-on-the-back praise that is vague:** "You did a great job of your explanation." **Changing the (success) subject:** "It was really powerful when you stopped mid-sentence when Chris interrupted you. I just wonder if you could have noticed it sooner."
Foundational	Link to learning	Between you, explain how the teacher's actions and decisions supported student learning.	"What was the impact on student learning?" "Your use of wait time appeared to work well. You gave a good 10 seconds for a rather complex question and the answers you got from the five students you asked indicated that they thought hard."	**Personal preference:** "I just really like to see a lengthy period of group discussion." **Pat-on-the-back praise that does not link to learning:** "You gave a good amount of time - a few seconds is always good."

Foundational or flexible	Technique	What it is	Examples	Non examples
Flexible	Meta moves 	Between you, highlight the effective methods the teacher is using to develop their practice when the coach is not there.	"I can hear you've been monitoring how this has been going. You've even tweaked it to make it work better for your context. These are mechanisms and methods to improve our practice." "How many classes have you been using this with?... That means you've been practising this technique multiple times this week. It's more likely to become part of your repertoire this way." "Take a moment to think back to the beginning of the year, what are the differences between your routines then and now? How have you achieved this?"	**Pat-on-the-back praise that is vague:** "Well done for changing your practice!"
Flexible	Prompt retrieval 	Ask the teacher to recall important ideas, e.g. their previous action step and success criteria, knowledge about how learning happens, etc.	"Remind me of the step and success criteria you were working on." "Which success criterion were you exemplifying perfectly when you said, "Pens down. Eyes on me"?"	**Praise that fails to push:** "The action step you've been working on is... The success criteria was..." "Remember the success criterion you were working on in particular was..."
Flexible	Sensitivity check 	Check the teacher knows what makes the technique 'work' by asking about the conditions for success.	"Every student was engaged in pair talk. What did you do before and during the lesson to make that happen?" "When in future will you be using that technique again?...Why?" "When wouldn't you use that technique?... Why?" "What if/imagine you don't get the answer you expect, what do you do?"	**Praise that fails to push:** "You've done such a fantastic job of getting pair talk to work in your lesson. Keep at it."
Flexible	Seesaw support 	Move between seeking the teacher's expertise and sharing your expertise depending on the weight of the teacher's knowledge in that moment. Seek first, then scaffold the question, then share.	"Why was your use of group work successful at that point in the lesson?" [Teacher is unsure] "Think about what they'd done before. You had explained and checked their knowledge. What impact did this have on the group discussion?" [Teacher can't answer well] "They had the knowledge to challenge each other's thinking because you used group work after your explanation and check for understanding."	**Praise that fails to push:** "It was brilliant how you got all the students discussing the quote and then went over to Yasmin to help her out. That felt like the right decision." **Playing 'guess what's in my head':** "What was the impact of the class discussion on student learning?... How did it support learning?... Think about the impact it had on student learning. How would you describe that?"

Example 1 Foundational techniques

Let's see an example of a coach using the foundational techniques.

Context

Coach Lisa has been working with teacher Jake, to improve his use of hinge questions to check for student understanding at key points in the lesson. The particular focus in their latest coaching cycle was on his choice of questions and interpretation of answers.

In this excerpt, coach Lisa ensures Jake knows why his hinge question was successful and attributes it to his own hard work.

Watch how coach Lisa uses the foundational techniques in this stage: zoom in, surface mental models, spotlight specifics, and link to learning.

Coaching Excerpt

Coach Lisa: Let's zoom in on the moment when you used that hinge question after explaining equivalent fractions. You asked, "*Which of these three fractions is equal to ¾?*" and showed three plausible answers with one wrong answer. Every student responded using their mini whiteboards.

Zoom in: coach focuses the teacher on a particular situation

What was your goal at that moment?

Surface mental models: coach asks about the teacher's situation goal

Teacher Jake: I wanted to check if they really understood before moving on. In the past, I'd just ask a couple of students, but now I get responses from everyone.

Coach Lisa: And when you were in the moment, what were you looking for and what did you notice?

Surface mental models: coach asks about actions and events to check the teacher's awareness and align their mental models if necessary

Teacher Jake: I was scanning quickly – first to see if most of them had the right answer, and then to pick out anyone who might need help. Most of them picked the right answer (B) but there were two students who wrote 'A'. I decided I could move on but made a mental note to support those two students later in the lesson.

Coach Lisa: Yes, I noticed that too - you were really embodying the success criteria of 'survey answers and respond proportionately'. With only a couple who didn't understand, you really efficiently supported them a few minutes later when you set the class on the next task.

Spotlight specifics: coach highlights specific evidence of the teacher's decision and actions

What did you do before and during the lesson to make the hinge question so successful?

Surfacing mental models: coach asks about the causes of the positive effects they saw from the hinge question

Teacher Jake: In my planning I worked hard to phrase the question clearly like we rehearsed last time. All the wrong answers were plausible and targeted likely misconceptions the students might have, so it really tested their understanding. Last time you saw me, the answers were too vague to really make any inferences about student understanding. I also think my instructions to students were clear too: "*When I say go and not before...*" We've worked on them before. I think it was the way I phrased the question. Really concise just as we worked on last time.

Coach Lisa: Yes, you've done a lot of work in your planning to make the hinge question really diagnostic. Your careful choice of answers had them thinking hard – you could see this as many of them were looking at the board and took a bit of time to answer. Those clear instructions feel like a habit now too. No one started before you said 'Go'. Great practice all round.

Spotlight specifics: coach highlights specific evidence of what the teacher did and the effect on students

Let's think about impact. How did your use of the hinge question support student learning?

Link to learning: coach asks the teacher about the impact on learning

Teacher Jake: I can catch misunderstandings before moving on, rather than finding out too late. It means some students don't get left behind. I can adapt my teaching appropriately (like you saw) because I was able to go and help those students later.

Coach Lisa: Exactly. Don't forget as well that the question is causing them to retrieve what they know and retrieval is great for consolidating that knowledge.

Link to learning: coach explains another way the hinge question supports learning

Example 2 Flexible techniques

Let's see an example of a coach using the flexible techniques.

Context

As in the example above, coach Lisa has been working with teacher Jake to improve his use of hinge questions to check for student understanding at key points in the lesson. The particular focus in their latest coaching cycle was on his choice of questions and interpretation of answers.

In this example, coach Lisa decides she can push Jake's thinking even further without overloading him.

Watch how coach Lisa uses the flexible techniques in this stage: prompt retrieval, meta moves, and sensitivity check.

Coaching Excerpt

Coach Lisa: Kick us off by recalling the action step and success criteria you've been working on.

Prompt retrieval: coach asks the teacher to retrieve the previous target

Teacher Jake: The action step was 'Before moving on to more complex ideas, check whole-class understanding of important knowledge using a hinge question so you can address gaps or misconceptions.' The success criteria are that hinge questions need to be clear and concise, with plausible answers that make students think, but also diagnostic enough that I can instantly interpret the responses. I also need to survey answers and respond proportionately.

Coach Lisa: That's it, brilliant. And with that in mind, let's zoom in on the moment when you used that hinge question after explaining equivalent fractions. You asked, "*Which of these three fractions is equal to ¾?*"' and showed three plausible answers with one wrong answer. Every student responded using their mini whiteboards.

Zoom in: coach focuses the teacher on a particular situation

What was your goal at that moment?

Surface mental models: coach asks about the teacher's situation goal

Teacher Jake: I wanted to check if they really understood before moving on to the more complex ideas. In the past, I'd just ask a couple of students, but now I get responses from everyone.

Coach Lisa: And when you were in the moment, what were you looking for and what did you notice?

Surface mental models: coach asks about actions and events to check the teacher's awareness and align their mental models if necessary

Teacher Jake: I was scanning quickly – first to see if most of them had the right answer, and then to pick out anyone who might need help. Most of them picked the right answer (B), but there were two students who wrote 'A'. I decided I could move on but made a mental note to support those two students later in the lesson.

Coach Lisa: Yes, I noticed that too. Which success criterion were you embodying when you made that decision?

Prompt retrieval: coach asks the teacher to retrieve a specific success criterion

Teacher Jake: I guess 'survey answers and respond proportionately'. Only two didn't get it so there's no need to reteach to everyone.

Coach Lisa: Yes, I agree that was a really sensible decision.

Let's think about how you made the hinge question work so well. What did you do before and during the lesson to make the hinge question so successful?

Surfacing mental models: coach asks about the causes of the positive effects they saw from the hinge question

Teacher Jake: In my planning I worked hard to phrase the question clearly like we rehearsed last time. All the wrong answers were plausible and targeted likely misconceptions the students might have, so it really tested their understanding. Last time you saw me, the answers were too vague to really make any inferences about student understanding. I also think my instructions to students were clear too: *"When I say go and not before..."* We've worked on them before. I think it was the way I phrased the question. Really concise just as we worked on last time.

Spotlight specifics: coach highlights specific evidence of what the teacher did and the effect on students

Coach Lisa: Yes, you've done a lot of work in the planning to make the hinge question really diagnostic. Your careful choice of answers had them thinking hard – you could see this as many of them were looking at the board and took a bit of time to answer. Those clear instructions feel like a habit now too. No one started before you said 'Go'. Great practice all round.

How did your use of the hinge question support student learning?

Link to learning: coach asks the teacher about the impact on learning

Teacher Jake: I can catch misunderstandings before moving on, rather than finding out too late. It means some students don't get left behind. I can adapt my teaching appropriately like you saw – I was able to go and help those students later.

Link to learning: coach explains another way the hinge question supports learning

Coach Lisa: Exactly. Don't forget as well that the question is causing them to retrieve what they know, and retrieval is great for consolidating that knowledge.

Let's make sure we really understand what makes hinge questions work for supporting student learning. What if you had asked a hinge question but your responses had been split three ways across the answer options, what would you have done then?

Sensitivity check: coach uses a 'what if' question to check the teacher really knows how to use the technique well

Teacher Jake: Interesting... If the responses were all over the place, I wouldn't have been able to move on because it'd show the class wasn't secure. I'd have to pause and reteach before checking again.

Coach Lisa: Exactly. A hinge question isn't just about checking – it's about deciding what happens next. You're making decisions based on what you see.

Thinking about the development of your practice in this area, which has been considerable, how did you manage to make these changes?

Meta move: coach asks teacher to highlight effective methods and ways of thinking they have used to improve their practice

Teacher Jake: I think two things really helped. First, I started monitoring the effect of my hinge questions – checking whether they actually gave me useful information. And second, I kept practising them in different lessons, tweaking the format to make them sharper. Sometimes it takes some careful planning to phrase questions to get short but meaningful answers for example.

Coach Lisa: That's brilliant. You weren't just applying the strategy, you were reflecting on its impact and refining it each time. Keep doing that and you're likely to keep improving.

Example 3 Seesaw support

Let's see an example of a coach using one specific flexible technique.

Context

Let's see a snippet of the secure success stage where coach Lisa adjusts her support to meet teacher Jake's needs. Lisa seeks Jake's expertise, scaffolds, and then shares her own when he is still struggling.

Watch how coach Lisa does this by using a flexible technique in this stage: seesaw support.

Coaching Excerpt

Coach Lisa: Kick us off by recalling the action step and success criteria you've been working on.

Prompt retrieval: coach asks the teacher to retrieve the previous target

Teacher Jake: The action step was 'Before moving on to more complex ideas, check whole-class understanding of important knowledge using hinge questions so you can address gaps or misconceptions.' The success criteria are that hinge questions need to be clear and concise, with plausible answers that make students think, but also diagnostic enough that I can instantly interpret the responses. I also need to survey answers and respond proportionately.

Coach Lisa: Great. And when you say 'diagnostic enough,' what do you mean exactly?

Seesaw support: coach seeks the teacher's expertise first

Teacher Jake: Um... I think it just means it shows who gets it and who doesn't?

Coach Lisa: Remember what we said last time about the answers we select for these questions and why?

Seesaw support: coach scaffolds to support the teacher

Teacher Jake: They have to be deliberately chosen to quickly work out what's wrong?

Coach Lisa: Yes, but let's refine that a little. A diagnostic hinge question doesn't just show right or wrong. It tells you why students might be struggling. That's why the wrong answers you choose are so important. They should reveal different types of misconceptions rather than just being random mistakes.

Seesaw support: coach shares their expertise rather than continuing to ask questions the teacher is unlikely to be able to answer

Coaching commentary

This is where we get meta and analyse the quality of the coaching in the examples above.

Below we explain how the coaches' use of techniques supports their teachers to understand, do, decide, and improve, i.e., to develop their adaptive expertise.

Understand
...key knowledge that helps solve persistent problems.

Do
...a repertoire of effective, efficient teaching techniques.

Decide
...on the best course of action using situation-sensitive mental models.

Improve
...continuously through an adaptive mindset and metacognition.

Understand

Better knowledge fuels better mental models. Coach Lisa supports Jake to develop his knowledge of hinge questions by **zooming in** to focus on just this one area of his practice. Later she makes sure he has a good understanding of the impact of his practice by **linking to learning**. She gets him to do this first and then she adds another way hinge questions support learning to make sure he hears all the benefits.

In example 2, Jake has to think hard because coach Lisa **prompts retrieval** of the action step and success criteria (his target from his last coaching cycle). We also see in example 3, coach Lisa **seesawing support** to share her expertise to make sure Jake properly understands the success criteria for hinge questions, developing his knowledge of effective teaching.

Do

Even though the secure success stage is not about developing the teacher's repertoire of techniques per se, it is about reinforcing what they are doing well. Coach Lisa does this through **spotlighting specific** actions: 'With only a couple who didn't understand, you really efficiently supported them a few minutes later when you set the class on the next task.'

Decide

Securing success is not just about reinforcing great actions but also the great decision-making that often sits behind them. Coach Lisa uncovers Jake's decision-making by **surfacing his mental**

model: she asks questions to surface his goal, awareness of actions and events, and cause and effect: 'What was your goal at that moment?', 'What were you looking for and what did you notice?', 'What did you do before and during the lesson to make the hinge question so successful?'

In example 3, coach Lisa uses the technique **sensitivity check** by asking Jake, 'What if you had asked a hinge question but your responses had been split three ways across the answer options, what would you have done then?' This checks that Jake knows how to adapt to different conditions, which is a hallmark of those with adaptive expertise. These questions are powerful for taking your teacher beyond the situation and into other plausible ones, checking and pushing their thinking to develop their mental models.

Improve

Meta moves are questions that elicit, or reinforce, great ways the teacher has developed their practice through using behaviour change mechanisms or habits of thinking such as testing and refining the approach. Coach Lisa uses a **meta move** when she asks Jake, 'Thinking about the development of your practice in this area, which has been considerable, how did you manage to make these changes?' He explains how he's monitored and adjusted his practice, which Lisa then reinforces. By explicitly discussing these methods, we can help teachers get better at getting better.[4]

Do this in your coaching

Let's look at how we can use these coaching techniques at the right time for the right reasons in our coaching.

Get started with these foundational techniques

When you're trying something new in your coaching, you need some foundational techniques to adopt. Try these techniques using one of the suggested sentence stems.

Zoom in:

- Let's focus on . . .
- Let's zoom in on . . .

Surface mental models:

- What was your goal?
- What happened?
- What do you think caused . . .?
- What did you do before and during the lesson to make this a success for student learning?
- What was your reason for doing/deciding . . .?

Spotlight specifics:

- It was brilliant when you said, '[exact quote]' because . . .
- You just said you made the decision to do [action]. This was appropriate at that moment because . . .
- Your decision to do [action] seemed like the right one at that moment because . . .

Link to learning:

- What impact do you think your action/decision had on student learning?
- After you decided to do [action], I noticed [evidence of positive impact on student learning] . . .
- How is this approach better for student learning than the previous one?

Adapt your coaching appropriately using flexible techniques

Have these flexible techniques in your coaching repertoire to use when needed.

Prompt retrieval:

- Remind us of the action step/success criteria you've been working on . . .
- What success criteria did you exemplify really well when you did/decided . . .?

Sensitivity check:

- What if a student [behaved in a different way, gave a different answer, etc.]?
- What if your goal had been [a different plausible goal from the current one being discussed]?
- When wouldn't you use this technique/success criterion?
- Imagine this scenario: [give a plausible alternative situation the teacher might encounter so they can simulate how they might decide and act differently].
- What different versions of this technique could you use? When are each of them appropriate?

Seesaw support:

- **Seek** the teacher's expertise by asking a question, e.g., 'When would you use a hinge question?'
- **Scaffold** the question with a narrower focus and more cues if they can't answer well, e.g., 'At which points in the lesson do you need to know what students understand before moving on?'
- **Share** your expertise if they can't answer well, e.g., 'We use hinge questions to specifically check for all students' understanding of an important idea that if misunderstood, would prevent them accessing the rest of the lesson. So we use hinge questions at critical "hinge" points in the lesson where the understanding of the rest of the lesson hinges on them understanding a key idea. In your lesson, this was . . .'

Notes

1 Boguslav, A. (2024) 'Parsing coaching practice: A systematic framework for describing coaching discourse,' *AERA Open*, 10, p. 23328584241263861.

2 Brooks, I. (2009) *Organisational behaviour: Individuals, groups and organisation*. Harlow: Pearson Education.

3 Ericsson, K. A. and Pool, R. (2016) *Peak: Secrets from the new science of expertise*. London: Bodley Head.

4 Lemov, D., Woolway, E., and Yezzi, K. (2012) *Practice perfect: 42 rules for getting better at getting better*. Hoboken, NJ: John Wiley & Sons.

Stage 2

Study the problem

In the **study the problem** stage, it's the coach's role to focus the teacher on a particular situation where they might better have supported student learning. However, this stage can feel really tricky, like walking a tightrope: too direct and you might offend the teacher; too indirect and you might confuse them.

To navigate this we need to remember that the coach at this stage does not (indeed cannot have) formed a concrete judgement about the problem. They need the teacher's perspective (mental model of the situation) before the problem can be fully understood. Plus, supporting the teacher to dig into the reasoning for their actions may be associated with improvements to their practice.[1] This may be because it means coaching meets the teacher where they are rather than making assumptions or skipping ahead. Coming into this stage then, the coach has a *hypothesis* about the problem, which has survived testing against evidence from the lesson, and they must hold this lightly.

The main activity in this stage is for the coach and teacher to piece together critical evidence to work out what the problem is. They need alignment on their versions of the situation to reach a shared mental model of what happened, what was significant about it and what they think the problem is. The temptation can be to skip ahead to discussing solutions . . . but solutions for what? This is why this stage is called *study* the problem. It reminds us to examine and understand it first, particularly what might be causing it. This is sometimes relatively clear and other times quite difficult to discern. Where it's difficult, making the teacher's thinking visible by mapping their mental model can be the key to gaining insight on the issue.[2] Indeed, there is evidence that experts in other fields spend time trying to best represent problems (whereas novices move more quickly to solutions).[3] Plus, spending time defining the problem to-be-solved may also make it more likely the teacher adopts the practice selected as a solution.[4]

It's here and throughout that we need to also stress a key point about building adaptive expertise: it's about doing the right thing at the right time for the right reason. This means having the most effective situation-sensitive mental model. Therefore, we are attempting to develop the teacher's (and often our) understanding of the *situation* – what it demands of a teacher and what decisions and actions might have caused suboptimal effects on student learning. This means focusing the *study the problem* stage on that situation and not narrowly on a technique itself. Of course it will

DOI: 10.4324/9781003465850-11

come back to what the teacher decided and did, but this can only be made sense of and is only a problem because it didn't work *in that situation*. So, we must start with the situation.

As we work to define the problem with our teacher, we must hold ourselves accountable to the most important goal: *what is best for student learning*. Seen through this lens, our efforts are targeted at defining the learning problem because this stands in the way of student learning. It's not us against each other - it's us against the problem.

Purposes

Here's what we want teachers to feel and know after this stage.

Awareness[5] and alignment: 'I can see what happened and how I was thinking in this situation. My coach and I share an understanding of this.'

Mental models are tacit, hidden even from their owners. We need to help the teacher surface their mental model of the situation so they can examine their thinking. We need to ensure there is agreement on what happened and what is significant about it. This may mean the coach changing their mental model and/or the teacher changing theirs. We must remember though, it is always about what is best for student learning.

Gain insight on the issue: 'I see the issue that occurred and the likely causes. I can explain why it impacted student learning.'

We need to make sure the teacher sees the issue in their teaching. We might help them have an insight or we might need to explicitly show them the issue we saw and check they understand it. Why is this so important? Or put another way . . . can't we just skip this and give them a solution? The reason it's so important is that actions happen in context. An issue is usually an issue for two overlapping reasons:

1. A teacher's decisions and actions didn't suit the contextual features of the situation. If we focus just on the action itself, e.g., 'You took the answer from a student with their hand up,' we are communicating that the action itself is wrong. But it's not *always wrong* to take a hand up. It depends on the contextual features and the goal in that situation. These contextual features aren't just about that moment either. Sometimes prior context affects the success of a teacher's decision, for example, they might try to implement a technique students aren't prepared for because the culture of the class isn't favourable.
2. A teacher's decisions and actions aren't in line with a powerful goal related to student learning. And, because context changes rapidly when you're teaching classes of students, teachers may need to adjust their situation goals quickly, i.e., 'go off plan but stay with intent.'[6]

If we focus on the teacher's actions without seeking to develop their mental model of the situation where the issue arose, we divorce the action from the context. Teachers will come away with an oversimplified understanding of good teaching: 'I shouldn't take hands up.' Rather than the situation-sensitive understanding that adaptive experts have: 'I shouldn't take hands up in this situation because . . .'

Trading one action for another doesn't support the teacher to develop a mental model that can best serve student learning in future. Examining the situation where the issue arose and developing a better mental model of that situation can.

State the problem: 'I can articulate the problem we are trying to solve.'

Discussing an issue can give us the illusion that we are both on the same page about what the problem is. If we state it concretely, we can be sure.

Pitfalls

Pitfalls are typical ways we can undermine this coaching stage. We need to know them so we can avoid them.

The vague opener:[7] 'How do you think the lesson went?'

Opening this stage of coaching with a broad question or statement is problematic:

1. It wastes time because it prompts the teacher to talk about multiple aspects of the lesson when you just want to focus on one.
2. It's unfair on the teacher because they know you have something in mind to discuss and aren't saying it.
3. Vague prompts are unhelpful for everyone and likely to be particularly unhelpful for less experienced teachers who tend to respond in equally vague ways.[8] They benefit from more specific questions.

Instead, zoom in immediately on the situation in the lesson where you got tripped up: 'Let's focus on the independent practice towards the end of the lesson.'

More than one problem: just like with the secure success stage, it's common to see coaches focusing on more than one problem they think they see in the teacher's lesson. This is likely to hinder your ability to develop your teacher's mental model of *any* problem (as there won't be time), demoralise, and potentially overload them. Remember, it's really hard for teachers to change their practice. Let's support them to do one thing better.

Catch yourself sneaking in additional issues by eliminating phrases like 'one more thing' or 'I think it will also be a quick win to . . .'[9] Highlighting more problems doesn't mean more change. In fact, it often leads to less.

Technique not situation: focusing solely on the execution of a teaching technique, divorced from context, is unlikely to support your teacher to do the right thing at the right time for the right reasons in future. If the problem appears to be the execution of a teaching technique, ensure the teacher understands the effect this appeared to have on student learning in that situation.

Skipping to solutions: this is one of the *biggest pitfalls* we see in this stage. Why?

1. Handing teachers solutions is unlikely to build their mental models of situations, which means they will struggle to use solutions appropriately and may not even have the awareness of the issue next time it crops up in their lessons.
2. We can't be sure a solution is right if we only have our mental model of the situation to go by: we need to understand the teacher's mental model too.
3. If we start by trying to understand the problem, the solution will be a better fit. Think of the problem and solution as two pieces of a puzzle that must fit together in the mind of your teacher. Ultimately this will make it more likely that you are both working on something that will impact student learning.
4. Asking the teacher about their understanding of the situation means you know their starting point. We know learning happens best, i.e., more meaningfully, when we activate and link the learners' prior knowledge.[10] You can coach for meaningful learning when you understand the teacher's current mental model.

But, what if it's the teacher that skips to the solution? Listen to them and then pull them back by saying something like, 'It's valuable for us to spend a few minutes defining the problem and its causes so we can decide on the best solution. Let's try and articulate exactly what we think it is first. Then we can see whether your solution is the best fit.'

Jumping to judgement: it's human to want to share our judgements. As coaches, we may mistakenly think it's our role. But our role is to develop the teacher's adaptive expertise: their ability to understand, do, decide and improve. Jumping to judgement closes doors to this development - it treats coaching as advice-giving instead.

Jumping to judgement prevents us from developing the teacher's mental model because we've skipped any analysis of the situation. It damages our relationship with them because judgement is off-putting and any questions we ask after will seem tokenistic as our minds are clearly made up. Judgement also goes against the notion of everyone having different mental models because the coach is assuming their mental model *is* reality. There is also the possibility that the issue we think is an issue isn't an issue at all!

So avoid using language that expresses judgement at this stage, even subtly:

'I want to focus on the independent practice where students couldn't follow *your lengthy instructions*.'

'Let's zoom in on the explanation of "climate change." *How clear was this*, do you think?'

'I noticed you asked a question and then *didn't give any time for students to process it.*'

You'll see from these examples that judgement comes when we start by interpreting rather than investigating the problem. So, what should we do instead? First off, we need the teacher's perspective: we must ask about their mental model: 'Let's zoom in on [situation]. Tell me what your goal was and what you did.' If surfacing their mental model does not help them see an issue, we can share the effects of their actions on student learning (what we noticed). We can do this because we collected neutral, non-judgemental evidence (stenographer not judge or jury!) when preparing for coaching (see Stage 0 Prepare for coaching by diagnosing need). If the teacher is really struggling to see an issue, despite a lot of evidence to suggest there is one, the coach can share their hypothesis.

Unaccountable thinking: this pitfall can happen when the coach or teacher decouples their thinking from what is best for student learning. It can come in a few different forms. The first is falling prey to personal preferences:

> I tend to get students to do some group work at that point in the lesson instead.
>
> I like to see checks for understanding at least every 10 minutes during a lesson.

The second is a bit more subtle than this. It's where coach or teacher seem to go with their gut but don't link it to student learning:

> I noticed the pair talk lasted five minutes. That felt too long. I'd suggest keeping it to two minutes.
>
> With your explanation, the pace could have been quicker.

(You'll notice these first two categories also commit the pitfalls of skipping to solutions and jumping to judgement!)

The final category of unaccountable thinking is where the coach or teacher makes excuses for what happened and these excuses leave them unaccountable to student learning:

> Coach: I noticed during the pair talk that after three minutes, four pairs had finished discussing the question and fallen silent. Did you notice something similar?
>
> Teacher: Yes but I'm not fussed if a few of them have to wait a few minutes for the others. They are the ones that tend to grasp it the quickest anyway.

What does the coach do here to keep thinking accountable? First off, it's important when contracting for coaching (see Stage 0 Set up coaching by contracting) to agree on the importance of keeping our thinking accountable to student learning. This gives coach and teacher permission to respectfully challenge each other if one or other falls short. Secondly, we need to model continually linking what we say to evidence from the lesson related to student learning and to principles from research about student learning. So the coach could say . . .

> Coach: Our ultimate goal is to maximise learning for all students. If some of them aren't thinking hard anymore, we know they won't be learning. We can do some small things to tighten up pair talk to make sure all of them are thinking hard throughout. Let's start by considering what led them to finish conversations early.

Playing 'guess what's in my head': asking questions can be powerful to support the teacher to have a moment of insight about an issue. However, we must avoid asking questions when the teacher actually needs us to seesaw support and share our expertise. You know you've got to this point if you are asking more and more focused questions and your teacher is not having the insight you wanted:

> Is there an issue with the action you took initially? . . . Did students react the way you wanted? . . . Did you want some of them to explain their answers in that way?

These wheel-spinning questions can eventually lead to a lack of trust because the teacher will come to think that your questions are motivated by a desire for them to guess what's in your head rather than genuine curiosity or attempt to engineer insight. Instead, notice when the teacher needs support and tell them what you think. Remember, as a coach, you have a valuable mental model of the situation. You are also non-judgemental and ground your analysis in what is best for student learning – this makes your mental model extremely useful. Telling the teacher what you saw or think does not make you a bad coach. If done at the right time, and when insights are rooted in evidence and student learning, it's good coaching.

Obscuring the issue: linked to the pitfall of playing 'guess what's in my head' is obscuring the issue. This can happen when coaches find it uncomfortable directing the teacher's attention to, or directly pointing out, an issue. The coach might obscure the issue by switching to things the teacher did well or minimising the issue rather than stating it clearly:

> I wonder . . . shall we look at how students came into the lesson? You did some great work around getting Ben to sit down actually. That's something I sometimes struggle with. But there was something . . . wasn't there . . . about the amount of time it took. I mean, we can't expect that class to sit down straight away and maybe that was better than normal, I don't know . . .?

Be clear to be kind. If the teacher is struggling to spot an issue you have seen that affects student learning, point it out non-judgementally by spotlighting specifics from the lesson and giving your clear interpretation: 'I want to zoom in on the start of the lesson where students entered the classroom. What was your goal? . . . What happened? . . . I noticed it took students six minutes to get in, sit down and start the task on the board. How is this affecting learning in your lesson?' This is another example of the coach holding the conversation accountable to student learning.

Coaching techniques

Use these coaching techniques to help your teacher **study the problem**.

Some techniques are foundational, i.e., we should always use them, and some are flexible, i.e., we should use them when appropriate, depending on the level of the teacher's expertise in the moment.

Foundational or flexible	Technique	What it is	Examples	Non examples
Foundational	Zoom in 	Focus on *one* situation to examine.	"Let's focus on your modelling of catching the ball and pivoting." "I want to zoom in on the point where you were giving feedback as you circulated during the independent task."	**The vague opener:** "Tell me about how you thought the lesson went." **More than one problem:** "I want to focus on the phonics input you did on the carpet and then how you shared objectives later on."
Foundational	Surface mental models 	Ask questions to surface the teacher's mental model of the situation: goals, actions and events, cause and effect and decision drivers. Share what you noticed and inferred if the teacher gets stuck.	"What was your goal in this situation?... And what did you do?... I noticed you gave the instructions as you walked in between desks." "What happened as you were giving feedback?" "What did you notice after you gave the instructions?" "What do you think caused that?" "What drove your decision to do [action]?"	**Jumping to judgement:** "You were focused on one student for too long and the rest of the class lost focus."
Foundational	Spotlight specifics 	Reinforce specifics from the situation that help to build a picture of what happened and what the problem might be.	"Don't worry that you can't remember. I've noted down that five students put their pens down. One minute later, five more did." "You said you noticed some students had written '1' on their boards. What did you do when you saw that?" "You said you tried to get Eliza to repeat Scott's answer. I noticed she couldn't do it and you said, "You need to listen Eliza." I wondered if it might also be because his answer was quite long. His answer was, "...""	**Jumping to judgement:** "Lots of students didn't follow your instructions because they weren't clear enough." "You noticed that some students had written '1' on their boards but you didn't do anything about it. Why?" **Obscuring the issue:** "There were five students writing. I guess they might still have been listening though."

Foundational or flexible	Technique	What it is	Examples	Non examples
Foundational	Identify the issue	The teacher may identify the issue for themselves when you zoom in and surface their mental model. If not, ask pertinent questions to generate insight or state what you think the issue might be (based on the evidence and linked to learning).	"You said your goal was to get students familiar with the causes of the war. You showed a video clip explaining them. We found about 8 of them couldn't pick out the causes. What was it about the video clip that might have contributed to this?" "I think the issue might be with your goal. You said you wanted students to come up with a prototype for their target audience. Given the level of discussion we heard, I wonder if the goal should first have been to develop their knowledge of these types of products. This might have given them more to discuss. What do you think?"	**Jumping to judgement:** "It didn't sound to me like you planned properly for that explanation." **Obscuring the issue:** "I wonder if the goal should first have been to develop their knowledge of these types of products. This might have given them more to discuss. But, then perhaps you felt they should know it?"
Foundational	Link to learning	Between you, explain how the issue impacts student learning.	"Why is it so important we address this issue?" "How might this be impacting student learning?" "We've noted that other students started to talk and look out of the window. There's learning time here that they are wasting."	**Unaccountable thinking:** "Your explanation took up too much time."
Foundational	Pin down the problem	After you've examined the situation and determined the issue, state and agree on the problem on two levels. 1. The problem as it impacted student learning. 2. a) The problem as related to Goodrich's teaching problems. b) The problem with the teacher's actions and decision-making.	"Let's articulate the problem we're seeing here. How does it impact student learning? Which of the teaching problems does it relate to? And what actions/decisions are we looking to change?" "It looks like we are saying that the problem is that students didn't have to think hard. This relates to the broader teaching problem of driving thought. We've concluded that the way you decided to ask the question may only have prompted one student to think hard."	**Obscuring the issue:** "So there's a problem with the way you did the explanation perhaps."

Foundational or flexible	Technique	What it is	Examples	Non examples
Flexible	Map mental models 	If you think the teacher may struggle to identify an issue, visually map out the components of their mental model for that specific situation, so you can examine their decision-making together.	"So based on what you've said, I've mapped your goal as 'check for all students' understanding' and we can see what we both noticed happening afterwards (actions and events) linked together by our cause and effect arrows. Let's map your reasons for your decisions (decision drivers) underneath."	**Skipping to solutions:** "Trust me when I say that students could get more out of your explanation if you use the example I'm about to show you."
Flexible	Meta moves 	Take opportunities to highlight the effective ways you and the teacher are thinking in order to work out the problem. This might include you 'showing your working', i.e., explaining how you formed and tested your hypothesis when observing the teacher.	"You really examined your decision-making there when you said you could see that your actions didn't meet your goal. This is the first step to improving it." "When I observed you, I noticed those two students coming in talking. My hypothesis was that they would be slow to start. It's important to test hypotheses though, so I wanted to share what was in their books five minutes in..."	**Skipping to solutions:** "OK, so you've said your explanation is the issue, what can we do about that?"
Flexible	Seesaw support 	Move between seeking the teacher's expertise and sharing your expertise depending on the weight of the teacher's knowledge in the moment. Seek first, then scaffold the question, then share.	"And what was the decision driver behind giving Michael feedback on that error?" (seek) [Teacher is unsure] "Why Michael specifically?" (scaffold) [Teacher can't recall] "My reflection was that you might have thought it was only Michael who was struggling with that question. Is that right?" (share)	**Playing 'guess what's in my head':** "Do you see an issue with how you gave the instructions?... Was there something about the order of them?... What do you think they didn't hear from you?"

Example 1 Foundational techniques

Let's see an example of a coach using the foundational techniques.

Context

Coach Sufian got tripped up when he saw teacher Leah's photosynthesis slide - he had a hunch there was too much information on it. He recorded what he saw, which enabled him to form the hypothesis that students hadn't listened to Leah's explanation and were trying to work out the images on the slide.

Watch how coach Sufian uses the foundational techniques in this stage: zoom in, surface mental models, spotlight specifics, identify the issue, link to learning, and pin down the problem to support teacher Leah to identify the issue.

Coaching Excerpt

Coach Sufian: Let's zoom in on your explanation of photosynthesis and the slide with the leaf diagram, that had the forest background, and the sunlight photo. Could we take another look at it?

Zoom in: coach focuses the teacher on one particular situation

Teacher Leah: *[Brings up the slide on the computer]*

Surface mental models: coach asks about the teacher's situation goal

Coach Sufian: What was your goal when you explained this slide?

Teacher Leah: I wanted to show how photosynthesis happens in nature, not just in a diagram. I thought the real images would make it more engaging.

Coach Sufian: Yes, that's understandable as otherwise it can feel quite abstract. Let's work out whether this happened. When you were explaining the diagram, what were students looking at?

Surface mental models: coach asks what events the teacher noticed

Teacher Leah: Probably the diagram… or maybe the photo? Not sure. There's a lot going on there, I guess.

Spotlight specifics: coach spotlights key evidence from the lesson that may indicate the issue

Coach Sufian: That's what I noticed too. Some were frowning at the board. I captured some specifics about what happened next: when you set the summarise task, one student asked, *"Which bit do we copy?"* and another *"Do we write about the forest?"* What does this suggest?

Identify the issue: coach asks this question after they've spotlighted key specifics to support the teacher to identify the issue

Teacher Leah: The images were maybe a bit overloading and they weren't concentrating on what I was saying. I didn't think about that. I thought more images would help, not distract.

Link to learning: coach holds their thinking accountable to learning

Coach Sufian: Yes I can see why. But let's think about what research suggests about using visuals. Cognitive load theory tells us that when we present too much visual information at once, students struggle to know where to focus and that can hinder learning.

Teacher Leah: Yeah, that makes sense.

Coach Sufian: So we can say that the learning problem seems to be that using too many images on the slide may have been overloading for students and they didn't listen properly to you. The teaching problem here would be the one we're working hard on already, 'optimising communication'.

Specifically, deciding to use all these images was driven by a desire to show them photosynthesis in the real world - a solid motivation - but showing all the images at once may have caused the problem.

So, to be clear, this doesn't mean it's wrong to use visuals. It's how we use them to convey ideas and avoid distracting students that matters.

Pin down the problem: coach states the problem clearly and makes sure the teacher doesn't overgeneralise and think visuals should not be used

Example 2 Foundational and flexible techniques

Let's see an example of a coach using the foundational and flexible techniques.

Context

Let's take a moment to look at what coach Sufian would do if teacher Leah really struggled to identify the issue. This next excerpt is a variation on the last one.

Notice how coach Sufian harnesses the power of the techniques **spotlight specifics** and **link to learning** to hold their conversation accountable to student learning and evidence from the lesson when teacher Leah struggles to see the issue. Sufian makes sure this does not feel like he's catching Leah out. He does this by explaining his process during observation (using evidence to form a hypothesis and then testing it against the evidence) – this is an example of the flexible technique **meta moves** where the coach helps the teacher understand how to *think* in order to improve. It also shows Leah that he hasn't jumped to judgement.

Watch how coach Sufian uses the foundational and flexible techniques in this stage: spotlight specifics, link to learning, and meta moves.

Coaching Excerpt

Coach Sufian: And when you were talking through that diagram, what do you think students were looking at?

Teacher Leah: The diagram, definitely. That's what I was talking about, and it was big on the screen. They didn't appear off task. I don't remember needing to stop and do a reset or anything.

Coach Sufian: Yes, I didn't notice you needing to do that for any behaviour issues. I noticed a group of students (two on the side table and two at the back) were frowning at the screen. It appeared as if they weren't sure what to focus on.

Spotlight specifics: coach highlights specific evidence to support the teacher to identify the issue

Teacher Leah: I'm not sure about that. They may have just been thinking about what I was saying.

Meta moves: coach 'shows their working' by explaining their thought process when forming a hypothesis and testing it against the evidence

Coach Sufian: I wasn't sure either. It was when I saw them frowning that I wondered if the slide might be distracting them – that was my hypothesis. I started to note down what was happening so we could work it out together. When you asked them to summarise, one student asked, *"Which bit do we copy?"* and another *"Do we write about the forest?"* This led me to think maybe they hadn't been listening, perhaps because they were distracted. What do you think?

Spotlight specifics: coach spotlights key evidence from the lesson that may indicate the issue

Teacher Leah: They like to do that sometimes... ask questions to stall the lesson a bit, I don't think it's about the slide.

Meta moves: coach involves the teacher in the process of identifying the issue by looking at the evidence

Coach Sufian: Totally fair – it could have been that. Let's follow the evidence. What happened when you asked them to label the diagram after?

Teacher Leah: Yeah a few couldn't do it fully I guess... And I think maybe some of them were the students you saw frowning. But I still think the images help. I've used them before and they've been fine?

Coach Sufian: Absolutely – and visuals can help. What we're digging into is how many, and how they're working together. Right now, there are three images doing three slightly different jobs, and that can overload working memory. Cognitive load theory tells us that if students are trying to figure out what's relevant, they can't listen properly to your explanation.

Link to learning: coach keeps the conversation rooted in what's best for student learning

Teacher Leah: So you're saying even if the images are good individually, together they might be too much? That might have been it.

Identify the issue: the culmination of spotlighting specifics, linking to learning and keeping it supportive using meta moves has helped the teacher identify the issue

Example 3 Flexible technique

Let's see an example of a coach using a flexible technique.

Context

Coach Amira got tripped up at the end of teacher Lewis' lesson when he asked the students a question and got poor responses despite what seemed like successful teaching earlier on.

Coach Amira formed the hypothesis that Lewis wanted deep thinking from students so he could check the depth of their understanding, but the way he asked questions only allowed for surface-level responses. She's holding her hypothesis lightly though and aims to surface and map Lewis' mental model so they can work to identify the issue together. She opts for mapping because it doesn't feel like a straightforward issue to uncover.

Watch how coach Amira uses a flexible technique in this stage: map mental models.

Coaching Excerpt

Zoom in: coach focuses the teacher on a particular situation

Surface mental models: coach asks about the teacher's situation goal

Coach Amira: Let's zoom in on the end of the lesson where you were asking children about the diary excerpt. What were you hoping to find out from the students at that point?

Teacher Lewis: I wanted to check their understanding to see if they recognised that it wasn't a diary entry.

Surface mental models: coach helps the teacher pin down their situation goal

Coach Amira: And when you say "understanding," what kind are we talking about – just spotting features or something more?

Teacher Lewis: More than spotting. I wanted them to think about whether it felt right for a diary, so not just the features, but the purpose of the writing too.

Coach Amira: Got it. So your goal was to efficiently check students' understanding of diary entries: both features and the purpose of the writing. Would you say that's accurate?

Map mental models: coach visually maps the teacher's mental model so they can examine it

Teacher Lewis: Yes, that's spot on.

Coach Amira: Great. Let's map that out.

That sounds like a strong goal at that point in the lesson as you'd taught them a lot and you wanted to do that final check before finishing. And so, what was the question you posed to them?

Teacher Lewis: I asked, "Does this feel like the end of a diary entry?"

Coach Amira: And how did you tell them to respond?

Teacher Lewis: Thumbs up or thumbs down. I wanted to check everyone quickly.

Surface mental models: coach asks about actions and events to check the teacher's awareness and align their mental models if necessary

Coach Amira: Okay. What did you do next?

Teacher Lewis: I asked *"Why not?"* and chose Maya to answer. She gave a vague answer. Then I asked Leo, but he didn't say anything. I ended up just giving them the answer myself.

Surface mental models: coach asks about the teacher's decision driver (the reason behind their action)

Coach Amira: What drove your decision to ask 'why not?' to a couple of students?

Teacher Lewis: I wanted to hear them explain how the extract on the board was different from a diary.

Map mental models: coach visually maps the teacher's mental model so they can examine it

Coach Amira: Ok, let's add to the map your actions and events, cause and effect and your decision drivers, so we can examine it more closely.
You started with a question: *"Does this feel like the end of a diary?"*
The response format you asked for was thumbs up/down. And the decision driver for that was because you wanted to quickly check everyone. Then you followed up with "Why not?" and asked individuals to explain. One gave a weak answer *('It doesn't sound like the diary from earlier')* the other didn't give an answer, and then you stepped in to explain it yourself. You asked this question to see if they could explain the difference between the extract and a diary entry given what you'd taught them.

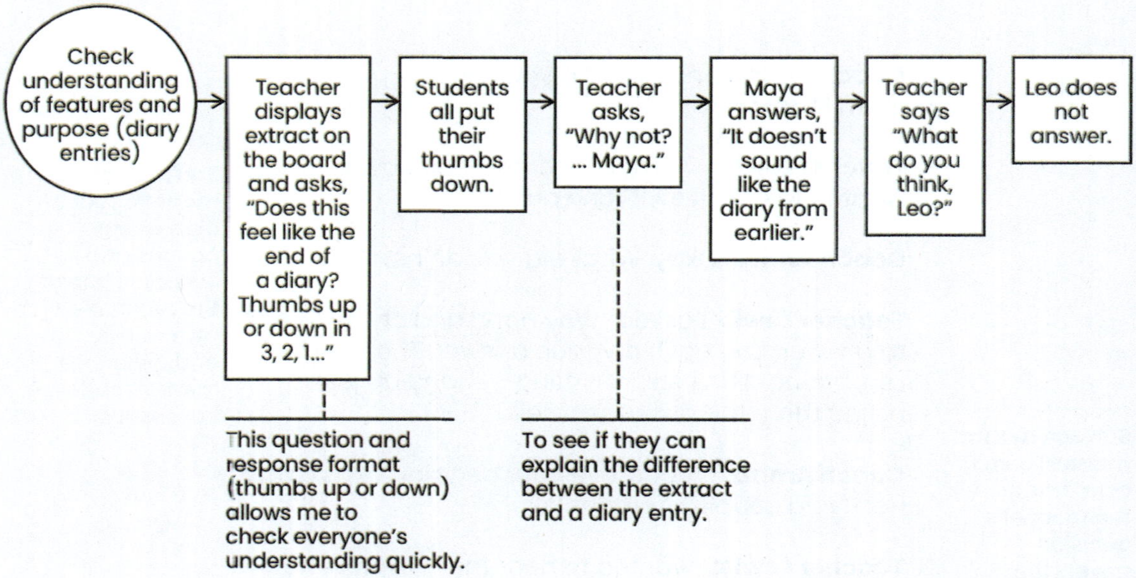

Teacher Lewis: Yeah, that's exactly how it went.

Coach Amira: And when you look back at the mapping there, how well do you think your actions supported your goal?

Identify the issue: coach asks a question designed to spark insight in the teacher about the issue

Teacher Lewis: *[Looks over the mapping]*. Actually... not very well, to be honest. The thumbs up or down gave me surface responses, and just asking them *'does this feel like a diary entry?'* was a bit vague. It wasn't really designed to get at whether they could articulate the purpose of the writing. I wanted a quick but deep check... but by choosing thumbs up or down, I prioritised quick over deep.

Coach Amira: Yes it looks like your action and decision driver there didn't align with your goal. But let's just check: what evidence do we have that this might be an issue?

[Coach Amira points to the end of the mapping where the students gave their answers]

Spotlight specifics: coach highlights specific evidence of the impact on student learning

Teacher Lewis: when I then asked *'why not?'*, they couldn't articulate it. They seemed a bit confused or taken off guard by the question.

Coach Amira: So you had a goal that needed depth, but the structure leaned more toward speed. Why is this an issue? Think about the impact on learning.

Link to learning: coach asks the teacher about the impact on learning

Teacher Lewis: Well... I don't think most of them actually had to explain or even fully form their thinking. Just a quick thumb up or down. And the ones who didn't get picked didn't get to practise reasoning at all. So I probably missed the chance to get them really consolidating their thinking on diary entries, and I definitely missed out on checking their understanding at that deeper level, which was my goal!

Coach Amira: That's a really thoughtful reflection. So, to sum up then: we think the learning problem is that students didn't have to think hard to respond to your question. This showed in their responses. The teaching problem then is around driving thought. You wanted to check deeper understanding but the format you used didn't call for that and so when you asked 'why?', students hadn't really prepared to answer in that way.

To be clear, thumbs up and down isn't a bad way to gather answers, but just didn't get you what you wanted this time around. Shall we work on what actions might better meet this goal? This will hopefully help you with these types of questions at the end of future lessons.

Pin down the problem: coach states the problem clearly and makes sure the teacher doesn't overgeneralise by thinking thumbs up and down is always the suboptimal decision

Teacher Lewis: Yes!

Example 4 Flexible techniques

Let's see an example of a coach using a different flexible technique.

Context

Let's take a moment to look at what coach Amira would do if she asks her question geared at helping Lewis identify the issue, but Lewis doesn't have the insight.

Watch how coach Amira uses a flexible technique in this stage: seesaw support.

Coaching Excerpt

Coach Amira: And when you look back at the mapping there, how well do you think your actions supported your goal?

Teacher Lewis: *[pauses]* I'm not sure... I guess... I don't know.

Coach Amira: That's okay, let's look carefully at our mapping. Your goal was to check their understanding of the features and purpose of diary entries: you asked the question, *"Does this feel like the end of a diary?"* and asked for thumbs up and thumbs down. What answers would you have needed to meet your goal?

Seesaw support: coach scaffolds their questions and spotlights specifics on the map to support the teacher to identify the issue

Teacher Lewis: Deeper. I wanted them to say that it isn't a diary entry because it wasn't written for the purpose of processing thoughts and the style wasn't expressive writing (like we'd discussed earlier).

Coach Amira: Right. So if we look at the question and response format, it didn't invite this thinking. The follow-up 'why' question didn't either as we can see from the responses, possibly because the question wasn't clear and/or they didn't have time to think about their answers. Take a moment to explain to me what the issue appears to be in relation to your goal and actions.

Seesaw support: coach decides to tell the teacher the issue so they can identify it

[coach points at the mapping]

Teacher Lewis: yes I see that now. In the moment, I was a bit confused about what I wanted I think. I now realise my goal was that deeper response and looking at my actions *[Lewis points to the mapping]* they didn't invite a deep response at all.

Example 5 Flexible techniques

Let's see an example of a coach using flexible techniques.

Context

Coach Daria and teacher Grant have been working on the goal of maintaining class attention for a few weeks in relation to different parts of the lesson. Coach Daria got tripped up when she noticed some students' attention slipping during whole-class questioning. She formed the hypothesis that the way Grant changed his questions may have led to the issue, so she recorded his questions and students' answers and behaviours (cause and effect) precisely when she mapped in preparation for coaching.

Watch how coach Daria uses a flexible technique in this stage: map mental models. Instead of mapping 'live' as coach Amira did in a previous example, coach Daria shares what she mapped when preparing for coaching. This is another way this technique can be used.

We join them now as they review a video clip from teacher Grant's lesson that shows the instance of whole-class questioning coach Daria wants to focus on.

Coaching Excerpt

Coach Daria: *[watching video]* So we've got this child here. What's she doing?

Zoom in: coach focuses the teacher on a situation in the lesson through their use of a video clip and questioning

Teacher Grant: Apparently she's looking down at her fingers… Yeah, this child is as well…

[They watch a little longer, then coach Daria pauses the video]

Coach Daria: Ok. So here's what I've done: I've mapped out what I thought was going on, and what I thought your mental model was of what was happening. Let's have a look through. If at any point you think, 'actually no, that's not why I was doing that', or 'I don't actually think that happened in that order', tell me and we can tweak it. I'm holding this lightly – this is my best guess at what you were thinking.

Surface mental models: as the coach presents a pre-prepared map, they are simultaneously surfacing mental models and checking with the teacher

Teacher Grant: Yes, sounds good.

Coach Daria: So, first: I thought your goal was to maintain attention during whole-class questioning. Was that right?

Map mental models: coach visually displays the situation goal they inferred when preparing for coaching

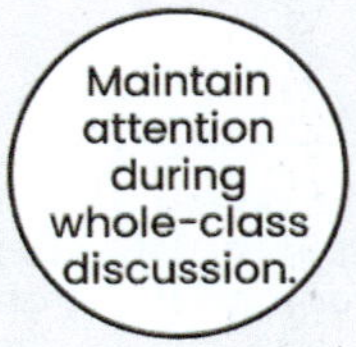

Teacher Grant: Yes, we've been working on that.

Coach Daria: Exactly, that was the goal we'd settled on last week too, which is great. We can go deeper into it.

Spotlight specifics: coach uses the exact language the teacher used

The first thing that happened was you posed this question: "Why does this not show one quarter?" Then you said, "Tracking...Elena."

The effect of this was that the whole class looked at Elena and appeared to be listening. Does that sound right?

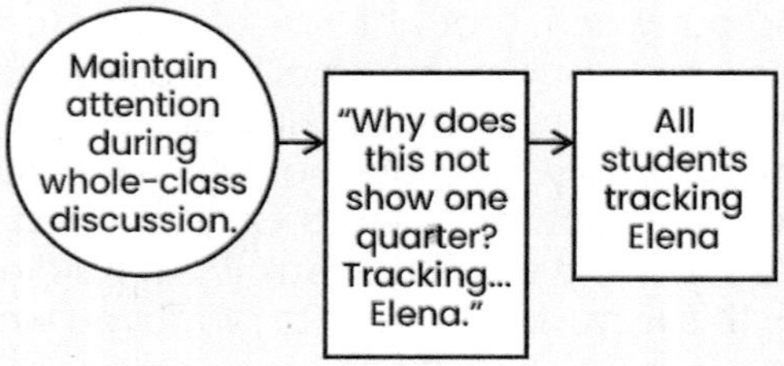

Teacher Grant: Yes.

Coach Daria: You followed up with a second question: "What fraction would be coloured in then, Elena?"

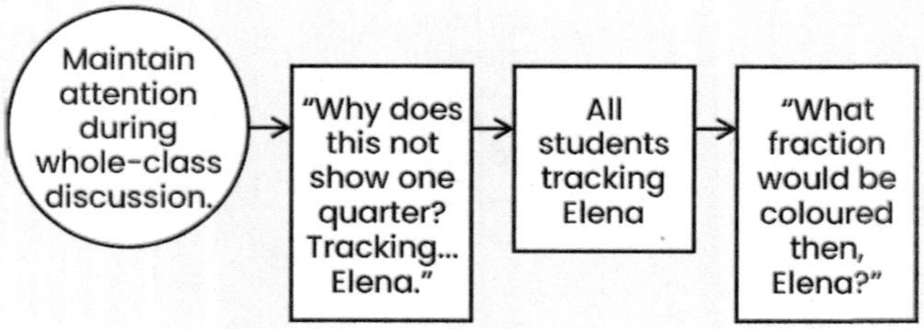

The context was that the fraction on the board wasn't one quarter (it was two quarters) and you were expecting her to say "two quarters."

Teacher Grant: Right.

Coach Daria: What's the difference between this question and the first one?

Identify issue: coach asks a question to generate insight about the issue

Teacher Grant: I didn't say, "Tracking, Elena" again (although they should still have been tracking her). And maybe I could have opened it up a bit more to others.

Surfacing mental models: coach attempts to surface the teacher's mental model of cause and effect

Coach Daria: What was the effect we saw on the video in relation to your goal of maintaining whole-class attention?

Teacher Grant: A couple were looking at their hands, so I didn't have the whole class at that point.

Spotlight specifics: coach keeps the conversation rooted in specific evidence from the lesson

Coach Daria: And about three or four others looked away I think.

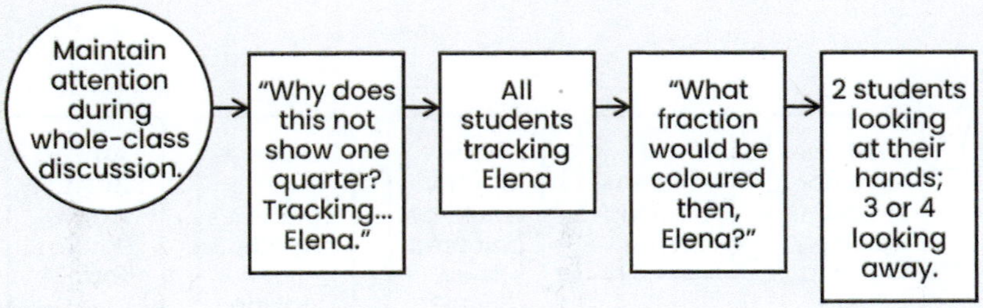

Ok, then you asked the third question: "Amelia, how many do we have in total?"

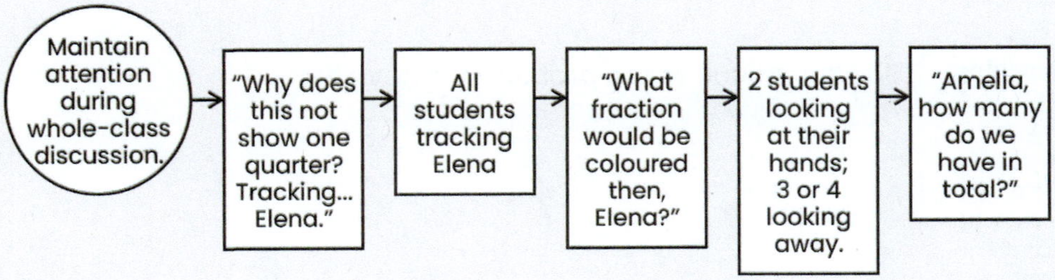

Identify the issue: coach asks a question to generate insight about the issue

What's the difference between that question and the first two?

Teacher Grant: Hmm... there's been a different pattern each time. I've not said "tracking Amelia" and actually I've not put Amelia's name last so that everyone has to think in case I choose them. I've tried to finish the questioning sequence quickly. I probably felt like I was losing them. But then you lose more learning when you're trying to finish it quickly.

Coach Daria: Really counterintuitive, isn't it. It's great how you surfaced your reason for your actions (trying to finish quickly) and reflected that it's actually a false economy, since fewer children are having to think hard. It's this surfacing and examining of your mental model that can help develop your decision-making in future. Let's map that on and the effect of that final question. I saw more students looking away (seven now) and two had picked up pencils.

Meta moves: coach reinforces an effective method of improvement, i.e., surfacing and examining their mental model

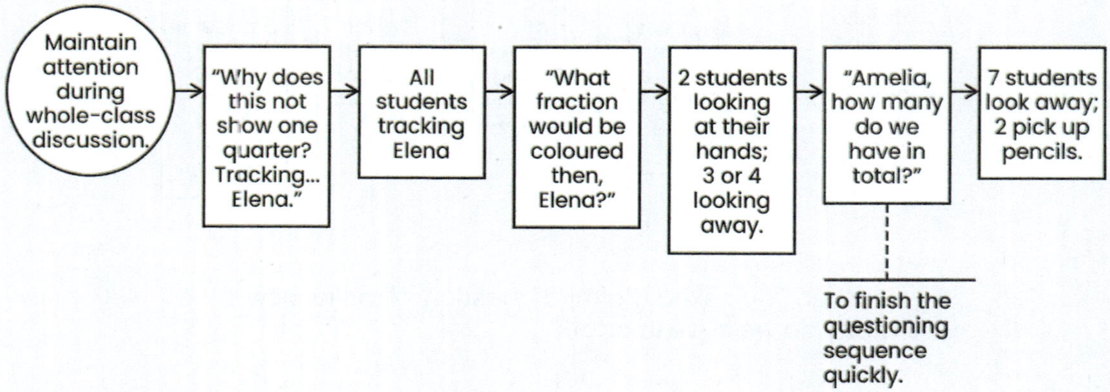

Link to learning: whilst pinning down the problem, the coach makes sure the teacher understands the impact on learning

So let's articulate the problem we have here. Let's start with the learning problem?

Teacher Grant: If the rest of the class aren't paying attention, they won't be learning.

Coach Daria: Exactly. So we stick with the teaching problem we've been working on: ensure attention. Specifically, by changing how you asked your questions (not asking students to track the speaker and not putting the name last in that third question) in order to speed up the questioning, some students showed visible signs that they weren't listening.

Pin down the problem: coach defines the problem in terms of the learning problem (above) and the teaching problem, plus the teacher's actions and decisions

Coaching commentary

This is where we get meta and analyse the quality of the coaching in the examples above.

Below we explain how the coaches' use of techniques supports their teachers to understand, do, decide, and improve, i.e., to develop their adaptive expertise.

Understand

...key knowledge that helps solve persistent problems.

Do

...a repertoire of effective, efficient teaching techniques.

Decide

...on the best course of action using situation-sensitive mental models.

Improve

...continuously through an adaptive mindset and metacognition.

Understand

Our coaches in these examples all use the technique **zoom in** to make sure they develop the teacher's knowledge of *one* particular situation. This technique avoids the pitfalls 'the vague opener' and 'more than one problem,' which can overload the teacher and prevent them developing a deep understanding of how learning occurs. In addition, all of the coaches **link to learning** (using a question or sharing their expertise) to develop their teacher's understanding of how a practice impacts student learning. For example, coach Amira directly asks teacher Lewis, 'Why is this an issue? Think about the impact on learning.' Link to learning also keeps the conversation accountable to what's best for students. Coach Sufian uses it with teacher Leah to support her to understand the issue: 'Right now, there are three images doing three slightly different jobs and that can overload working memory.'

The coaches ensure they **pin down the problem** by the end of this coaching stage. Stating it specifically helps ensure both coach and teacher agree. And, by articulating it both in terms of learning and teaching, the teacher can develop their understanding of how their actions impact student learning as well as a deeper understanding of the learning and teaching problems themselves.

Do

At this stage of coaching, our coaches are not developing their teacher's ability to do a technique – this begins in the next stage. This stage is about examining the actions the teacher did take in context, often to check if they are aligned with a powerful goal and had the effect the teacher wanted.

Decide

You'll notice that this stage of coaching (study the problem) contains a lot of techniques geared at surfacing and examining the teacher's mental model to work out the problem.

All of our coaches use the technique **surface mental models** to understand the teacher's decision-making in the situation they've focused on. They do this by asking about the teacher's goal, then their awareness of actions and events. This helps them assess the teacher's mental model of the situation: is their goal a good one linked to learning? Are they aware of what happened or did they miss anything? The teacher often volunteers the decision drivers behind their actions and sometimes their understanding of cause and effect. If not and where relevant, coaches can also ask about these components of their mental models.

Coach Amira finds teacher Lewis to have quite an accurate recollection of what happened and he's open about his decision drivers. She moves quickly to support him to **identify the issue** by getting him to reflect on his mental model: 'How well do your actions support your goal?'

However, sometimes teachers need support to surface their mental model or identify the issue. Teacher Leah was struggling to see the issue and kept explaining the evidence away. Coach Sufian found the evidence compelling so he used **spotlight specifics** to keep Leah's thinking accountable to the evidence from the lesson: one student asked, "What do we copy?" and another "Do we write about the forest?" Quoting evidence could feel like trying to catch the teacher out though. To avoid this, coach Sufian uses the technique **meta moves**, where he shares the thinking he did to prepare for coaching. He's tentative but clear: 'I wasn't sure either. It was when I saw them frowning that I wondered if the slide might have been distracting them . . .' This models to the teacher how to *think* in order to understand the problem. At no point does Sufian fall foul of the pitfalls 'playing guess what's in my head,' 'obscuring the issue,' or 'unaccountable thinking.' He maintains a steadfast focus on the specific evidence from the lesson throughout to help Leah see the issue with her decision-making.

Teacher Lewis struggled to identify the issue too. He wasn't explaining the evidence away (like teacher Leah) - he just couldn't work out what the issue might be. In this instance, coach Amira used the technique **seesaw support**. First she scaffolded her question (using the mapping she had done of his mental model) by asking a more focused question and ultimately by sharing her expertise, so he could identify the issue.

Coaches Daria and Amira use the technique **map mental models** to -

1. Check their hypothesis about the issue and
2. Support the teacher to identify the issue.

This technique may not be necessary if the teacher is able to identify the issue just by surfacing their mental model (hence why it's a flexible coaching technique). Coach Amira uses it because she wants to check her hypothesis that Lewis's goal doesn't match well with his actions. Mapping means they don't have to hold all the components in mind and allows her to point Lewis to the map to help him gain insight. In contrast, coach Daria opts to expose her mapping (from her coaching preparation) because she wants teacher Grant to spot the lack of consistency between his questions as the probable cause of the lack of attention. Without the mapping, Grant would have to hold this in mind, taking up the cognitive capacity he needed to examine his mental model and identify the issue.

Improve

The technique **map mental models** serves another function too. The coach visually represents the necessary components of the teacher's mental model of the situation to aid them in examining it and identifying the issue. This practice of surfacing, representing, and examining is a key sense-making exercise that can support teachers to overcome the knowing-deciding-doing gap. In other words, as well as an aid for identifying issues, mapping helps teachers understand what it takes to improve their decision-making and practice.

Another technique to support teachers to understand how to improve is **meta moves**. We've touched on how coach Sufian uses it to 'show his working out,' i.e., explain his tentative thought process when observing Leah. This models to Leah how to *think* in order to improve. Coach Daria explicitly reinforces teacher Grant's thinking (surfacing and examining) when she says, 'It's great how you surfaced your reason for your actions . . . It's this surfacing and examining of your mental model that can help you develop your decision-making . . .' By highlighting and reinforcing the ways teachers think in order to improve, coaches help teachers to get better at getting better.[11]

Do this in your coaching

Let's look at how we can use these coaching techniques at the right time for the right reasons in our coaching.

Get started with these foundational techniques

When you're trying something new in your coaching, you need some foundational techniques to adopt. Try these techniques using one of the suggested sentence stems.

Zoom in:

- Let's focus on . . .
- Let's zoom in on . . .

Surface mental models:

- What was your goal? . . . I thought it might be . . .
- What happened? . . . I noticed . . .

- What do you think caused X? I think . . .
- What was your reason for doing/deciding X? . . . I thought it might be . . .

Spotlight specifics:

- I noticed three students put their hands up straight away . . .
- What did you notice about the words Reshma used in her answer?
- Then you asked the question, 'Isla, what is the mass of the block?'

Identify the issue:

- We noticed students lost attention during that series of questions. What do you think might have caused that?
- Your goal was to get everyone's attention but your reason for giving the instructions right away was to move on with the lesson. The issue we identified might stem from your actions and decision drivers being at odds with your goal.
- So, thinking about the actions you took, who is doing the most cognitive work? . . . What evidence suggests this might have been a problem?

Link to learning:

- What do we think the impact was on student learning?
- This may be an issue for students with weaker prior knowledge because they aren't going to naturally make the link between last lesson and this lesson.

Pin down the problem:

- Now we've worked out what we think it is, can you sum up the learning problem and the teaching problem that may have caused it?
- So we have said that the problem is related to ensuring attention: putting the name first means other students get to switch off because they don't think they will be asked.

Adapt your coaching appropriately using flexible techniques

Have these flexible techniques in your coaching repertoire to use when needed.

Map mental models: The coach asks questions to surface the components of the teacher's mental model of the situation: goal(s), actions and events, decision drivers, and understanding of cause and effect. The coach visually represents the teacher's mental model of the situation so it can be examined.

Meta moves:

- My hypothesis was that the question on the worksheet took it a step further than your modelling, so I thought they would struggle. I gathered evidence from their answers and noticed . . .

- By identifying the issue with your actions and goal, you've done a great job of examining your decision-making. This is crucial for identifying the issue as accurately as we can.

Seesaw support:

- **Seek** the teacher's expertise by asking a question, e.g., 'How might this impact student learning?'
- **Scaffold** the question with a narrower focus and more cues if they can't answer well, e.g., 'Think about the impact it had on their ability to complete the independent task.'
- **Share** your expertise if they can't answer well, e.g., 'If we don't create space for students to process new information in relation to what they already know, even if they are listening to you, they may not really be understanding it.'

Notes

1 Witherspoon, E. B., Ferrer, N. B., Correnti, R. R., Stein, M. K., and Schunn, C. D. (2021) 'Coaching that supports teachers' learning to enact ambitious instruction,' *Instructional Science*, *49*(6), pp. 877-898.

2 Parrish, S. (2023) *Clear thinking: Turning ordinary moments into extraordinary results*. London: Penguin.

3 Pretz, J. E., Naples, A. J., and Sternberg, R. J. (2003) 'Recognizing, defining, and representing problems,' *The Psychology of Problem Solving*, 30(3), pp. 3-30.

4 Walsh, M. E., Witherspoon, E. B., Schunn, C. D. and Matsumura, L. C. (2023) 'Mental simulations to facilitate teacher learning of ambitious mathematics instruction in coaching interactions,' *International Journal of STEM Education*, 10(1), p. 9.

5 The language of awareness and insights is drawn from Goodrich, J. (2024) *Responsive coaching: Evidence-informed instructional coaching that works for every teacher in your school*. Woodbridge: John Catt.

6 Ward, P., Gore, J., Hutton, R., Conway, G., and Hoffman, R. (2018) 'Adaptive skill as the *conditio sine qua non* of expertise,' *Journal of Applied Research in Memory and Cognition*, 7(1), pp. 35-50.

7 Thank you to Anna Jordan, Senior Deputy Headteacher at Derby High School, for this phrase.

8 Dmitrenko, N., Panchenko, V., and Shkola, I. (2025) 'The role of reflection in the teaching practicum of prospective English language teachers,' *Journal of Cross-Cultural Education*, (5), pp. 38-45.

9 Author Sarah Cottinghatt was particularly guilty of sneaking in extra issues and solutions using this phrase.

10 Ausubel, D. P. (2012) *The acquisition and retention of knowledge: A cognitive view*. Dordrecht: Springer Science & Business Media.

11 Lemov, D., Woolway, E., and Yezzi, K. (2012) *Practice perfect: 42 rules for getting better at getting better*. Hoboken, NJ: John Wiley & Sons.

Stage 3

Specify the step

This stage, **specify the step**,[1] is a crucial part of the coaching process. This is the stage where the goal for the teacher is stated in clear and specific terms. This is vital, as teachers, like all learners, have limited working memory capacity. If coaching is vague or tries to address too many areas at once, it overwhelms rather than supports. Goals must be *granular*[2] to avoid overloading the teacher and enable change to happen, but what is overloading depends on the current capabilities of each teacher.

Specifying the step helps the teacher focus on one small, actionable change, reduces ambiguity and decision fatigue, and forms the focus for the rest of the coaching process. Without specifying the step, coaching becomes subjective and hard to implement. A vague goal like 'improve questioning' is much less helpful than 'ask a cold-call question and follow up with probing questions.' But we can go even more granular and specific than this by stating concretely when, what, and why. This not only specifies the step for the teacher but is a framework for building their mental model of the practice so they know how to do the right thing at the right time for the right reasons.

Furthermore, clear steps create a shared understanding between a coach and teacher, as it ensures both parties are working towards the same visible behaviour. When a step is specific and observable, it's also easier to monitor whether it has been implemented, celebrate success, and decide if it's time to move on to the next stage of improvement.

By this point in the coaching conversation, the teacher is invested in the change because they can see the problem. However, if the step is granular and achievable, this is also more likely to motivate them to believe they can make the change and be successful in doing so. Experiencing success with small steps builds momentum for change over time.

Coach and teacher are looking for the best step to solve the problem they've studied - this may well be the one the coach has already planned in Stage 0 Prepare for coaching by diagnosing need, or they may land on a different one during the conversation. Action steps can be to improve a teacher's *performance* of a technique or they can be to support a teacher's *planning*. Let's again be clear on the difference between the two:

Performance action steps: action steps that involve in-lesson teaching techniques, e.g. action steps about delivering explanations, questions, responding to students' answers, managing behaviour, etc.

DOI: 10.4324/9781003465850-12

Planning action steps: action steps that involve developing a thought process when planning, e.g. action steps about planning lesson learning goals, retrieval questions, hinge questions, planning to increase challenge, etc.

However, categorising these types of action steps can be problematic. This is because performance action steps will usually involve some scripting (planning) and planning action steps will often also eventually be executed (performance). For example, a planning step might involve scripting some modelling for students. The corresponding performance step might be about delivering the script using 'my turn, our turn, your turn' with a strong teacher voice. Setting both the planning of the modelling and the delivery as one action step may not be granular enough to avoid overloading your teacher. This means making a decision about whether the problem you have studied is best remedied by the planning or performance step. But remember, coaches can also plan to coach on a series of steps over time too, so not choosing one doesn't mean it won't ever be coached on.

Let's look at the purposes of the 'specify the step' stage in more detail.

Purposes

Create clarity: 'I get what I'm meant to do . . . on paper.'
We need to make sure that teachers are clear what they need to do next. A clearly defined action step and success criteria remove a lot of ambiguity. Rather than vague goals like 'improve questioning,' the teacher knows what to do next. This clarity helps the teacher *begin* to understand what to do to improve. Their mental model is like a blueprint: after this stage, they should know what to do 'on paper.'

Obviously observable: 'I feel motivated because my coach will be able to observe the progress I am making.'
A good action step is measurable. Both coach and teacher can see whether it's been implemented and whether it made a difference.

Same page: 'Both me and my coach are working towards the same thing.'
A specific action step ensures that both the coach and teacher are working toward the same outcome. It avoids miscommunication and helps maintain trust.

Pitfalls

Pitfalls are typical occurrences that can undermine this coaching stage.

Over- and under-specifying the step: an action step that is too micro or procedural can lose sight of the intent behind the practice. For example, if a coach asks a teacher to just 'stand on the left side of the board while giving instructions' this would definitely miss the broader goal of improving clarity and authority during transitions. This could just lead to teachers complying without understanding, which may lead to robotic practice that lacks professional judgement. As demonstrated in the rest of this book, coaching cannot become tick-box or performative if we want to improve decision-making and cultivate adaptive expertise. Yet, under-specifying the action step can also be an issue. Indeed, if steps are too vague, it leaves the teacher struggling to know exactly what they need to do. It can sometimes also fall into a 'Captain Obvious fallacy' where teachers are told they need to do something, which they already knew they had to do and the coach's support makes it no clearer how they take the step, or exactly what that step looks like. For example, 'Be more commanding when you give instructions' or 'Make your explanations easier for students to grasp.' This is the equivalent of telling a footballer to score more goals, or a surgeon to save more lives. Instead, specifying the step (when, what and why) as well as the success criteria will help the teacher gain clarity on what they need to do.

No success criteria: without success criteria, neither the coach nor the teacher knows how to do the action step. This leads to vague expectations and makes it harder for the coach to show a model and the teacher to rehearse meaningfully (both later stages of the coaching conversation - 'see the step' and 'simulate the step'). If there's no agreed standard or outcome, feedback becomes subjective or inconsistent because teachers are held to secret standards. Neither coach nor teacher can know if there's progress and coaches can't give specific, actionable feedback. This means teachers will struggle to feel a sense of achievement. Avoid coaching feeling like guesswork rather than growth work and pair the action step with clear and concise success criteria.

Missing the most important step: sometimes it can be hard to see the wood for the trees and the specified step targets a symptom, not the root cause. This might look like a coach advising that a teacher improves their checking for understanding, yet the classroom culture is not conducive to them doing this. This could become a problem, as it just leads to superficial change and the teacher's efforts might not translate into better learning. This causes frustration for both the teacher and the coach. Instead, view Goodrich's teaching problems[3] as a hierarchy:

- Ensure attention
- Optimise communication
- Drive thought
- Gather and give feedback
- Ensure consolidation

Generally speaking, evidence you have of a problem higher up the hierarchy (e.g. with 'ensure attention') will be more fruitful to address than one lower down. Of course, there will be exceptions - sometimes you might decide to stick within a problem lower down because it is where the teacher has been working for a while and you want to deepen that understanding - but as a rule of thumb, go upstream.

Unaccountable thinking: if the coach does not explain why the step matters, or discuss how it, or the success criteria, connect to student learning, the teacher may not understand why it's likely to be beneficial. For example, if the step specified is to use gradual release (often now referred to as 'I do, We do, You do') to help students master a skill, without an understanding of how it supports cognitive load, it may lead to shallow implementation. In the long run, this also reduces teacher agency and adaptability, as they will not be able to use the specified step at the right time, for the right reasons.

Ignoring complexity: by this point in the conversation, coaches and teachers have a good sense of what the problem might be. But complexity means we can't be certain. This means we cannot guarantee that the action step set will definitely solve the problem. Having adaptive expertise means holding ideas lightly, accepting that we need to hypothesise, test, monitor, and evaluate. So avoid being certain that the action step will work. Instead, be clear that it will be a process of implementation that will need to be closely monitored by the teacher and coach.

Over directing or under supporting: it is important to carefully diagnose how much support the teacher needs to specify the step. This is not as simple as just assuming that a teacher will be able to specify their own step if they have been teaching for a long time or that they won't have any good ideas if they are relatively new to teaching.

Experienced teachers may struggle to specify a step because knowing how to teach and knowing how to break down teaching are two different types of expertise (hence why this book is all about how to coach!). If they were the same, then every great teacher would automatically be a great coach. Even very experienced teachers may need a lot of support from a coach when it comes to setting an action step and success criteria. Similarly, newer teachers may not always need to be told the step. They may have ideas of their own. Coaches can always ask the teacher what they think would work and of course, hold any ideas accountable to what is best for student learning.

As knowledge of teaching strategies and success criteria develops across the school and between coaches and teachers, teachers may feel more confident co-constructing the action step and success criteria with the coach. A good rule of thumb is that we seesaw support: we seek the teacher's expertise, scaffold (if we think this will help) and then share our own.

Coaching techniques

Use these coaching techniques to help your teacher **specify the step**.

Some techniques are foundational, i.e., we should always use them and some are flexible, i.e., to be used when appropriate, depending on the level of the teacher's expertise in the moment.

Foundational or flexible	Technique	What it is	Examples	Non examples
Foundational	When what why 	Always use the structure 'when, what, why' for writing an action step so that steps help build mental models.	When diffusing off task behaviour, use proximity to remind students of your presence because this is non-threatening and unlikely to disrupt learning in the lesson.	**Underspecifying the step:** Pre-empt off-task behaviour.
Foundational	Meta moves 	Check the teacher understands how the step is likely to solve their problem. Emphasise the ways of thinking such as hypothesising, testing, monitoring, iterating and evaluating.	"We hypothesised that students aren't able to improve from the feedback because they don't understand it. How is this action step around whole-class specific feedback likely to help solve this problem?" "What will we see that might suggest it's working?"	**Ignoring complexity:** "This step will solve the problem and we'll see all students behaving as they should."
Foundational	Spell out success 	State concretely the success criteria for the step.	"The success criteria for this action step on using 'turn and talk' are – • A clear prompt question and goal for the talk task. • Roles for both students where each have to talk • Circulate with purpose: circulating the room and listening out for misconceptions and key words. • Structured sharing: cold call specific students for curated conversation."	**No success criteria:** "Now we've got the action step, we're ready to see a model..."
Foundational	Link to learning 	Check the teacher understands how the success criteria are likely to support learning.	"Why is the success criteria 'circulate with purpose' important to support learning?"	**Unaccountable thinking:** "That is just good teaching."

Foundational or flexible	Technique	What it is	Examples	Non examples
Foundational	Precision and decision	Be clear on which success criteria need to be adhered to (precision) and which can be contextualised and adapted (requiring a decision) - crucially, check or state how to make the decisions around these success criteria.	"You'll see from the success criteria that it's important when using 'show me' boards to check for understanding that all students put them up at the same time. This is something we are precise with, so that students are less likely to copy each other's answers and we get their answer. However, how you respond based on what you see might vary. We need to make a decision here..." "You'll see from the success criteria that greeting students at the classroom door is a precision success criterion. This is so they have a warm welcome, and we can remind them of what to do. But what you say when you greet them is up to you - it requires a decision. We'll look at a few examples when I model it to you next and you can see what sounds natural and useful for you and your students."	**Too precise:** "You'll want to do all of these success criteria in the way I'm about to show you." **Hiding expert decision-making:** "We need to make a decision about which check for understanding technique we use. Just pick the best one."
Flexible	Seesaw support	Provide the action step/success criteria when the teacher needs you to. Co-construct it if the teacher has the expertise.	"A possible solution is a 'do now' task at the start of the lesson to create a purposeful climate for learning." Coach: "What could we do to create a smoother start?" Teacher: "How about a 'do now' task?" Coach: "How would that solve the problem?" Teacher: "Students have a clear routine at the start of the lesson and work to do from the get go." Coach: "That makes sense. Let's create an action step for that using the 'when, what, why' format..."	**Over directs or under supports:** The coach either always provides the action step and success criteria without asking the teacher or leaves it to them to come up with when they don't have the expertise to do so.

Example 1 Foundational and flexible techniques

Let's see an example of a coach using foundational and flexible techniques.

Context

Coach Yuvraj is working with teacher Alex who is new to the school and in his second year of teaching. Alex has been finding it challenging to ensure all students pay attention and to maintain this for the whole lesson. Yuvraj supports Alex throughout by providing the action step, success criteria, and breaking down their questions to support Alex to answer. This is deliberate, since Yuvraj sees Alex needs this support.

Watch how coach Yuvraj uses the foundational techniques in this stage: when what why, link to learning, spell out success, and precision and decision, as well as the flexible technique, seesaw support.

Coaching Excerpt

Coach Yuvraj: What are your thoughts on an action step that would work to solve the problem we think you're facing around ensuring all students are paying attention?

Seesaw support: coach seeks the teacher's expertise first, scaffolding the question by reminding the teacher of the problem they hypothesised, then sharing their expertise when the teacher struggles to answer

Teacher Alex: I'm not sure exactly. I think I need a good routine like I see from other teachers.

Coach Yuvraj: I agree. Here's an action step I think would work to solve the problem we think you're facing around ensuring all students are paying attention:

- *When* you need all students' attention...
- *What* you'll do is stand where you can be seen, use a clear call for attention, and only move on when every student is visibly attending.
- *Why*? Because having everyone's attention makes it more likely they'll all listen to the next part of the lesson and not waste lesson time asking you what they should be doing.

When what why: the coach has prepared an action step that tells the teacher when to do it, what to do and links it to learning with the 'why'

How might that solve the problem we hypothesised?

Teacher Alex: Well, we said that students might be asking me what to do because they haven't listened to the instructions properly. Our hypothesis was that this happened because there wasn't a clear call for their attention before the instructions. So that action step is all about me devising one and making sure it works to get everyone's attention before speaking. I think that sounds good.

Meta moves: coach gets the teacher thinking about how the action step might solve the problem. The emphasis is on key ways of thinking about improving such as hypothesising, testing and evaluating

Coach Yuvraj: How would we know if it has worked?

Teacher Alex: I guess we'd ultimately see visible signs of them all paying attention to me and we'd see them following instructions without having to ask me to repeat them?

Coach Yuvraj: Yes I agree. When you test this out in your lessons, we'll hopefully see these benefits. So now we've got the action step, let's look at what makes it work. Here are the four success criteria. Have a read:

- **Consistent cue**: use the same signal every time, so it becomes a routine.

Spell out success: coach makes the action step clearer by stating granular success criteria

- **Concrete concise instructions**: tell them exactly what "attention" looks like. For example: *"3…pens down. 2…eyes on me. 1… sitting up straight."* This helps them get it right.
- **Visible position**: stand where you can see all of them and they can see you. That helps your signal carry and helps you scan.
- **Scan**: after your cue, actively scan the room. This makes it feel like it's urgent they follow your cue.

Link to learning: coach has selected a success criteria they suspect the teacher needs to understand the most and asks the teacher to explain why it matters

Talk to me about why the consistent cue matters for creating a routine?

Teacher Alex: Routines rely on consistency. I want students to know what to do really quickly, so I can get them focused.

Link to learning: coach asks a question to drill down into the impact on student learning

Coach Yuvraj: Yes. How will this support learning?

Meta moves: coach gets the teacher thinking about how the action step might solve the problem. The emphasis is on key ways of thinking about improving such as hypothesising, testing and evaluating

Teacher Alex: Routines support learning because children know what to do and it's easier to behave in this productive way they are used to. This means we can spend more time on learning.

Seesaw support: coach has asked the question a couple of different ways and the teacher has given good reasons but not all the reasons, so the coach shares their expertise

Coach Yuvraj: Exactly that. Plus, if we keep these routine aspects of lessons the same, it also has the benefit of spotlighting the things that do change in the lesson – the learning content. This is what we want students thinking hard about. Not 'what behaviour does my teacher expect of me?'

Teacher Alex: Ah ok so it supports behaviour and learning. That makes sense.

Coach Yuvraj: Yes, nicely put! So as ever, the success criteria require some precision, which means we need to stick to them. But there are elements that require decisions so we can personalise to you and your class. Our school have a consistent cue – a countdown – for getting students' attention. This is precise for us, so that all students experience the same routine. But, there are aspects that require decisions too. I sometimes use a silent countdown when students are doing group work so I don't have to shout over them and strain my voice. I also vary the instructions depending on what they are doing. I just need to make sure they are actually concrete and concise!

Precision and decision: coach gives the teacher a clearer understanding of how to use this technique by stating what requires precision and what requires decisions. Coach explains how they make these decisions

I'll show you a model of what I tend to do and we'll discuss what would work for you for the success criteria that require decisions when we plan for rehearsal...

Example 2 Foundational and flexible techniques

Let's see a second example of a coach using foundational and flexible techniques.

Context

Coach Diana and teacher Fran have a hypothesis that the problem she's experiencing is related to 'driving thought.'[4] This is because Fran is seeing that students are struggling to retain the ideas she's teaching them even within a lesson. Diana and Fran suspect this is because she is waiting until the near the end of the one-hour lesson to do any sort of consolidation task. They decide that these consolidation tasks should be more frequent and shorter to enable students to think hard at key points in the lesson. Coach Diana seesaws support, moving between asking open questions to give Fran a go at devising her action step and providing her with scaffolding too.

Watch how coach Diana uses all of the foundational techniques for this stage: when what why, link to learning, spell out success, precision and decision, and meta moves as well as the flexible technique, seesaw support.

Coaching Excerpt

Coach Diana: Let's try putting that into a clear step you could use stating when you'd do it, what you'll do and why. Just like the other steps we've worked on in the past. Let's both take a moment individually to write down what we think.

When what why: the coach scaffolds the teacher's creation of an action step using when what and why

Seesaw support: coach allows the teacher space to try constructing the action step

[Diana and Fran take a minute to write down their thoughts]

What have you got?

Teacher Fran: When I've got to logical points in my lesson, What I'll do is give students a short task that gets them using the knowledge straight away. Why? So they have to process the idea actively before it fades.

Coach Diana: That works and mine is similar actually. I think we just need to be clearer about the 'when' because 'logical point' feels a little too subjective. When should we use these tasks? Think back to the lesson itself. When did you say you should have used one?

Seesaw support: coach asked focused questions to get the teacher to write a clearer action step

Teacher Fran: After I explained the process. But I guess sometimes it's after I've explained a key concept too or clarified one they struggled with in their homework. So, we can change 'logical points' to 'key processes and concepts'?

Coach Diana *[writes]*: *When I've explained key processes and concepts in my lesson.*

Meta moves: coach prompts the teacher to think about how the action step is likely to solve the problem and emphasises how they will monitor for signs of success or otherwise

Nice. How is this likely to solve the problem we identified earlier? And, how will we know if it has?

Teacher Fran: I'm strategically inserting points where students need to process the important stuff I've taught them. Hopefully they should then be able to use these ideas to think really hard at the end of the lesson. I guess we will know if they have a high success rate on the questions in the final task. At the moment they are really struggling just to recall what we've done earlier in the lesson. They'll also be able to tackle some of the stretch questions, which I deliberately make contextually different (a different acid is involved in the reaction than the one discussed for example).

Coach Diana: Yes, these are the measures of the success of this approach: can they recall the ideas better at the end of the lesson and use them in more complex ways? You'll be monitoring for this as you try it out and of course, I'll come back in to observe.

Now we need to make it more specific by stating the success criteria – the ingredients that make this step 'work'. You've already pointed us towards some of the areas we need to unpack here by using particular phrases in the action step. First, you use the words "short task": we need to think how long (roughly) these consolidation tasks should take. Secondly, you've said "using the knowledge": what kinds of tasks might these be? Finally, something we haven't touched on yet is how you might monitor students' answers?

Seesaw support: coach scaffolds how to devise success criteria by pointing the teacher to the areas of the action step that need more granular definition

Teacher Fran: Ok. I think realistically in an hour's lesson, with time at the end for extended practice (albeit not as much), each consolidation task should be less than 5 minutes. The type of task will vary but it will be to summarise in their own words or apply what I've just explained – not copy stuff down. This will get them thinking hard. The final point around checking… I'm lucky as there's only 12 of them, so I'll circulate to check but I'll have my checklist of things I need to see in their answers so I know what I'm looking for.

Spell out success: coach formulates success criteria based on what the teacher has suggested.

Coach Diana: Ok so, how about these success criteria:

1. **Timed and Targeted:** Each task is under 5 minutes and clearly linked to the specific idea or process just taught.

2. **Apply or summarise:** Tasks ask students to apply or summarise what's just been taught – not just copy.

3. **Whole-Class Check:** Use an appropriate whole-class check such as circulating and checking against key points you need to see in their answers.

Any tweaks or anything I've missed?

Seesaw support: coach returns to the teacher, seeking their expertise and sign off

Teacher Fran: These are good. I think let's add one about me planning these in advance. I won't come up with good ones in the moment.

Coach Diana: Great catch. Let's add a fourth:

4. **Planned in Advance:** Consolidation tasks are pre-planned as part of lesson design.

Why do you think the 'whole-class check' is going to be so important for these consolidation tasks?

Link to learning: coach makes sure teacher understands why a key success criteria is important for student learning

Teacher Fran: I think because the content is always really new. It's not only to consolidate what they've heard or seen but a great opportunity for me to check they don't have any fundamental misconceptions. This is useful actually because before, I'd only find this out at the end of the lesson.

Coach Diana: That's potentially a major win for addressing those issues early and not letting them affect the rest of the lesson.

Precision and decision: coach prompts the teacher to think about which elements are precise (must be done in a particular way) and which require decision-making

So, which elements of the action step are going to be precise (stay the same) and what's going to require some decision-making when you plan for these tasks?

Teacher Fran: We're fully precise on 'timed and targeted' I think. They must be less than 5 mins or I won't cover the material I need to, and they have to be targeted at the key processes and concepts because it's not worth spending time on other things. More decision-making is needed around the type of activity I choose. This will really depend on the content and quite how new it is for them. Summarising in their own words might be most useful when the content is pretty new as I need to see if they've grasped it. Also I need to make a decision around the type of check I do.

Coach Diana: On what basis will you decide on the type of check you use?

Teacher Fran: I think it will depend on the nature of the consolidation task. I think generally it will be circulating because it will often be short answer questions, but I could also get them to use whiteboards for quick questions where they are writing out a formula for example.

Coach Diana: Great analysis of precision and decision there. Let me show you a model of my thought process in planning for this step using our success criteria.

Coaching commentary

This is where we get meta and analyse the quality of the coaching in the examples above.

Below we explain how the coaches' use of techniques supports their teachers to understand, do, decide, and improve, i.e., to develop their adaptive expertise.

Understand
...key knowledge that helps solve persistent problems.

Do
...a repertoire of effective, efficient teaching techniques.

Decide
...on the best course of action using situation-sensitive mental models.

Improve
...continuously through an adaptive mindset and metacognition.

Understand

In the *specify the step stage* of coaching, steps should be granular, clear, actionable, and specific. In the first example, coach Yuvraj supports the teacher to have a clear understanding of what they need to do by using the coaching technique **when what why** to specify the step in granular terms, as well as when to use it, and the desired effect. The coach also needs to check the teacher understands why it is important for student learning. Both coaches use the technique **link to learning** to achieve this.

Co-constructing action steps and success criteria is a great idea for teachers with the expertise to give it a go. Providing support with this can empower them to do it themselves. In example 2, Diana uses the technique **seesaw support** in various ways to support Fran to draw on her knowledge of great teaching to come up with the action step and co-create the success criteria. For example, Diana gives Fran space, time, and the **when what why** structure to support her to write out an action step. She asks targeted questions to ensure it's as clear as it needs to be. Diana then asks open questions about parts of the action step that can be turned into success criteria. This ensures that Fran is given the chance to articulate her mental model and also motivates and empowers her to feel that she is an active participant in the coaching. This wouldn't have been right for Yuvraj and teacher Alex because Alex's idea was very vague. If Yuvraj had tried asking questions (even closed ones), it would have been a slow, frustrating, and potentially overloading process for Alex.

Do

Both coaches move their teachers a little bit closer towards understanding how to do the step themselves by using the technique **spell out success**. Defining granular success criteria gives teachers a sense of what it means to execute it well. Of course, they still need to see a model and rehearse it themselves to develop their ability to do it.

Decide

By also addressing which success criteria need **precision and decisions**, the teacher understands where they need to make decisions and how they should make them. For example, coach Yuvraj explains that he varies the technique (calling for attention) during group work to avoid having to shout over students, and he varies the instructions so they are appropriate to the context. Explaining his decision drivers is going to be powerful for Alex when she needs to make these decisions herself.

Improve

The coaches use the technique **meta moves** when they ask the teachers in these excerpts how the action step is likely to solve the problem they hypothesised about in the previous coaching stage, *study the problem*. Note the language they use is tentative ('likely') and the coaches emphasise their method for improvement: hypothesising, testing, monitoring, iterating, and evaluating. Using **meta moves** is important because it models and reinforces the habits of thought coaches want teachers to get into so that they can improve their teaching.

Do this in your coaching

Let's look at how we can use these coaching techniques at the right time for the right reasons in our coaching.

Get started with these foundational techniques

When you're trying something new in your coaching, you need some foundational techniques to adopt. Try these techniques using one of the suggested sentence stems.

When what why:

- When (spotlight the point in the lesson)
- What (name the strategy)
- Why (state the reason/desired effect of the strategy)

Meta move:

- How is this step likely to solve the problem we hypothesised?
- How will you monitor if it's working?
- The proxies of success we are likely to see are . . .

Spell out success:

- Here's the success criteria for doing this action step well . . .
- An effective use of show me boards to check for understanding includes . . .

- Let's each take a moment to write down the success criteria we think would go with this action step, i.e., how it should be done to have the best effect on student learning, solving the problem we hypothesised.

Link to learning:

- What impact do you think [success criteria] could have on learning?
- Why is this so important for learning, do you think?
- How is this likely to affect learning?

Precision and decision:

- We need precision on keeping the language concise to prevent overloading students, but we make decisions on when to pause to ask the question. We'll base that decision on what the core concepts in the explanation are and how complex we think these are for the students.
- Which parts of the success criteria do we need to be precise with and why? Which can you be more flexible with? How do we make the decision about how to use them?

Adapt your coaching appropriately using flexible techniques

Seesaw support:

- **Seek out** the teacher's expertise by asking a question, e.g., 'How does this success criteria support learning?'
- **Scaffold** the question with a narrower focus and more cues if they can't answer well, e.g., 'How would this be more likely to secure attention?'
- **Share** your expertise if they can't answer well, e.g., 'Yes, you're right that you could scan the whole room from that vantage point but don't forget it also helps you secure attention because all students can see you as well.'

Notes

1 We are indebted to Steplab for their high-quality and extensive codification of action steps and success criteria, which have supported us in our coaching work (and in writing about coaching for this book).

2 Sims, S., Fletcher-Wood, H., O'Mara-Eves, A., Cottingham, S., Stansfield, C., Goodrich, J., Van Herwegen, J., and Anders, J. (2025) Effective teacher professional development: New theory and a meta-analytic test. *Review of Educational Research*, 95(2), pp. 213-254.

3 Goodrich, J. (2024) *Responsive coaching: Evidence-informed instructional coaching that works for every teacher in your school*. Woodbridge: John Catt.

4 Goodrich, J. (2024) *Responsive coaching: Evidence-informed instructional coaching that works for every teacher in your school*. London: John Catt, p. 234.

References

Goodrich, J. (2024) *Responsive coaching: Evidence-informed instructional coaching that works for every teacher in your school*. London: John Catt, p. 234.

Sims, S., Fletcher-Wood, H., O'Mara-Eves, A., Cottingham, S., Stansfield, C., Goodrich, J., Van Herwegen, J., and Anders, J. (2025) 'Effective teacher professional development: New theory and a meta-analytic test,' *Review of Educational Research*, 95(2), pp. 213–254.

Stage 4

See the step

This stage is called **see the step**. It is the part of the coaching session where the coach models the action step (and/or uses a video model) to highlight the success criteria to the teacher. So, why not call this stage of coaching, 'modelling'? 'Modelling' means showing a conception of quality. This is crucial, but the term **see the step** captures more than that. It's about teachers seeing a conception of quality and understanding the important features of a practice. It's the next stage of building their mental model of effective practice by providing them with a 'functional image' of better.[1] Importantly, it's also about them seeing the features of the model that are less important and can be tailored to their context.

Let's look at the purposes of the **see the step** stage.

Purposes

Develop a mental model: 'I see what I am aiming for.'

We need to make sure that teachers have a concrete example of what they are aiming for so that they are able to build their mental model of the teaching practice. This involves knowing what the target practice looks like and which parts are most important (the success criteria). The **see the step** stage helps the teacher create an animation in their mind of what it means to do the technique. Their mental model is improving as they move from thinking about the action step on paper (static and scarce) to the model (dynamic and detailed).

Understand the difference: 'I understand what I need to change in my practice.'

We need to help teachers understand the success criteria of a practice – the components that really help the practice to achieve its aim. Crucially, success criteria are a framework teachers can use to compare to their current practice and then pinpoint the necessary change. As coaches, we can support them to see and understand this difference.

Pitfalls

Pitfalls are typical occurrences that can undermine this coaching stage.

DOI: 10.4324/9781003465850-13

Falling for familiarity: sometimes, coaches can feel that modelling is unnecessary. When you have explained something that you understand really fluently and the teacher seems to grasp the idea really clearly, it can feel like modelling would be an insult to their intelligence. This temptation should always be avoided. Teachers may well understand what they need to do *on paper*, they may even be confident that they can do it or even have a really clear mental simulation of it being done in their heads. But, familiarity gives the illusion of knowing. There is no substitute for being absolutely certain that teachers know precisely what they are aiming for and they can only get there by experiencing a high-quality model. Plus, the questions you ask after modelling will ensure they understand why the modelled practice is likely to be effective.

Skip success criteria: avoid providing a model of the performance or planning action step without first breaking down what the teacher will see. We want to avoid saying, 'OK, I'm going to model setting up "think, pair, share" so watch carefully and tell me what you think." This doesn't direct the teacher's attention; it just gives them a vague focus, 'tell me what you think.'

It's important for the teacher to see the technique 'think, pair, share' being executed in full but their attention needs to be focused on the key success criteria that make it successful. This makes it more likely that they will be able to understand and later rehearse the practice. Here's a better example: 'OK, I'm going to model "think, pair, share" now. As I model, look out for the way I circulate during the thinking time. This helps everyone feel accountable for doing the thinking that I want them to do." This example makes it really clear to the teacher where their attention should be and what they should notice.

A cursory nod: avoid a cursory reference to the success criteria and instead, ensure that enough time is spent on understanding them and why they are important *before* showing the model. Then, make them unmissable *during* the model and spotlight key ones *afterwards*. We call this coaching technique 'wrap-around success criteria' because the success criteria feature before, during, and after. For example, rather than saying, 'OK, watch how I pause and then name the student, step away and scan the room' say, 'It is really important that you notice how I pause after asking the question (one of our success criteria). This provides enough time for every student to do the thinking before I name one student to answer the question. As I do the model for the first time, watch out for the length of my pause and consider why I've paused for that long.'

Wishy-washy modelling: modelling is to give your teacher a clear concept of how to do the action step well, i.e., a clear concept of quality. Sometimes coaches go through the motions when they model – perhaps they are self-conscious or think their role is just to give the teacher 'an idea' of what to do. Avoid this wishy-washy modelling and show your teacher a clear conception of quality by making each success criterion unmissable in your modelling and model multiple times if needed. A good rule of thumb is that you should be able to repeat your model again exactly as you did it. If you can't, it means you don't have a clear conception of quality, so it's unlikely your teacher will either.

Over-modelling: teachers need to be able to focus on the success criteria of the model and they have limited cognitive resources with which to do this. Therefore, model only the practice that you want the teacher to focus on. Avoid adding extra bits to your model. For example, if you are modelling an explanation, go straight in with that. Don't model how you would get the class's attention first. Likewise, stop the model at the end of the explanation. Don't go on to show how you would then check for understanding following your explanation. Over-modelling can quickly cloud the focus.

Skipping modelling for planning action steps: it can be easy to see modelling as something we do for performance action steps and not for planning ones. Imagine we've agreed to work on this action step around planning exit tickets:[2] *When you want to assess student understanding at the end of a lesson, plan questions about the main learning in the lesson so that you can check students' understanding and adjust future instruction accordingly.*

This is a planning action step and requires knowledge of our subject/phase to do well. But, we shouldn't assume that just because we don't teach our teacher's class or subject that we can't model it. They can still benefit from hearing our thought process as we model the step using the success criteria in the context of our own subject or phase. Teachers can benefit from being able to see the coach's thought processes as much as their actions. For example, 'Tomorrow, I am teaching a Year 7 maths class and we will be working on adding fractions with different denominators. The first success criterion of our action step is to "select key knowledge to target in the exit ticket." The key knowledge in this lesson is converting both denominators to the same number by using the lowest common multiple of the two denominators, so there has to be a question on this in the exit ticket . . .'

Here, the important learning for the teacher is not the question that is asked but the reasons why that question is asked. They will only grasp this from a model of the thought process.

Hypothetical modelling: 'Here's what I'd do. I'd stand up at the front and scan the whole room. Then I'd . . .' Here, the coach is saying what they *would* do rather than modelling what *to* do. Hypothetical modelling isn't effective modelling. In fact, we probably shouldn't even call it modelling. It's not helping the teacher gain a concept of quality. Make your modelling as realistic as possible by getting up and doing it (for performance action steps) and using real materials (for planning action steps).

Too precise: when you model, you're showing the teacher one version of how to do the action step well. It's important for them to recognise that they can copy your model later when they rehearse and in their own teaching when this is appropriate or they may want to contextualise your model based on sound reasons related to their context. Stopping or stifling this will make your modelling too precise. Often, there are aspects of the success criteria the teacher will need to make decisions about, with your support, so the technique will work in their context.

For example, a coach models how to plan and enact a circulation route around the classroom exemplifying the success criterion 'plan your route.' They circulate to the students who need more support first because the coach finds those students often need a little support to get started. They are clear with the teacher that this is a success criterion that requires a decision, i.e., the teacher can do it differently depending on what's best for their students. Later in the coaching conversation the teacher says they find the students who often need more support need to be left alone in the first few minutes of a task to get to grips with it and get started. It's best that she plans her route to reach them later.

Coaching techniques

Use these coaching techniques to help your teacher **see the step.**

Some techniques are foundational, i.e., we should always use them and some are flexible, i.e., to be used when appropriate, depending on the level of the teacher's expertise in the moment.

Foundational or flexible	Technique	What it is	Examples	Non examples
Foundational	Zoom in	Model the agreed action step.	"Now we've discussed the success criteria, watch how I model self-interrupt..."	**Over-modelling:** "Let's look at an example of self-interrupt. I'll start by getting students' attention before the explanation where Billy interrupts me..."
Foundational	Wrap around success criteria	Make success criteria unmissable: 1. Before you model, prime the teacher to see the success criteria. 2. As you model, demonstrate every success criterion clearly and when appropriate, point them out. 3. Spotlight specific success criteria after the model.	**Before the model:** "I'll model setting up paired talk now. You'll notice that I do three things: 1. Use the sentence stem, 'When I say go...' 2. Use lean language. 3. Pause before saying 'go'." **During the model:** The coach clearly models the success criteria. If needed, during the model: "OK, when I say go (note the sentence stem I used there), I am going to invite partner A to share their ideas with partner B. Partner B is going to listen (note how I kept that instruction really lean). Partner A, you will turn to partner B and begin your idea sharing with 'I think...' .... (note the pause) ... Go" **After the model:** "You saw me use the sentence stem 'When I say go...' What effect is this likely to have on student behaviour?"	**Skip success criteria:** "Let's dive straight in with the model..." **Wishy-washy modelling:** "So what I might do now is..."

Foundational or flexible	Technique	What it is	Examples	Non examples
Foundational	Spotlight specifics 	Make sure that you ask the teacher about specific success criteria after the model. Particularly focus on success criteria they are likely to find hard to spot, difficult to understand, or that are very different from their current practice.	"What did you notice about the justifications I gave for my vocabulary choices in the model I just showed you?" (the coach asks about this because it is something that is really different from the teacher's current practice). "What did you notice in relation to 'Lean language'?" (this is likely to be a success criterion the teacher will have struggled to spot as it is less obvious).	**A cursory nod:** "Ok so you probably saw what you needed to see there."
Foundational	Link to learning 	Make sure the teacher understands how the success criteria will support student learning.	"Why is the length of the pause so important in terms of learning?" "The length of the pause is so important because it signals to the class that interruptions are not acceptable and reduces the chance of further interruptions to learning."	**A cursory nod:** "The success criteria are the important parts."
Flexible	Precision and decision 	In the previous stage, specify the step, you will have discussed which success criteria need to be adhered to (precision) and which can be contextualised and adapted (requiring a decision). In this stage, you may need to highlight how you made decisions around certain success criteria for your model and/or reinforce the reasons for why some success criteria are precise.	"Remember we said that deciding how long to pause for requires a decision because it depends how challenging the question is likely to be for my class? What did you notice about how long I paused for in my model?" "We said that the success criteria 'stand where everyone can see you' must be precise because we need all students to see your signal. Where did I stand? Where would you need to stand in your room?"	**Too precise:** "You'll want to copy my model exactly." **Hiding expert decision-making:** "I decided to use cold call to check for understanding."
Flexible	Seesaw support 	Move between seeking the teacher's expertise and sharing your expertise depending on the weight of the teacher's knowledge in the moment. Seek first, then scaffold the question, then share.	"What did you notice about how I used wait time in that model?" [Teacher is unsure] "How long did I pause for?" (Scaffolding the question) [Teacher can't say] "I paused for 4 seconds as the question is likely to be hard for my students."	**Playing guess what's in my head:** "What did you notice about how I used wait time in that model?... What about the length of pause?...How many seconds would you say?"

Example 1 Foundational techniques

Let's see an example of a coach using the foundational techniques.

Context

Coach Gabby has been working with teacher Terry on 'optimising communication.'[3] In the lesson that coach Gabby observed, teacher Terry provided a completed model for his students. He then analysed what made it good and asked them to have a go at doing their own. At the point that we are joining the conversation, coach Gabby has helped teacher Terry to understand that live modelling would be more effective because it would allow him to model his choices, including rejections, and this would make it more likely that students produce their own high-quality work by mimicking his thought processes.

Watch how coach Gabby uses the foundation techniques for this stage: zoom in, wrap around success criteria, spotlight specifics, and link to learning.

Coaching Excerpt

Coach Gabby: OK Terry, let's look at an example of modelling your choices live as you are making them, so that students understand the thought process you are using to make your selections and rejections.

Zoom in: coach directs teacher's attention to the action step they are going to focus on

Teacher Terry: Yes, sounds good.

Coach Gabby: As I model the technique, I want you to have a look for these four success criteria:

Wrap around success criteria: coach introduces the success criteria that they want the teacher to focus their attention on during the model

[Gabby reads the success criteria they agreed in the specify the step stage]

- **Clear**: ensure that the choices you exemplify have several plausible options so that students see the importance of the selection.
- **Scan**: scan over your shoulder in between every second word so that students know 100% attention is expected.
- **Narrate**: narrate the options so that students understand that different words have different advantages or disadvantages.
- **Reasons for rejection**: explain the reasoning for rejecting the word or phrase that is not chosen so that students understand the process and not just the outcome.

Focus particularly on the 'narrate' success criteria as this was quite different from your current practice.

Teacher Terry: OK, got it.

Coach Gabby: *[Stands up at the board]* OK everyone. I am going to write my model and I want you to notice how I use really carefully chosen verbs to communicate a sense of chaos.

Wrap around success criteria: coach ensures the success criteria are clear throughout the model

[Gabby writes] ***The boat***

Hmmm. I have a choice to make here about my verb. I could choose 'tipped' because when boats are on water and the water is rough, they do tip to one side or the other. I could also use 'rocked' because that would show the boat moving from side to side... I think I will choose 'lurched' though because 'tipped' and 'rocked' are both too gentle and I am trying to create a sense of chaos. 'Lurched' is more of a chaotic, exaggerated movement than 'tipped' or 'rocked'.

[Gabby writes] ***The boat lurched forward*** *[Gabby scans]* ***and the*** *[Gabby scans]* ***waves crashed*** *[Gabby scans]* ***against the*** *[Gabby scans]* ***wooden sides****. [Gabby scans]*

Wrap around success criteria: coach makes reference to the success criteria they used at the end of the model

Coach Gabby: OK, so within that, I was clear with my model by planning to show them plausible options, I scanned deliberately, I narrated the options and my reasons for rejection. Let's think about one of my success criteria in more depth now - narrate. How did you see me do that and in what way is that different from your current practice?

Spotlight specifics: coach asks the teacher about a specific success criterion that is quite different from their current practice

Teacher Terry: You said that you had a choice and then you talked about the merits of each of the options before then explaining why you were opting for 'lurched'. At the moment, when I do it, I don't really explain the advantages or disadvantages of the options.

Link to learning: coach asks teacher why this is such a good thing to do for learning

Coach Gabby: That's right. Why is that such a powerful thing to do for learning?

Teacher Terry: It really helps to show students that as writers, they have choices and they are decision makers. It might encourage them to see the importance of independent thought.

Spotlight specifics: coach asks teacher to reflect on another of the success criteria. The importance of it in terms of making the technique effective could easily be missed

Coach Gabby: In relation to success criteria 2 - reasons for rejection, tell me what you noticed.

Link to learning: coach pushes teacher to think about what the significance of this success criterion is for learning

Teacher Terry: I saw that you gave a really clear explanation as to why you were rejecting 'tipped' and 'rocked', not just an explanation of why you chose 'lurched'.

Coach Gabby: Excellent spot. Why might this be effective for student learning?

Teacher Terry: Because students need to engage in the thinking behind what they are doing and that includes rejecting some options in favour of others, but they really need to have a strong rationale for why they are choosing one over another. By modelling reasons for rejection, it makes it explicit for the students.

Example 2 Flexible techniques

Let's see an example of a coach using the flexible techniques.

Context

We are about to see an alternative version of example 1. In this example, when coach Gabby asks Terry what he has noticed about the success criterion 'reasons for rejection' in her model, his answers suggest he hasn't really understood. Coach Gabby provides more support to help him.

Watch how coach Gabby uses the flexible techniques for this stage: seesaw support and precision and decision.

Coaching Excerpt

Coach Gabby: In relation to success criteria 2 - reasons for rejection, tell me what you noticed.

Teacher Terry: You stated some less effective options.

Coach Gabby: What did you notice about how I did this?

Teacher Terry: I'm not sure...

Coach Gabby: I narrated clearly why I was rejecting 'tipped' and 'rocked' (the reason for my decision). Watch me model again and this time, I'll explain what I am doing as I do it.

[Stands up at the board]

OK everyone. I am going to write my model and I want you to notice how I use really carefully chosen verbs to communicate a sense of chaos.

[Gabby writes] The boat

Hmmm. I have a choice to make here about my verb. I could choose 'tipped' because when boats are on water and the water is rough, they do tip to one side or the other. I could also use 'rocked' because that would show the boat moving from side to side. I think I will choose 'lurched' though because 'tipped' and 'rocked' are both too gentle and I am trying to create a sense of chaos'. 'Lurched' is more of a chaotic, exaggerated movement than 'tipped' or 'rocked'.

[Gabby steps out of role]

Here, I am saying why I won't choose tipped or rocked, not just why I will choose lurched. What's likely to be the effect of this?

Seesaw support: coach provides greater support to teacher to really help them see the important features of the action step

Teacher Terry: Ah I see, yes. It's not just about showing them how to pick the best verb but how to make decisions about rejecting other ones.

This is likely to be particularly useful to them because I sometimes support them with word banks - banks of verbs to choose from. This will make their decisions more thoughtful and effective.

Precision and decision: coach explains why the success criterion requires decisions by the teacher. This ensures the teacher knows to make it bespoke to each model he does

Coach Gabby: Great point about the word banks! This success criterion, reasons for rejection, is one we have to make decisions about because there will be different reasons for rejecting poorer choices with every model we do. For example, if we were modelling using different sentence structures to create a sense of chaos, our reason for rejecting a sentence structure wouldn't be generic ('it's not as effective for creating chaos') - it would be tailored to the model we are doing (e.g. 'a long compound sentence here won't be as effective as a simple one because...').

Coaching commentary

This is where we get meta and analyse the quality of the coaching.

Below we explain how the coaches' use of techniques supports their teachers to understand, do, decide, and improve, i.e., to develop their adaptive expertise.

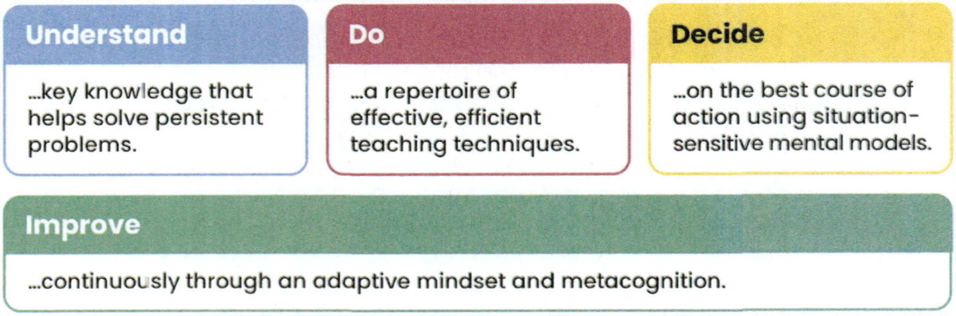

Understand

Knowledge is developed in this stage through developing understanding of how a teaching practice is likely to improve student learning. This happens through seeing high-quality models and paying attention to their success criteria. Coach Gabby supports teacher Terry to understand the practice of live modelling (during teaching) by **zooming in** on this part of his practice only. She also uses the technique **link to learning** to ensure Terry is building his knowledge of how the practice is likely to benefit students. For example, when discussing the success criteria 'narrate' she checks Terry understands why it is likely to be powerful for student learning. When Terry struggles to understand the success criterion 'reasons for rejection,' Gabby **seesaws support** by re-modelling and pointing out the success criterion explicitly in her model then re-checking he understands why it is important.

Do

In the *see the step* stage, coaches are building their teachers towards being able to enact the practice themselves. Coach Gabby uses the technique **wrap around success criteria** to make the success criteria unmissable: Terry is aware of them before so he knows what to look for, he sees them during the model and after too. Gabby checks he understands the purpose of specific criteria that are different from his current practice or easy to miss by **spotlighting specifics**. This helps him to build his mental model of what he needs to do when he rehearses and ultimately, when he applies the action step in his practice.

Decide

Not every success criteria is precise, i.e., done in the same way as the model or the same way each time the technique is enacted. Many success criteria will require decisions. Coach Gabby supports

Terry to understand this in example 2 by pointing out that the 'reasons for rejection' success criterion will be different each time even when modelling a very similar task to students. This is an example of a coach using the technique **precision and decision**.

Improve

Modelling is a key mechanism of effective professional development that coaches can use to help teachers close the knowing-doing gap.[4] Coaches like Gabby make high-quality modelling a mainstay of their coaching practice, and this signals to their teachers the importance of accessing and analysing great models of practice they aspire to, that may solve the problems they are experiencing, when they are working to improve.

Do this in your coaching

Let's look at how we can use these coaching techniques at the right time for the right reasons in our coaching.

Get started with these foundational techniques

When you're trying something new in your coaching, you need some foundational techniques to adopt. Try these techniques using one of the suggested sentence stems.

Zoom in:

- Let's focus on/zoom in on our action step . . .
- Let's look at an example of . . .

Wrap around success criteria:

- During my model, watch out for these success criteria . . .
- What did you notice in terms of this success criteria?
- Which success criteria did you see me use?

Spotlight specifics:

- What did you notice about how I . . .?
- Notice how I . . .
- Often this particular criterion is overlooked, so watch for this in the model . . .

Link to learning:

- What impact do you think [success criterion] could have on learning?
- Why is this so important for students?

Adapt your coaching appropriately using flexible techniques

Precision and decision:

- This criterion should always be done like this because . . .
- The flexibility in this criterion is . . .
- We need to make a decision about . . .
- You base your decision on . . .

Seesaw support:

- **Seek** the teacher's expertise by asking a question, e.g., 'How might this impact student learning?'
- **Scaffold** the question with a narrower focus and more cues if they can't answer well, e.g., 'Think about the impact it had on their ability to complete the independent task.'
- **Share** your expertise if they can't answer well, e.g., 'If we don't create space for students to process new information in relation to what they already know, even if they are listening to you, they may not really understand it.'

Notes

1 Kochmanski, N. and Cobb, P. (2023) Identifying productive one-on-one coaching practices. *Teaching and Teacher Education*, 131, p. 104188.

2 Lemov, D. (2010) *Teach like a champion: 49 Techniques that put students on the path to college*. San Francisco: Jossey Bass.

3 Goodrich, J. (2024) *Responsive coaching: Evidence-informed instructional coaching that works for every teacher in your school*. London: John Catt.

4 Sims, S., Fletcher-Wood, H., O'Mara-Eves, A., Cottingham, S., Stansfield, C., Goodrich, J., Van Herwegen, J., and Anders, J. (2025) 'Effective teacher professional development: New theory and a meta-analytic test,' *Review of Educational Research*, 95(2), pp. 213–254.

Stage 5

Simulate the step

Simulate the step is the stage where the teacher rehearses the action step. This is so they start to lay the foundation for habit change in their planning and teaching. We've said many times how incredibly difficult it is to change our behaviours. Rehearsal is likely to be a key mechanism to bridge this knowing-doing gap[1] and evidence suggests it doesn't just help teachers adopt the practice but adapt it appropriately too.[2]

The rehearsal process does something very important for our teacher's mental model of the action step. They move from seeing it modelled by the coach (an animation of sorts) to embodying it for themselves. The **specify the step** and **see the step** stages are about making the tacit actions of a teacher explicit. **Simulate the step** is where the teacher begins to internalise the explicit and make it tacit for themselves.[3]

Rehearsing isn't just 'having a go.' It's systematically working on a focused area of practice to get it right in calm conditions. This is similar to the notion of deliberate practice, which is not just showing up and trying something out, but a form of practice that involves pushing beyond one's comfort zone, working towards well-defined, specific goals, focusing intently on practice activities, receiving and responding to high-quality feedback, and developing a mental model of expertise.[4]

The coach has a crucial role to play, watching the rehearsal carefully with the success criteria in mind, providing feedback to support the teacher to rehearse well and helping them to avoid embedding errors.

The reason we've called it **simulate the step** is because this captures both the rehearsal the teacher does and the coach's role to simulate the effects of the teacher's decisions and actions. Simulation therefore elevates rehearsal because it takes the teacher beyond the 'now' and provides them with feedback as if they were doing it for real. Simulation also captures the idea that the coach can change the conditions of rehearsal (e.g. to add plausible complexity for the teacher), so the teacher can rehearse this too.

Drawing these points together, we can see that the coach's role in this stage is threefold:

1. To ensure rehearsal meets the concept of quality shown in the model and lays solid foundations for habit formation. This often means giving specific feedback linked to success

DOI: 10.4324/9781003465850-14

criteria to ensure the teacher does not embed errors and practises until they can't get it wrong.[5]

2. As a 'feedback loop' for the teacher's actions and decisions. This may mean exemplifying the effect of the teacher's actions for performance action steps (e.g. acting as students) or prompting the teacher to simulate the effect of their planning on students for planning action steps (e.g. 'Let's think through how Akhil and Mason are likely to respond to that task.').
3. As the creator of multiple contexts. If the teacher can cope with complexity, the coach can vary conditions of rehearsal so they can rehearse their decision-making and varied response.

Let's look at the purposes of the **simulate the step** stage.

Purposes

Embody the step: 'I know how it feels to do this technique well, albeit out of context.'

The teacher's mental model develops further as they now know how it feels to enact the step well. They are explicitly using the success criteria to guide their actions and decisions, albeit out of context. With each stage of coaching, their mental model is improving and in this stage, the technique is internalised as the teacher tries it themselves.

Kick-start automaticity: 'I feel like this is becoming automatic.'

When teachers talk about the action step, they understand it in its component parts and that the parts combine to have the desired effect. When they watch a model, they develop a vision for tying together the component parts. When they simulate the step, they feel which parts of the step they can chunk together and automate and which parts still require their explicit attention. The more they rehearse, the more automated the step becomes and the more aware the teacher can be of necessary adaptations. While incomplete in the early stages, this sense of automaticity begins to develop from the first rehearsal run.

Realising importance: 'I couldn't have foreseen the importance of that aspect.'

When teachers imagine themselves doing the action step, this begins to build a picture of what they are aiming for in their minds. However, the picture is incomplete. There are details of every action step that teachers are likely to only notice when they actually come to rehearse it. This could include the importance or the difficulty of a particular success criterion or the realisation that executing the step in a particular way is important.

Prepare for reality: I know how to adapt it to real-life conditions.'

For some teachers, they will be able to add complexity to the technique by factoring in plausible real-life adaptations they might need to make.

Pitfalls

Pitfalls are typical ways we can undermine this coaching stage. We need to know them so we can avoid them.

Skip rehearsal: if teachers and/or coaches have not rehearsed before, it can feel daunting. The idea of standing up and 'pretending' to teach in front of a colleague could be completely alien to a teacher, and the task of watching a colleague go through this discomfort is only marginally easier. Plus, rehearsal comes towards the end of the coaching conversation, so it's easy to accidentally run out of time. This can lead to skipping rehearsal altogether. Avoid this. There's such a strong rationale for rehearsal. Actually doing the right thing at the right time for the right reasons in lessons relies on enacting the action step during coaching to lay those foundations for habit formation and the capacity to adapt. We'll address how to scaffold rehearsal to overcome the discomfort.

Apologise for rehearsal: there is no denying that for some teachers and coaches, rehearsal can feel awkward. Exposing your teaching to a colleague requires a willingness to be vulnerable, and this can amplify this sense of awkwardness for teachers when it comes to rehearsal. The awareness of the requirement to assume vulnerability can lead some coaches to apologise for rehearsal. For example, 'I know it's super awkward but let's just bite the bullet and get it done.' While this seems like empathy and collegiality, it undermines the value of rehearsal and reduces it to a necessary task rather than a valuable tool for professional development.

Instead, exhibit professional enthusiasm for rehearsal to reinforce the message about its value. This will need to be pitched right for the teacher. For example, saying, 'I can't wait to see you try this given the impact we think it will have on the students. Let's do some rehearsal.' will work for a teacher who is already on board with it, whereas, 'There's such value in you trying this with my support. We'll take it step by step and put it all together only when you're ready.' might be better for a teacher who is reticent.[6]

Ram-home rehearsal: the flip side of apologising for rehearsal is to force it on teachers who are understandably nervous and wary of doing it: 'It's daft to be nervous – I've explained how doctors, musicians, and sports people do it. How else do you plan to get better?' Whilst we don't want to lower our expectations, we shouldn't be callous or condescending either. Be patient with your teacher (and yourself). Scaffold rehearsal by doing things such as ensuring they are comfortable rehearsing from a script or rehearsing sitting down before moving to rehearsing in a way that is closer to the reality of teaching.

The wrong focus: for rehearsal to be most effective, it needs to prepare teachers for something they are actually going to do or plan for in an upcoming lesson. Sometimes, driven by a desire to get on with the actual act of rehearsal, coaches suggest the teacher rehearse a past situation: 'Let's go back to the explanation you gave in the lesson and have another go.' Or a hypothetical situation: 'OK so let's rehearse. Imagine it's a maths lesson and you're teaching about . . . say . . . long multiplication.' Neither of these supports the teacher in the future, which means teachers are less likely to put it into practice. By using a *genuine upcoming lesson*, coaches create an opportunity for teachers to use the action step soon. Plus, it will likely save time preparing for the upcoming lesson. So, make sure rehearsal is forward focused, i.e., for an upcoming lesson.

Failing to plan, planning to fail: because we want rehearsal to prepare teachers for the reality of teaching, we need to help them plan it carefully so that we can be sure that they have thought through as many plausible issues as possible. If rehearsal isn't planned, teachers are likely to be consciously deciding what to do and say *during* the rehearsal itself. This reduces the attention they are able to pay to executing the success criteria. Not planning rehearsal also makes it less likely that the teacher will execute it well, reducing the possibility of them gaining confidence from the rehearsal and about the value of rehearsal.[7] So, always make sure you support your teacher to plan for the rehearsal. This may mean scripting what they will say or gathering the resources they need for an upcoming lesson so they can rehearse an aspect of their planning.

Hypothetical rehearsal: because rehearsal can be uncomfortable at first, your teacher may lapse into just explaining what they would do: 'So, I would get the quote up on the board and start underlining the key words .... Just as we shouldn't hypothetically model to our teacher ('Let's talk about what I *would* do ...'), we shouldn't allow them to hypothetically rehearse either. Hypothetical rehearsal is not rehearsal – it's just a chat. If the teacher is working on a performance action step, they need to embody it by getting in role (as themselves teaching) and rehearsing it. If it's a planning technique, they need to talk through their thought process as they actually plan. This is why it's so important to be forward-focused: it makes rehearsal useful and realistic.

Allow poor rehearsal: too often coaches accept rehearsal attempts that are not quite as good as they could be, i.e. not all success criteria are done well. The teacher therefore won't have embodied the action step and laid the foundation for habit change. Instead, create a culture where your teacher expects feedback from you to tweak what they do so they are spot on.

Coaches can also allow poor rehearsal to *run on*. This happens when the teacher does some smaller things sub-optimally and the coach doesn't jump in to support until the end of the round of rehearsal. For example, if the teacher is rehearsing how to design questions for an independent task (a planning action step) and one of the success criteria is 'be concise,' the coach should step in immediately and give the teacher feedback to support them to make their questions more concise rather than wait until they've planned them all. Another example would be if the teacher is practising scanning the room and giving non-verbal reminders and they are not scanning deliberately (one of the success criteria). The coach can pause the rehearsal to give the teacher a quick reminder to scan obviously just like they saw in the model.

Just-right rehearsal: perhaps because rehearsal can feel a little odd at first, coaches might end the rehearsal stage *just* as the teacher gets the technique right. But remember, rehearsal is to lay the foundations for habit formation. To achieve this, teachers need to rehearse beyond right; ideally, they need to rehearse until they can't get it wrong. This purpose should be shared with the teacher as it may feel strange to be asked to 'go again' despite hitting the mark two or three times already. Aim for three consecutive correct rounds of rehearsal for performance action steps – more perhaps when the technique is short. For planning action steps, you redo bits as you go and there often aren't usually whole rounds of re-practice.

Stay in the comfort zone: teachers might get the action step right pretty quickly, i.e., in one or two 'rounds' of rehearsal. It's tempting to end rehearsal there. Where the teacher gets it right and locks it in quickly with a few rounds of perfect practice (or for planning action steps, one great round off the bat), add in plausible complexity to the rehearsal to push them out of their comfort zone and maximise their learning. In chapter 3, we said coaches can coach any teacher with any level of expertise if we look at it as adding more if-then branches to their mental models, i.e., developing their situation-sensitive mental models. The coach, as curator of contexts, can ask the teacher, or suggest themselves, a plausible complexity to add into the rehearsal. Plausible complexity may involve undesirable behaviour by students, different answers from students, unexpected levels of prior knowledge (less or more), etc. The key is the complexity must be likely or there isn't much point rehearsing it and the teacher won't have a chance to use it in their practice either.

Vague or waffly feedback: 'Good job there.' 'Try that again I think.' 'OK, that works. Let's move on.' Vague feedback doesn't help your teacher to know what to keep doing or what to do to improve. Keep feedback specific and actionable so your teacher learns from it. Similarly, avoid waffly feedback that goes on and on detracts from the main message and takes up valuable time the teacher could be using to re-rehearse. Keep feedback concise and specific.

Unaccountable feedback and secret standards: when watching rehearsal, the coach needs to ensure the teacher rehearses to the concept of quality they've modelled earlier. Anything less and the teacher needs (and deserves) the coach's specific actionable feedback to rehearse it right. Sometimes though, the coach offers random feedback on rehearsal based on personal preference or some unspecified criteria not linked to learning: 'Actually, I think you need to smile more at that point.' This is problematic for two reasons. First, it breaks the coach's promise to root their feedback in what is best for student learning. Secondly, it introduces a secret set of criteria on which the teacher is judged - this may well undermine trust and is at odds with coaching for adaptive expertise because a key facet of this is to develop the teacher's understanding of how to *improve* at their role. Introducing secret standards communicates to teachers that they will never learn how to get better at getting better.[8] They will think that good practice is understood only by their coach. Instead, keep feedback tied to the success criteria wherever possible. Occasionally, as the teacher rehearses, you realise there are things you need to add to the success criteria. Discuss this openly with them so they know what to do and why. You may also need to model it too.

Leaving feedback hanging: so, you've given some feedback to the teacher after a round of rehearsal and they've nodded and agreed. It *feels* as if you can move on to the final stage of coaching. Don't do this yet. Leaving feedback hanging means you can't be sure the teacher has understood it and they certainly haven't embodied it yet. Make sure after any piece of developmental feedback, your teacher 'goes again' to put it into action.

Coaching techniques

Use these coaching techniques to help your teacher **simulate the step**.

Some techniques are foundational, i.e., we should always use them, and some are flexible, i.e., we should use them when appropriate, depending on the level of the teacher's expertise in the moment.

Foundational or flexible	Technique	What it is	Examples	Non examples
Foundational	Clean but close	Make sure that rehearsal is 'clean' in that it takes place in an environment where there is no risk of distraction. Make sure that rehearsal is 'close' by making it as realistic as possible. For example, using real lesson materials or ensuring the teacher stands up and enacts the action step as they would in the lesson.	"Before you start rehearsing, where exactly will you be standing when you do this for real?" "Let's get out your lesson resources for your next reading lesson with year 3."	**Hypothetical rehearsal:** "Don't worry about standing up – just run through what you'd say."
Foundational	Plan forward-focused rehearsal	Always plan for rehearsal. Help the teacher to plan the precise time they will use it in an upcoming lesson.	"When are you next teaching? Is there an opportunity to use 'show me' boards in that lesson? When in the lesson would that be?" "Great, you've got the resources for next lesson. Let's figure out what the independent task is likely to be."	**The wrong focus:** "Looking back to the lesson I saw then, let's rehearse doing that part differently."
Foundational for performance action steps	Between-rounds feedback	After a round of rehearsal, spotlight a specific success criterion that the teacher has done well and (often but not always) one they can improve next round. Re-model success criteria when this might help remind the teacher of what good looks like. **Note:** for action steps that focus on planning, between-rounds feedback is unlikely to be used. Instead, just-in-time feedback (see below) is the type of feedback that is most often given.	"I noticed how you stepped back as you posed the question. This was great for opening the student's answer up to the whole room." "Next time try pausing for the full three seconds we decided were necessary to give students time to think hard. Let's do that together to feel how long it is."	**Vague feedback:** "Try to be clearer when you explain the group 1 elements." **Secret standards:** "Try that again and this time I wonder if you could pick up the pace towards the middle of the modelling."
Foundational	Link to learning	Support your teacher to understand why what they are doing is likely to support student learning.	"Why is it so important to ensure that the feedback you give as you circulate is actionable?" "What impact does giving students time to jot down ideas before paired talk have on learning, do you think?" "Targeting the most important knowledge with the questions you plan means you'll check the key ideas and know how to adjust your instruction. You don't have time to check everything so isolating the most important ideas is key."	**Unaccountable feedback:** "I really like to see it done that way."

Foundational or flexible	Technique	What it is	Examples	Non examples
Foundational	Go again	Encourage the teacher to do multiple rounds of rehearsal to rehearse beyond good. Whenever you give developmental feedback, make sure the teacher goes again immediately.	"Let's go again, this time with a slightly longer pause after the name." "Run it again but this time use that pointing gesture as you say who you want them to track." "OK, let's go again to really lock in the change..."	**Leaving feedback hanging:** "So that's what I think you can do better. Let's move on." **Just-right rehearsal:** "You've just about got it. Nice work. Let's wrap this up."
Flexible for performance action steps Foundational for planning action steps	Just-in-time feedback	For planning action steps, coaches can give just-in-time feedback to support teachers in the moment to enact the action step better. This is short specific feedback the teacher acts upon immediately. Between-rounds feedback may not be appropriate for many planning action steps. For performance action steps, sometimes teachers need micro reminders to prevent them from encoding the wrong practice. Then, they can quickly 'go again' to get it right.	"It was effective when you planned to break down the process into those four steps. 'Break down' is one of the key success criteria. Now, let's phrase step 2 more concretely (another of our success criteria) by stating what students should do?" "I'm just going to jump in there. Remember, our success criterion 'scan deliberately'? [Coach moves their head to re-model it]. Let's go again."	**Allow poor rehearsal:** [Coach thinks]: "They've almost got it right. I won't give them feedback on that." **Leaving feedback hanging:** "Remember to scan as you wait. But don't worry, I'm sure you will when you're doing it for real." **Waffly feedback:** "OK, I'm going to jump in here if you don't mind. You'll remember from my model that I scanned really deliberately over my right shoulder as I was modelling that piece of writing. That was super important because it holds students accountable for paying attention as I write so they aren't just seeing the outcome but also the process that leads to that. When you just did it a moment ago, the scanning was there but it wasn't very deliberate so I think some students might not even see you doing it and then you just don't quite get that attention gain which is a real shame because what you're writing is great!"
Flexible	Scaffold rehearsal	If teachers are nervous or reluctant to rehearse, support them to build up to full rehearsal. Choose from a range of scaffolds: 1. Do it sitting down first. 2. Encourage them to read from the script until confident. 3. Do some back-and-forth repetition of the script with them. 4. Rehearse small parts, building up to the whole.	"Let's try it sitting down first." Coach: "OK, let's start by just passing the execution of the action step back and forth. I'll go first then you copy." "How much money is left after the visit to the shop... Hugo?" Teacher: "How much money is left after the visit to the shop... Hugo?"	**Ram-home rehearsal:** "Rehearsal is really important. Research shows it's the best way to get better so come on, up you get."

Foundational or flexible	Technique	What it is	Examples	Non examples
Flexible	Add complexity 	Once teachers have rehearsed the action step thoroughly and well, coaches may introduce plausible challenges so teachers can rehearse their responses.	"Let's run it again but this time, let's plan and rehearse how you'd respond to an unexpected answer. I'll be the student and I'll give you the answer 'I don't know'." "You've just planned a task to get students thinking really hard about the key ideas. Now imagine an earlier check for understanding shows they don't have the prior knowledge we thought they would. How would that alter your plan?" "Let's think about what could realistically happen to change how you'd execute this step. What would it be?"	**Stay in the comfort zone:** "You nailed that really quickly. Let's move on." **Implausible complexity:** "How would you do that differently if a pigeon flew into the room and distracted the class?"
Flexible	Seesaw support 	Move between seeking the teacher's expertise and sharing your expertise depending on the weight of the teacher's knowledge in the moment. Seek first, then scaffold the question, then share. But, do not skip planning for rehearsal or skip rehearsal itself.	Coach: "Remembering the model, what's the next thing you do?" Teacher: "I'm not sure..." Coach: "The success criteria is 'choose plausible distractors' – what does this mean?" Teacher: "Ah, yes! It means answers that could be correct and target possible misconceptions."	**Failing to plan, planning to fail:** "I think you've got the idea. Jump in and rehearse." **Skip rehearsal:** "You seem like you understood the model really well, so I don't think we need to rehearse."

Example 1 Foundational and flexible techniques

Let's see an example of a coach using the foundational and flexible techniques for a performance action step.

Context

Coach Hameed has been working with teacher Sarah for three months. Sarah is in her first year of teaching. Recently, coach Hameed and teacher Sarah have been working on 'driving thought'[9] with students so they think hard and remember more. Their most recent action step was –

> *After teaching a concept, ask students questions that allow them the opportunity to use their new knowledge to think deeply about the concept so that they are able to connect it to relevant existing knowledge.*

In the lesson coach Hameed observes, teacher Sarah completes her whole-class input and poses a series of thoughtful questions that encourage the students to think hard about the new concept they have been taught. Coach Hameed is tripped up by the fact that teacher Sarah names the student who she wants to answer the question before asking the question itself. This makes him think that the students who had not been picked to answer might not engage in the thinking teacher Sarah wanted them to do at all. As the students are set off on independent practice, coach Hameed goes to three students who had not been picked to answer questions and asks them the same questions that teacher Sarah had posed to other students. None of the students are able to give an immediate answer, suggesting that they hadn't previously done the deep thinking when teacher Sarah had posed the question.

Coach Hameed planned to coach Sarah on the following *performance* action step and success criteria:

Action step	Success criteria
When posing questions to drive student thought about new content, pose the question before naming the student to answer so that all students have the opportunity to think deeply about the content.	• **Question then name**: pose the question and then name the student so all students engage in thinking. • **Pause before you name**: leave an appropriate pause after posing the question and before naming the student so all students have thinking time. • **Scan deliberately**: during the pause, scan the room deliberately to communicate an expectation that all are thinking. • **Step away**: as you name the student to answer, step away from that student so other students know the response is to everyone and the answerer has to speak up.

At the point of the conversation in the excerpt, coach Hameed has modeled the action step, and they have analysed his model using the key success criteria. They are about to start rehearsal.

Watch how coach Hameed uses the foundation techniques for this stage: clean but close, plan forward-focused rehearsal, between-rounds feedback, go again, and link to learning, as well as the flexible techniques, scaffold rehearsal, just-in-time feedback (flexible because this is a performance action step), and add complexity.

Coaching Excerpt

Coach Hameed: OK, so just to recap the success criteria:

- Question then name
- Pause before you name
- Scan deliberately
- Step away

Let's plan for rehearsal. When will you be cold calling in an upcoming lesson?

Plan for forward-rehearsal: coach supports the teacher to plan to rehearse the action step for an upcoming lesson, scripting what they will say

Teacher Sarah: Next lesson I'm doing a bit of a recap on the effects of the writer's use of metaphor, so I'll do some questioning around that, and I want everyone to think hard about it.

Coach Hameed: Great. What question will you ask?

Teacher Sarah: "What is the purpose of the metaphor in this sentence?"

Coach Hameed: Great, write that down so we don't forget it.

[Sarah writes]

So, our first success criterion (question then name) is about putting the name after the question. Who will you ask?

Teacher Sarah: I'll ask Gary, I think, as he's a good barometer for what the class understands. So I'll say, "What is the purpose of the metaphor in this sentence? Gary."

Coach Hameed: Great. Our second success criterion is 'pause before you name' and we said this requires some decision-making. What's the appropriate amount of time to pause to get the thinking you want from the class and Gary's best answer?

Teacher Sarah: After seeing your model, it's longer than I thought! I think 5 seconds is good.

Coach Hameed: Let's just pause for 5 seconds and see how that feels...

[pauses for 5 seconds]

Teacher Sarah: Yes that's good. That gives them time to think, but they won't find the question so hard they need longer, so 5 seconds is good. Then, looking at the success criteria, I need to use my really obvious scanning and remember to step away from Gary as I say his name.

Coach Hameed: Brilliant. We've planned each success criterion for a question you'll ask in an upcoming lesson. Are you ready to rehearse?

Teacher Sarah: OK...I'll be honest, I'm really nervous about doing this. It's not you, it's me just not wanting to get it wrong.

Coach Hameed: Wrong isn't important but nervous is. What is it that you're nervous about getting wrong?

Teacher Sarah: It's this thing of making sure the name goes after the question. I really see why that's so important, but I just think I'm going to fall back into old habits.

Scaffold rehearsal: coach supports the teacher to do it sitting down first with the script. Once she is used to saying it, she can get into teacher mode

Coach Hameed: That's really important to acknowledge that risk. The best way to build new habits is to start to create the grooves for them to fall into. The best way to do that is to get to a point where we rehearse in a way that is as close to reality as possible but we don't need to start in the most realistic way - we can build up to it.

Let's start with just a few repetitions of the question you've planned with the student's name at the end and that 5 second pause you decided on. I'll go first, then you, then me, then you - we'll just take it in turns sitting down. I'll get in role and ask the question as if I am you. Ready?

Teacher Sarah: Yes!

Coach Hameed: What's the purpose of the metaphor in this sentence... Gary?

[Hameed gestures to Sarah that it is her turn]

Teacher Sarah: What is the purpose of the metaphor in this sentence... Gary?

Coach Hameed: What is the purpose of the metaphor in this sentence... Gary?

Teacher Sarah: What is the purpose of the metaphor in this sentence... Gary?

Coach Hameed: One more time...

Teacher Sarah: What is the purpose of the metaphor in this sentence... Gary?

Coach Hameed: That's great! Super smooth. Give it a try stood up but keep the script with you. If you need to read it before starting, do that.

Clean but close: coach prompts teacher to rehearse without the script to make rehearsal as close to real teaching as possible

Teacher Sarah: *[stands up]* What is the purpose of the metaphor in this sentence... Gary?

Coach Hameed: That's really good. The delivery of the question was very confident. OK, so now, try again without the script.

Just-in-time feedback: coach provides a micro piece of feedback to remind the teacher to do one of the success criteria

Teacher Sarah: What is the purpose of the metaphor in this sentence...

Coach Hameed: *[hand raised]* Just jumping in for a second... try again and remember to scan really deliberately here.

Teacher Sarah: What is the purpose of the metaphor in this sentence... *[pauses and scans]* Gary?

Between-rounds feedback: coach gives teacher feedback on their round of rehearsal. This is longer than just-in-time feedback as the coach wants to check the teacher remembers the importance of the success criterion she missed

Coach Hameed: Scanning was top drawer – really deliberate. OK, let's reflect on the success criteria. The only one we still need to incorporate is 'step away'. Why is that so important?

Teacher Sarah: Ah, yes... I forgot to step away, didn't I. It's really important because it sends a signal to everyone else that the conversation isn't just between Gary and I but between everyone.

Link to learning: coach ensures the teacher understands why this success criterion is so important

Coach Hameed: That's it. It's really important for the rest of the students to know that it isn't a one to one conversation even though you have chosen one child to give an answer. Let's go again and this time, build in that 'step away' criterion.

Teacher Sarah: What is the purpose of the metaphor in this sentence... *[pauses and scans]* Gary?

[steps away]

Between-rounds feedback: coach gives teacher feedback on their round of rehearsal as a whole before the next round

Coach Hameed: So good. You had the name last, the pause, the scanning and the stepping away.

Let's go again a few more times...

Go again: coach prompts the teacher to rehearse until she can't get it wrong

[Teacher Sarah is encouraged to go again three more times even after she has correctly executed the technique]

Coach Hameed: That's great. Really nice step away to open up the conversation. You've become really fluent with this action step now. Let's consider an additional, plausible complexity. Your goal is for all students to be held accountable for thinking. When you name the answerer (in this case, Gary), what do you want the rest of the class to be attending to and thinking about?

Add complexity: coach adds a layer of complexity to the teacher's planning by getting them to think about a plausible next step and supporting them to rehearse it

Teacher Sarah: I want them to be attending to Gary and thinking about his answer so they can build on it.

Coach Hameed: Yes. But, what risk do we run if we do cold call the way we just rehearsed?

Link to learning: coach helps teacher to see the potential impact on student learning

Teacher Sarah: I guess there's no encouragement for them to listen to the speaker and take in what he's said?

Add complexity: coach adds a layer of complexity to the teacher's planning by getting them to think about a plausible next step and supporting them to rehearse it

Coach Hameed: Right. So, building on what we've worked on in our coaching before now, what can we do to better ensure students listen to the answerer?

Teacher Sarah: Ah yes! We say 'tracking Gary' rather than just Gary?

Coach Hameed: Yes! That way, it's way more likely that all students will listen to what Gary has to say. I'm excited for this. Let's give it a go.

Go again: coach prompts the teacher to lock in the change

Teacher Sarah: What is the purpose of the metaphor in this sentence... *[pausing and scanning]* Tracking...Gary? *[steps away]*

Coach Hameed: Spot on. Try that three more times to really lock the 'tracking' element in.

[Teacher Sarah rehearses three more rounds]

Coach Hameed: I thought that worked really well and it's great to see you using techniques in tandem to meet a powerful goal. Do you feel like this moves you a bit closer to your goal? If so, in what way?

Teacher Sarah: Definitely. It makes it really hard for anyone to opt out of thinking at any point in the questioning.

Example 2 Foundational and flexible techniques

Let's see an example of a coach using the foundational and flexible techniques for a performance action step.

Context

Coach Tayla coaches teacher Katie who is a primary teacher with over twenty years' experience. Katie is enthusiastic about coaching and likes to have the opportunity to explain her teaching decisions to colleagues. Recently, coach Tayla and teacher Katie have been working on the teaching problem 'gathering and giving feedback'[10] and teacher Katie's most recent action step was:

> *When students are working on independent practice, circulate so that students can receive timely feedback on potential misconceptions.*

In the lesson that coach Tayla watched, teacher Katie's circulation route was in place. However, coach Tayla got tripped up when she saw teacher Katie spend around two minutes giving detailed feedback to one particular student. When teacher Katie had finished giving this feedback, she had only 30 seconds of circulation left before the end of the independent task, so she did not complete her circulation route. Coach Tayla then went to check on the student who teacher Katie had spent lots of time with. She asked the student a question with the same structure as the one that teacher Katie had spent time giving feedback on. The student was unable to answer the question independently - evidence that teacher Katie's feedback may not have improved the student's understanding.

Coach Tayla plans to coach Katie on the following *performance* action step and success criteria:

Action step	Success criteria
When students are doing independent work, give short, actionable feedback so that students take responsibility for their own improvement and so that all students receive feedback.	• **Lean language:** keep language concise and straightforward so that students can focus on the action. • **Indicate where:** support the student to spot the error or misconception. This can be directly showing them or giving them a clear hint. • **Clear action:** finish feedback with an actionable instruction so that students are more likely to remember what to do.

At the point of the conversation in the excerpt, coach Tayla has modeled the action step, they have analysed key success criteria from the model, and teacher Katie is about to rehearse.

Watch how coach Tayla uses the foundation techniques for this stage: clean but close, plan forward-focused rehearsal, between-rounds feedback, go again, and link to learning, as well as the flexible techniques, just-in-time feedback (flexible because this is a performance action step), scaffold rehearsal, and add complexity.

Coaching Excerpt

Coach Tayla: OK, we have the room set up as it would be for your lesson. Is that right?

Teacher Katie: Yes, that's right. The tables are organised as I usually have them for that group, and I always teach from my flip chart where it is right now.

Coach Tayla: And those five key students all have mini white boards at their desks?

Teacher Katie: Yep, their white boards are at their places as if they were sat there.

Clean but close: the room is set up as it will be for the lesson so it as realistic as possible

Coach Tayla: Great. In that case, let's think forward. When are you next teaching the class and which topic are you teaching?

Teacher Katie: I have that class again on Thursday morning and it's the next lesson in the sequence. I'm teaching them about long multiplication.

Coach Tayla: OK, so do you have the questions that they'll be working on independently?

Teacher Katie: Yes, I've got them here.

Coach Tayla: OK, so what is the most likely misconception or error they'll make?

Plan forward-focused rehearsal: coach supports teacher to plan for an upcoming lesson

Teacher Katie: The first one will be a calculation error with the times tables. Because there are quite a few steps involved, they often end up thinking quite hard about where they are up to in the method and then they make a routine error in multiplication.

Coach Tayla: OK, and let's plan for that misconception. Is there another likely misconception?

Clean but close: coach prompts the teacher to think of a realistic misconception

Teacher Katie: Definitely forgetting to put the 0 down as a placeholder on the second row of calculation.

Coach Tayla: OK great. So, let's just plan the feedback you would give to each of those errors. Remember our success criteria and look back at them as you plan your feedback.

Teacher Katie: For the calculation error, I'd say: "*There's a calculation error on this row somewhere for you to find and fix*". I think that's a 'clear action' for them (one of our success criteria for this action step) and it satisfies the success criterion 'indicate where' because I'm saying which row it is on.

Plan forward-focused rehearsal: coach supports teacher to plan how to implement the action step in detail

Then, for the second misconception, I'd circle where the 0 (place holder) has been missed because one of the success criteria for this action step is 'indicate where', so they are clear on what to correct - if I don't do this, I'm not sure they will be. I'd then say: "*check your calculation for a correction here*" I think overall my language was pretty lean there.

Coach Tayla: OK, let's put 5 white boards around the room that have completed long multiplication examples on them. Three of them will have those misconceptions embedded within the answers but I won't tell you which three. Then, as you circulate, you'll rehearse giving that feedback for each one. How does that sound?

Teacher Katie: Sounds good.

[Coach sets up the whiteboards]

Coach Tayla: OK, let's have a go at rehearsing this using the script to support you. Comfortable to start?

Scaffold rehearsal: coach supports rehearsal so that the teacher builds up to rehearsing without the script

Teacher Katie: Yes, ready to go.

[Teacher Katie rehearses by circulating the room, looking at each whiteboard and responding as she has planned depending on

whether there is a misconception and which misconception she sees. Then, as she builds her confidence, she begins to give feedback that is not on the script]

Teacher Katie: *[rehearsing giving feedback]* Remember, we want to make sure all the answers are checked carefully so that there aren't any silly mistakes. I can see a couple in here already. Don't worry about that but see if you can spot them, correct them and apply that to other questions.

Just-in-time feedback: coach intervenes to prevent the teacher slipping back into old habits

Go again: coach indicates that the teacher needs to act on the feedback straight away

Coach Tayla: Just jumping in for a moment. Remember the first success criteria? Try again and this time, keep your language lean.

Teacher Katie: Ah, yes, of course, OK, let me run that part again.

[Teacher Katie rehearses again and keeps her feedback lean]

Coach Tayla: Your language is much leaner - well done! You're executing the feedback well every time. The feedback you're giving is always actionable so students know what they need to do. Have another go and this time, try without the script.

Scaffold rehearsal: coach waits for the appropriate time to remove the script scaffold, i.e., when the teacher is getting it reliably right

Teacher Katie: OK.

[Teacher Katie rehearses. For a couple of 'students' though, Katie appears to forget to finish with a 'clear action' as per the success criteria]

Between-rounds feedback: coach gives feedback tied to the success criteria for the technique and that is more detailed than just-in-time feedback to support the teacher to rehearse right

Coach Tayla: Even without the script, your language is now lean. And, you're indicating where the error is. There were a couple of students where you forgot to end with that clear action. Remind me of the importance of this?

Link to learning: coach asks the teacher to remind them both why a success criteria is so important for student learning

Teacher Katie: OK, yes, it is a key part of what makes feedback effective: students need to use it. In this instance, I want to get them actioning my feedback immediately because these are errors they need to notice and correct themselves over time. Actioning the feedback will help them close the gap between their current performance and the desired goal.

Go again: coach makes it a clear expectation that the teacher will rehearse again to implement her feedback

Coach Tayla: That's it. If it's not acted upon, then it's not high-quality feedback. Now, take a quick look back at the script for how you said you'd phrase this actionable feedback and we'll go again.

[Teacher Katie looks back at the script then gets up and rehearses by circulating the room again and spending a short time on each of the white boards giving feedback as if the students were there and had the planned misconceptions. She ends all her feedback on a clear action for students]

Go again: coach encourages additional rounds of rehearsal to reinforce the practice

Coach Tayla: Spot on in that round. OK, let's get really fluent with that by doing another round of rehearsal.

Teacher Katie: OK, great.

[Teacher Katie rehearses for another round]

Coach Tayla: OK, you've nailed that. I even noticed in that last round, your language got even leaner. For example, you said, "check for a calculation error to fix" and pointed at the line. You're putting more of the thinking on them. Let's push this a bit further now. How many times would you need to see an error before you thought it would be best to give whole-class feedback?

Add complexity: coach supports teacher to think through the different branches of the mental model they may need to use so they can respond sensitively and appropriately to plausible situations

Teacher Katie: Maybe... three or more in a group this size?

Coach Tayla: Three or more will trigger you to think there's a pattern emerging. I might suggest that it depends on some other factors too. For example, if I saw three errors but they were all from students who had missed the previous lesson, I wouldn't stop the whole class but I might pull them in together and teach them while the others get on with independent practice.

Teacher Katie: Ah, yes, that makes sense. There's a clear reason why those three might have isolated errors.

Coach Tayla: Let's capture this decision-making process.

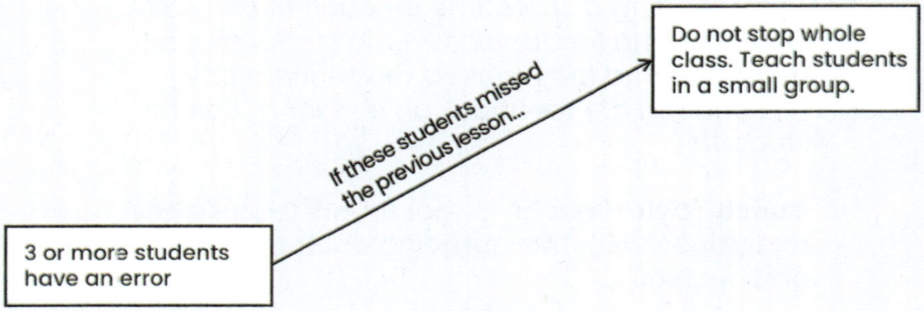

Coach Tayla: Are there any other variables?

Teacher Katie: Yes, if all the students I see often find the subject challenging, I might ask them to do some more straightforward questions, make a note of the errors and come back to them at another time when I have more time available to devote to teaching them the concept as well as the method.

Coach Tayla: That's a really good point. That's another connection between students we want to consider. Let's map this on.

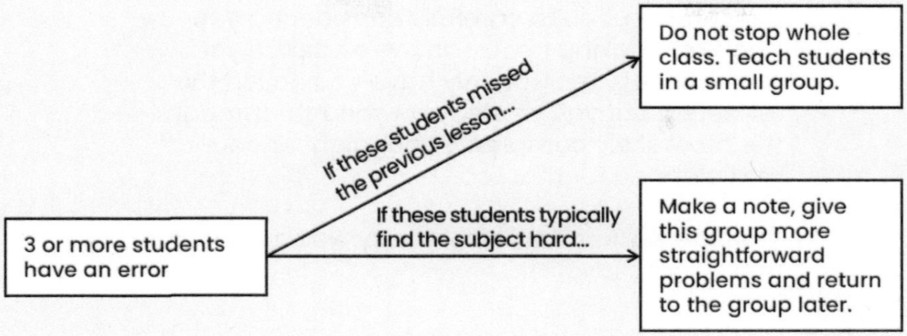

Coach Tayla: What circumstances would prompt you to pull everyone together for whole-class feedback?

Teacher Katie: I think if there was no obvious common feature between the three or more students as I've described then it's likely to be the way I explained it to everyone that's the cause of the problem. I'd bring them together for whole-class feedback then, I think.

Coach Tayla: Let's map on that third branch.

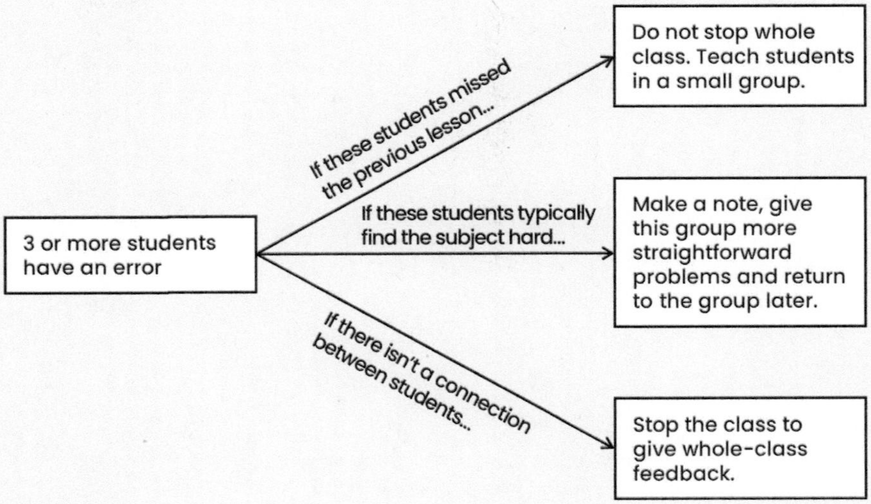

Coach Tayla: I really like the way you've thought this through. You're carefully considering your decision-making based on the evidence you might encounter. Not only have you nailed the rehearsal but you've also now thought through the most likely complexity you might encounter and planned for that too.

Teacher Katie: Yeah, I feel pretty well prepared now, I must say.

Example 3 Foundational and flexible techniques

Let's see an example of a coach using the foundational and flexible techniques for a planning action step.

Context

Coach Olly has been working with teacher Paula on 'driving thought'[11] and teacher Paula's most recent action step was:

> *When designing activities, ensure that students are required to apply the concept that they have been taught about in the lesson so that they can embed and process the knowledge they have learned.*

In the lesson that coach Olly watched, teacher Paula had given students an activity that required them to use some of what they had learned in the lesson. However, coach Olly got tripped up when he noticed that the activity did not allow students an opportunity to draw together and make connections between knowledge taught in the lesson. He noted that students' responses did not show the depth of understanding stated in Paula's lesson learning goals.

Coach Olly planned to coach Paula on the following *planning* action step and success criteria:

Action step	Success criteria
When designing an independent task, include the opportunity for students to make connections between different concepts so that the task enables students to think deeply.	• **Identify concepts:** identify the key concepts that you want students to make connections between before you design the task so you can ensure they are all present. • **Write response:** be clear on the quality of answer you want from students including the connections you want them to make by writing out the response yourself. • **Plan a task that prompts connection:** design the questions/task that will get students to make the connections. • **Scaffold success:** plan additional scaffolds where appropriate to support students so that they can make the connections.

At the point of the conversation in the excerpt, coach Olly has modeled the action step by thinking aloud as he planned questions that would cause students to draw connections. He did this for an upcoming lesson in his subject - maths. We join the conversation as coach Olly and teacher Paula begin to plan for teacher Paula's rehearsal for an upcoming lesson for year 7 in her subject - English.

Watch how coach Olly uses the foundation techniques for this stage: clean but close, plan forward-focused rehearsal, link to learning, and go again, as well as the flexible techniques, just-in-time feedback and seesaw support.

Coaching Excerpt

Coach Olly: OK, so talk to me about the lesson in the next few days that you want to plan an activity for.

Plan forward-focused rehearsal: coach helps teacher identify an upcoming lesson that provides an opportunity to apply the action step

Teacher Paula: I have a lesson on persuasive writing where I want them to have a go at writing a persuasive paragraph. We've worked hard on building knowledge of the topic as well as persuasive techniques and their effects on the reader.

Coach Olly: Why is that the lesson you want to use?

Teacher Paula: There are lots of different ideas about persuasive writing that I've taught them and so I need to set up a task that enables them to actually use those concepts together.

Coach Olly: That sounds like a good rationale. So to make sure this rehearsal is useful for you and allows you to see the impact of the step quickly, I want you to plan for the lesson specifically - what is it they are writing persuasively about?

Clean but close: coach prompts the teacher to think carefully about the specifics in the upcoming lesson to keep rehearsal 'close'

Teacher Paula: It's a speech about climate change. The audience are global leaders. We've been learning about this alongside how to write persuasively.

Coach Olly: Great. Let's just recap the success criteria before you dive into rehearsing your thinking around the design of that task:

- Identify concepts: identify the key concepts that you want students to make connections between before you design the task so you can ensure they are all present.
- Write response: be clear on the quality of answer you want from students including the connections you want them to make by writing out the response yourself.
- Plan a task that prompts connection: design the questions/task that will get students to make the connections.

- Scaffold success: plan additional scaffolds where appropriate to support students so that they can make the connections.

OK, over to you to think aloud as you plan this, similar to how I did in my model for you just now. Keep your thinking rooted in the success criteria - I might jump in occasionally to help you with this.

Teacher Paula: OK, so for this lesson on persuasive writing, I want students to connect the persuasive techniques we've worked on: start with a strong opinion, direct address, emotive language, and facts and statistics and use them to create a powerful persuasive argument about climate change (which we've been reading and thinking a lot about). That's me doing the first of our success criteria: identify concepts.

Just-in-time feedback: coach prompts the teacher to justify their decision around the concepts she has chosen

Coach Olly: Why those techniques in particular?

Teacher Paula: Because they each do something different: facts give credibility, emotion creates urgency, and direct address puts responsibility on the reader. But I've noticed students often use just one or two and miss the opportunity to combine them purposefully. If they can intentionally use them together, their writing will be much more persuasive.

Coach Olly: Those sound right to me then. Next, you write the response to ensure you understand what you want from students. We said this was really important because you have to be clear on the connections you need to see them making if you are to deliberately support them to do the same.

Link to learning: coach reminds the teacher of why a success criteria is so important. The coach does this because writing the response is a lengthy task and he wants the teacher to understand the value of their effort here

Teacher Paula: Yes, let me give this a go.

I'll start with a strong opinion...

"Global leaders must act now to tackle climate change before its effects become irreversible."

That's clear and urgent and it sets the tone. Then I want to bring in facts:

"According to the United Nations, the planet's average temperature has already increased by 1.1°C, leading to more frequent and intense natural disasters."

Coach Olly: That sounds spot on. You said you also want them to use emotive language. How are you thinking about doing this?

Teacher Paula: I think I need to focus on the consequences for humans - perhaps specifically children:

"If nothing changes, children in low-lying countries could lose their homes, their schools and their futures."

That feels powerful. And now, I want to end on a call to action, so this is where I'll use direct address:

"If you don't act now, you will be remembered as the leaders who let the world burn."

You know what, putting that last line in really helps me see how those techniques combine. I knew they worked individually and possibly together, but writing this helped me see that direct address has a real emotional impact, especially after the factual, logical build up.

Coach Olly: That's a brilliant insight and exactly the kind we want students to have. The rehearsal's doing its job here: helping you clarify the thinking you want from students in putting all these ideas together. What about our next success criterion then, 'plan a task that prompts connection'?

Just-in-time feedback: coach reinforces the insight the teacher has and links it to the power of the rehearsal they are doing

Teacher Paula: OK, so for the task I could write -

"Write a persuasive speech convincing global leaders to act on climate change. Start with a strong opinion and use emotive language, direct address, and facts and statistics to make your message urgent and compelling."

Just-in-time feedback: coach interjects in a timely way to get the teacher to rethink the wording of the task so it meets the success criteria

Coach Olly: It's got the techniques in there but remember that this task needs to prompt connection as the success criterion says. At the moment the techniques are just listed. Is there a way to signal to students that the purpose is to combine them for effect? Recall with my model earlier, I directly wrote this into my task so students knew what I was expecting from them. Try it again but prompting this from students.

Go again: coach phrases it as an expectation that the teacher will act on this feedback immediately

Teacher Paula: Ah yes, I can see it reads like a checklist. I'll revise it to make the goal more about how they should use the techniques together.

How about -

"Write a persuasive speech convincing global leaders to act on climate change. Combine techniques such as a strong opinion, emotive language, direct address, and facts and statistics in different ways until you work out the formula that makes your message powerful and convincing."

This is actually quite an interesting way to phrase it because it's actively encouraging experimentation and drafting and redrafting. This is something I've been trying to encourage with them for a while now. I never thought to bake it into the task instructions.

Link to learning: coach uses an opportune moment to ensure the teacher understands the value of what she is doing

Coach Olly: Brilliant to hear! This action step should support that longer-term goal too then. It's making me think that what you want is decision-making from students and that's what your task invites them to play around with. With that in mind, how do you think getting students to connect those techniques and experiment in this way is going to benefit student learning?

Teacher Paula: I think if they use techniques in isolation, they treat them like checklists: one rhetorical question, one statistic... done. But when they connect them, they're thinking about why their choices matter. Like how a fact followed by emotive language creates a powerful contrast and combination because it's compelling on both logical and emotional levels, and then direct address is more poignant because they've built a logical case first. That's what real writers do. They are learning about the power of the techniques and also the craft of writing.

Coach Olly: That's right. You're shifting them from using them superficially to strategically! That's how they start to write with purpose. Now we also need to think about scaffolds for those that might need them so they can experience success. That's our final success criterion: scaffold success. What do you think?

Seesaw support: coach seeks the teacher's expertise first

Teacher Paula: *[thinks]* Gosh. I'm not sure what's best to give them here.

Coach Olly: Let's work it out together. What might students find difficult when trying to combine those techniques?

Seesaw support: coach scaffolds the question, breaking it down to first think about what students might struggle with

Teacher Paula: Some students will be fine and others may struggle to hold in mind what the techniques mean and how to start them off.

Coach Olly: So, if some students are likely to forget what the techniques mean or how to get started, what kind of scaffold would remind them and help them begin writing?

Teacher Paula: Sentence starters I think. They act as a prompt for what each technique means and also give them a way into the paragraph.

Coach Olly: OK, let's try planning those and check whether we think they'll work for the students that need them.

Teacher Paula: For 'start with a strong opinion': "I strongly believe that…"

For 'facts and statistics': "According to recent data…"

For 'emotive language': "Think of the families forced to flee their homes…"

For 'direct address': "You have the power to…"

Coach Olly: They sound useful and I can see how they would remind and support. Let's plan a few more so there's a choice in there for them. More than one will also support them to better understand the technique if they're shaky on it…

Coaching commentary

This is where we get meta and analyse the quality of the coaching in the examples above.

Below we explain how the coaches' use of techniques supports their teachers to understand, do, decide, and improve, i.e., to develop their adaptive expertise.

Understand	Do	Decide
...key knowledge that helps solve persistent problems.	...a repertoire of effective, efficient teaching techniques.	...on the best course of action using situation-sensitive mental models.

Improve
...continuously through an adaptive mindset and metacognition.

Understand

Even though the *simulate the step* stage is mainly about the coach supporting their teacher to enact the action step, it is still important to continue to develop their understanding of why it is important for supporting student learning. All the coaches in these examples use the technique **link to learning** to ensure their teacher understands the purpose and value of particular success criteria for the action steps they are rehearsing. For example, coach Hameed prompts teacher Sarah to explain why the success criterion 'step away' is so important when executing cold call. He chooses this one in particular because she initially forgets to do it and he wants to ensure that she knows why it is likely to support students.

Do

The *simulate the step* stage is primarily there to develop the teacher's ability to enact the step and bridge the gap between knowing and doing. Most of the coaching techniques are geared towards greasing the wheels and steering rehearsal towards success. The coaches set up rehearsal so it is most useful using two key techniques: **clean but close** and **plan forward-focused rehearsal**. Coach Tayla ensures rehearsal is clean (no students) but close (as close to reality as possible) by making sure the classroom is set up just as teacher Katie usually has it since she will be rehearsing circulating the room. Coach Olly supports teacher Paula to plan for an upcoming lesson on persuasive writing so she can use the action step immediately and see the impact. It will also save her on planning time!

During rehearsal, the coach has the responsibility for supporting their teacher to rehearse well and rehearse right. Coach Hameed works with teacher Sarah to **scaffold rehearsal** carefully so she can do it well. They do it sitting down first, taking it in turns, then with the script and then finally without the script. Coach Hameed is reassuring and takes it at Sarah's pace.

All of the coaches use feedback tied to the success criteria to support their teachers to rehearse the right actions and thought process. **Just-in-time feedback** is used flexibly when rehearsing performance action steps to nudge the teacher to do something they already know about but have forgotten. For example, coach Tayla uses just-in-time feedback to nudge Katie to keep her language lean and coach Hameed used it to remind Sarah to scan deliberately. In both instances these were small tweaks the teachers knew how to do but had forgotten.

In contrast to performance action steps, **just-in-time feedback** is fundamental to planning action steps because the coach is guiding the teacher's thinking as they rehearse. For example, coach Olly gives immediate feedback on teacher Paula's attempt at the success criteria 'plan a task that prompts connection' because her task didn't explicitly do this yet. There are also no 'rounds' of rehearsal for planning action steps so just-in-time feedback is the core form.

The second form of feedback is **between-rounds feedback** for meatier feedback that may need discussing further. The coaches in the performance action step examples use it to reinforce the teacher's great practice and dig into a success criterion in more detail to ensure they understand its value and how to do it better in the next round. In all instances with any type of feedback, it is never left hanging. The coaches usually start their feedback with 'try again' to prompt the teacher to action it straight away. This coaching technique is called **go again** and it is also useful for ensuring your teacher rehearses beyond perfect until they can't get it wrong the way coach Hameed has teacher Sarah do when she rehearses her cold call action step. This helps lay the tracks for habit formation, which will free up the teacher's cognitive capacity to focus on cues that suggest they need to adapt what they are doing.

Decide

Teachers need to see themselves as decision makers. This is important because no two situations are ever identical and so teachers need to be able to navigate complexity and decide what to do to meet the challenges of the situation. Coach Hameed helps teacher Sarah to prepare for a plausible consequence by **adding complexity** to her rehearsal. Coach Hameed allows teacher Sarah to use her experience to combine the techniques of cold call and track the speaker (which she had previously worked on), **seesawing support** to allow her greater responsibility in this context. They were then able to rehearse this additional complexity.

In a different scenario, coach Tayla **adds complexity** when she asks, 'How many times would you need to see an error before you thought it would be best to give whole-class feedback?' She then supports teacher Katie to think through her decision-making about which feedback technique to use when depending on key contextual factors. Even though they are not able to rehearse those different pathways during coaching, the discussion supports Katie to mentally simulate and be more prepared for the decision-making she will need to do in her lessons. Adding complexity keeps action steps rooted in real life and supports teachers to further develop their mental models.

Improve

Supporting teachers to understand how to improve their practice is vital for ensuring they aren't dependent on their coach. In this stage of coaching, it is helping the teacher see the power of rehearsal for improving their practice. This hinges on coaches using the techniques discussed so far really well. For example, if a coach's feedback is specific, accurate, and actionable and they ensure the teacher goes again, the teacher should experience success and see the value of rehearsing. For example, rehearsal supports teacher Paula to have an insight about teaching persuasive writing: 'You know what, putting that last line in really helps me see how those techniques combine. I knew they worked individually and possibly together, but writing this helped me see that direct address has a real emotional impact, especially after the factual, logical build up.'

Encouraging your teacher to **go again** to rehearse the action step beyond perfect (when appropriate) through multiple rounds of rehearsal can also have a similar effect because they begin to feel how effortless it is becoming. Showing the teacher how to **add complexity** to their practice by combining techniques to address plausible, more challenging, situations is also a powerful way to model to a teacher how they can develop their mental models.

Do this in your coaching

Let's look at how we can use these coaching techniques at the right time for the right reasons in our coaching.

Get started with these foundational techniques

When you're trying something new in your coaching, you need some foundational techniques to adopt. Try these techniques using one of the suggested sentence stems.

Clean but close:

- Let's get stood up so . . .
- We'll use materials for your next lesson because . . .

Plan forward-focused rehearsal:

- When are you next teaching . . .
- What opportunity do you have to use this action step . . .

Between-rounds feedback:

- Let's talk about the success criterion . . . What makes it important?
- The way you did . . . was effective because . . .

Link to learning:

- What makes . . . so effective?
- How does . . . impact on student learning?

Adapt your coaching appropriately using flexible techniques

Have these flexible techniques in your coaching repertoire to use when needed.

Scaffold rehearsal:

- Let's start by . . .
- For round one, let's try . . .

Just-in-time feedback:

- Just jumping in for a moment . . .
- Can I stop you momentarily . . .

Go again:

- Try again and this time . . .
- Let's run that again . . .

Add complexity:

- If something is going to go wrong, what is it most likely to be?
- What if . . .?
- It's likely that . . . will happen. Let's rehearse how to respond.

Seesaw support:

- What are your thoughts on . . .
- My suggestion would be . . .
- I think that the key factor is . . .

Notes

1 Sims, S., Fletcher-Wood, H., O'Mara-Eves, A., Cottingham, S., Stansfield, C., Goodrich, J., Van Herwegen, J., and Anders, J. (2025) 'Effective teacher professional development: New theory and a meta-analytic test,' *Review of Educational Research*, 95(2), pp. 213–254.

2 Mancenido, Z., Hill, H. C., and Coppersmith, J. G. (2023) 'Practice-based teacher education pedagogies improve responsiveness: Evidence from a lab experiment,' *EdWorkingPaper*, pp. 23-873.

3 Nonaka, I. and Takeuchi, H., (1995) *The knowledge creating company: How Japanese companies create the dynamics of innovation.* New York: Oxford University Press. We are indebted to Jon Gilbert, Professional Learning and Improvement Director at Two Counties Trust for recommending this paper.

4 Deans for Impact (2016) 'Practice with purpose: The emerging science of teacher expertise,' Deans for Impact. Available at https://www.deansforimpact.org/tools-and-resources/practice-with-purpose-the-emerging-science-of-teacher-expertise (Accessed: 23 April 2026).

5 Lemov, D., Yezzi, K., and Woolway, E. (2012) *Practice perfect: 42 rules for getting better at getting better,* 1st edn. San Francisco: Jossey Bass.

6 The Steplab team model this approach time and again: not apologising and exhibiting enthusiasm instead.

7 CEO and co-founder of Steplab, Josh Goodrich, stresses the importance of planning for rehearsal, which is crucial to rehearsing usefully.

8 Lemov, D., Woolway, E., and Yezzi, K., 2012. *Practice perfect: 42 rules for getting better at getting better.* John Wiley & Sons.

9 Goodrich, J. (2024) *Responsive coaching: Evidence-informed instructional coaching that works for every teacher in your school.* London: John Catt.

10 Goodrich, J. (2024) *Responsive coaching: Evidence-informed instructional coaching that works for every teacher in your school.* London: John Catt.

11 Goodrich, J. (2024) *Responsive coaching: Evidence-informed instructional coaching that works for every teacher in your school.* London: John Catt.

Stage 6

Sustain the step

Behaviour *resists* change. Even though, up to this stage, we have employed many mechanisms to help the teacher bridge the knowing-doing gap (such as managing cognitive load, goal setting, instruction, modelling, rehearsal, etc.),[1] it's one thing to rehearse a technique in a low-stakes environment; it's another to enact it mid-lesson with real students. That's why this stage of coaching, **sustain the step**, is just as important as any other. We can't let coaching fizzle to a finish just because some of the meatier stages are over. Doing so fails to recognise that for the teacher, the biggest challenge is not engaging in the coaching conversation, but using the technique in their practice.[2] Plus, evidence shows us that specific action planning may support teachers to overwrite less effective cue-response associations with better ones.[3] This is why it's crucial to plan specifically for implementation of the step in the teacher's practice.

Why call it *sustain* the step and not embed the step? Unlike 'embedding,' which implies replicating the rehearsed step in the teacher's lesson, *sustaining* acknowledges the need for small, context-sensitive adaptations. A teacher who practises using a countdown, for instance, may find it looks different in the classroom than it did during rehearsal. What matters is not perfect replication, but holding the success criteria in mind and flexing to fit the moment.

This chapter explores how we can coach the teacher to plan intentionally for implementation, including how to navigate predictable barriers. This will give them the best chance of improving their practice and positively impacting student learning.[4]

Purposes

Here's what we want teachers to feel and know after this stage.

Develop better defaults: 'I use this practice at the appropriate time, every time.'

Teachers need to feel they can use the techniques they've rehearsed at the right time for the right reasons in their teaching to develop better defaults in their practice.

DOI: 10.4324/9781003465850-15

Monitor progress: 'I know what I might see if the step is or isn't solving my problem.'

The teacher knows what to look out for if the action step is or isn't having the desired effect on student learning (the proxies of success or failure) and how they might alter their practice where appropriate.

Pitfalls

Pitfalls are typical ways we can undermine this coaching stage. We need to know them so we can avoid them.

Accepting ambiguity: don't accept a vague plan for using the action step, such as, 'I'll probably try it next week before you come in again,' or 'I'll try to be clearer next time I do it.' Remember, behaviour resists change, especially under stress. We need to plan specifically for change if it is to happen. Crucially, this means planning when the teacher will do it so they have clear cues for the behaviour. These specific commitments make it more likely the teacher will use the action step in their practice.

So, turn ambiguity into concrete commitment by insisting the teacher plan exactly when they will implement the action step: 'I will try it on Friday with year 1 just after phonics when I do the whole-class input.'

Overlooking obstacles: with the best will in the world, the teacher's intentions to implement the action step can be thwarted by predictable barriers like a lack of time, assessment lessons, etc. Concrete commitments are a good start, but we make them even more powerful when we plan how to overcome predictable barriers.[5]

When we're fired up about our teacher trying a step, it can be hard to make our brain go to a place where failure is possible. Simply asking, 'What could go wrong?' may be met with 'Nothing really' or 'I don't know.' Instead, do what is called a *pre*-mortem.[6] A *post*mortem is where you look back at what happened and try to work out what went wrong. A pre-mortem is similar except you do this *before* you carry something out. It helps plan for those predictable barriers. In a pre-mortem, it isn't enough to ask, 'What could go wrong?' For a pre-mortem we must transport ourselves mentally into the future. Here's what the coach asks:

> Coach: Let's do our pre-mortem. Next time we meet, imagine you tell me you haven't been able to do this step in your teaching. Why? Let's both take a minute to write down our answers . . . OK, what do you have?
>
> Teacher: I've got a couple actually. The first is that I don't set aside time to plan my explanation carefully, cutting out the waffle, and I end up doing it off the cuff. It'll almost certainly be too long-winded if it isn't planned.
>
> Coach: How can we make sure this doesn't happen? . . .

By transporting the teacher into a future failure (and by both taking time to think), it's more likely you'll consider and plan to overcome predictable barriers so the action step has more of a chance of success.

Poor proxies: after coaching happens, teachers take on the role of implementing the action step as part of what Joyce and Showers (1982) term 'a second stage of learning.'[7] An important mechanism comes into play here: self-monitoring.[8] This is where the teacher takes responsibility for tracking the success, or otherwise, of implementation so they can adapt their practice if necessary. But this can't happen if the teacher doesn't know what to look out for or is looking for poor proxies of better student learning. For example, they may assume because students look busy that they are learning or they may think that simply doing the action step is enough to assume success without looking for the potential effect on student learning.

Get ahead of poor proxies by ensuring the teacher understands what they are likely to see and hear that allows them to infer the action step is, or isn't, successful. This may be evidence from student responses, from their work and it may be over a longer timeframe than just one lesson.

There are other benefits to ensuring the teacher can self-monitor effectively. If the teacher can see the action step is working, this adds value not just to their teaching but to their belief in the coaching process. It also focuses the teacher on the effects of the changes to their practice, and as we know, cause and effect are the building blocks of mental models.

Coaching techniques

Use these coaching techniques to help your teacher **sustain the step**.

Some techniques are foundational, i.e., we should always use them, and some are flexible, i.e., we should use them when appropriate, depending on the level of the teacher's expertise in the moment.

Foundational or flexible	Technique	What it is	Examples	Non examples
Foundational	Execution plan	Prompt the teacher to state specifically when they will execute the step. Often this will be the upcoming lesson they rehearsed the step for during the simulate the step stage.	You want this level of specificity from your teacher: "I will make sure I give a minute for all students to write down their thoughts next lesson in response to the key question around the meaning of the quote." "Next lesson, I will plan in the check for understanding question straight after my modelling."	**Accepting ambiguity:** "I'll be giving that a go soon." "I really want to try that out with one of my classes."
Foundational	See signs	Identify the proxies the teacher is likely to see if the action step is or is not supporting student learning.	"What might we hear from students' answers if this action step is doing what we want it to? What about if it isn't? What will we do?" "What differences do we expect from students' behaviour?... What might we see/hear?" "What time frame will it take for us to see improvements in their work do we think?"	**Poor proxies:** "Students should find the work easy." "As long as you do it as we rehearsed, students should benefit."
Foundational	Seal the gaps	Predict and shore up the potentially leaky parts of the teacher's plan to implement the step.	"Imagine we meet in two weeks after I've observed you again and you haven't been able to implement this step. What happened?"	**Overlooking obstacles:** "I just can't wait to see this next time I observe. I'm sure it will be a great success."
Flexible	Meta moves	Between you, highlight the effective methods the teacher is using to make sure the action step is implemented and sustained when the coach is not there.	"By setting such a specific commitment for when you will use the step, you're making it much more likely it will happen." "It's not easy to predict potential issues with implementing the step but by flagging the one you have done, we can plan to prevent it.".	**Accepting ambiguity:** "So, you think a barrier might be a lack of time. I guess we can't do much about that and you'll just need to do your best. "
Flexible	Seesaw support	Move between seeking the teacher's expertise and sharing your expertise depending on the weight of the teacher's knowledge in the moment. Seek first, then scaffold the question, then share.	"When will you be using this action step specifically?..." (seek) "In which lesson and at which point of the lesson will you be doing this next?..." (scaffold) "I suggest you try it out at the point when..." (share)	**Accepting ambiguity:** "Don't worry if you can't think specifically how you'll implement it. We'll just see how you get on."

Example foundational and flexible techniques

Let's see an example of a coach using the foundational and flexible techniques.

Context

In the current coaching conversation, coach Leo and teacher Amelie have been working on the teaching problem 'optimising communication.'[9] More specifically, helping students better link new literary concepts to prior knowledge rather than introducing them through definitions. Amelie's actions step (which Leo has modelled and Amelie has rehearsed) is -

> *When discussing new literary terms, start by activating students' relevant prior knowledge and explicitly linking this to the new idea so they can begin to make the term meaningful.*

Watch how coach Leo uses the foundational and flexible techniques for this stage: execution plan, see signs, seal the gaps, meta moves, and seesaw support.

Coaching Excerpt

Coach Leo: We've worked hard to specify the step, see it and simulate it. Now we need to make sure it transfers into your teaching practice. We need to make an execution plan. When, specifically, will you use this step next?

Execution plan: coach prompts the teacher to think about when they will use the action step

Teacher Amelie: Just as we rehearsed, I think: next lesson I need to remind them of the term 'soliloquy' because we're moving to the balcony scene. We've touched on it when Romeo does his soliloquy about Rosaline in an earlier scene but it's still quite a new term and I'm not sure they really grasped it, so I'll plan to activate their prior knowledge of that. It was so good to rehearse doing this!

Execution plan: coach prompts the teacher to make their execution plan very specific

Coach Leo: When exactly is that in your lesson?

Teacher Amelie: Good question. We have a 'do now' activity then it's straight after that and before I introduce the new scene. So, my execution plan is to activate prior knowledge after the do now and just before introducing the balcony scene.

See signs: coach asks the teacher to identify proxies for success

Coach Leo: Perfect. What signs would tell you that linking to prior knowledge is supporting student learning in the way we've discussed?

Teacher Amelie: When I check for understanding and when they do the written task, students should be writing about the term accurately. At the moment, they aren't using the literary terms well at all.

See signs: coach asks the teacher to identify very specific proxies for success

Coach Leo: Tell me about that written task. What would you expect to see them write?

Teacher Amelie: I'd see answers like, "Romeo's soliloquy in the balcony scene reveals his innermost thoughts about Juliet. As it's his second one about love, it also reveals this as a theme of the play…"

Coach Leo: Great. And what signs would you see if this action step isn't working yet?

See signs: coach asks the teacher to identify signs the step isn't working yet and they will need to do something else to sustain the step

Teacher Amelie: They will use the term in a surface-level way: "Shakespeare uses soliloquies. Romeo says..."

Coach Leo: Right, and what would you do then?

Teacher Amelie: I'd step in and specifically direct their attention to the connection again: "We have said that Romeo has already done a soliloquy about Rosaline. Think about what we said the power of this was. Shakespeare has given Romeo another soliloquy about Juliet, why?"

Coach Leo: Nice. By identifying those proxies for success and failure, you know what to look out for to monitor the effect of this step and make sure it works for your students. This monitoring is an important and effective way of ensuring the changes to your practice happen and help.

Meta move: coach highlights a key way the teacher is bridging the knowing-doing gap

But we know, even with the best intentions, it's hard to make sure we implement changes to our practice. Let's imagine (as we always do) that we meet again after your next observation and you haven't implemented this step as planned, what happened?

Seal the gaps: coach and teacher consider what might prevent the teacher implementing the step

[Leo and Amelie take time to think]

Teacher Amelie: If I'm short on time, I might revert to old habits and forget to use what we rehearsed.

Coach Leo: So, how can we make sure you remember?

Seal the gaps: coach ensures the teacher plans to overcome the potential barrier

Teacher Amelie: I think I'll add the word 'Activate' to the bottom of my slide that has the explanation prompts on it. This will remind me to make the link.

Coach Leo: That sounds like a good plan as it's a really strong cue to remind you to do it. The barrier

I thought of was that you are pushed for time in the lesson. Let's say the 'do now' activity at the beginning takes a while and you feel like you can't spend time activating the relevant prior knowledge so you skip it convincing yourself they remember it and crack on with the new stuff. Could this happen? If so, what do you do to prevent it?

Seal the gaps: coach shares what they think might prevent the teacher implementing the step

Teacher Amelie: Yes, it definitely could... I'm not sure what to actually do about that though. There's so much to cover.

Seesaw support: coach shares their expertise to scaffold the teacher's thinking about how to overcome the barrier

Coach Leo: I think your slide idea will help with this. But I also think you need to keep the activating of relevant prior knowledge nice and snappy so it becomes unskippable: it's important and it's short. This means delivering it just as you scripted during rehearsal and not adding extra stuff.

Teacher Amelie: Yes. I need to activate the relevant prior knowledge quickly. In fact, if I'm really pushed for time I could even alter it so instead of asking, "when does Shakespeare use a soliloquy earlier in the play?", I'll cut to, "Shakespeare uses a soliloquy in Act 1 scene 2 when Romeo tells the audience about his feelings for Rosaline. What is a soliloquy? Why is a soliloquy a powerful device to use here?"

This gets them straight to the thinking I need. It's not very important for them to remember the scene.

Coach Leo: Yes. Be judicious with the questions or explanation you give. Ok, let's fix a time for the next observation...

Coaching commentary

This is where we get meta and analyse the quality of the coaching in the examples above.

Below we explain how the coaches' use of techniques supports their teachers to understand, do, decide, and improve, i.e., to develop their adaptive expertise.

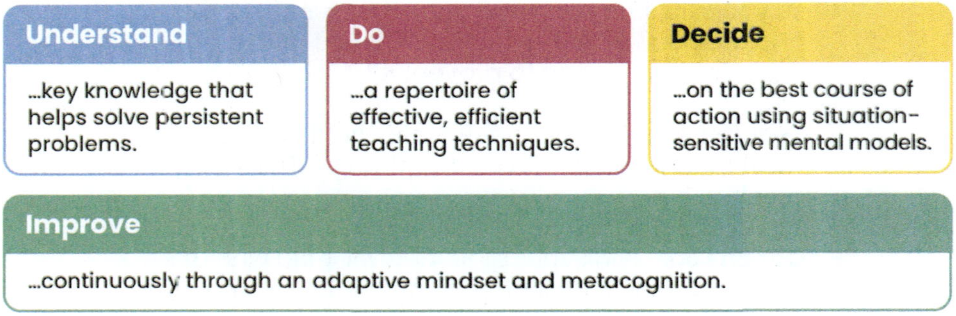

Understand

At this stage of coaching the coach has already developed the teacher's understanding of why the technique is likely to support learning.

Do

The technique **execution plan** makes it more likely your teacher will do the technique in their lessons because they have set a *specific* intention to do the action step at particular points in upcoming lessons. Coach Leo doesn't allow Amelie to be vague about her execution plan; he prompts her to be really specific as to when she will use the step.

Similarly, **seal the gaps** is a coaching technique that ensures all predictable and preventable reasons the teacher might not implement the step are planned for. Coach Leo makes sure both he and his teacher think about these possible gaps so they give the teacher the best chance of implementing the new practice. When Amelie struggles to think how to overcome Leo's suggested gap, he **seesaws support** to offer a general suggestion (keeping the activation question/explanation short), which she is then able to contextualise more specifically.

Decide

Coach Leo supports Amelie to make better decisions about her practice using the technique **see signs**. By identifying proxies for success or failure, your teacher should be more attuned to cues in the environment that cause them to make adaptations to their practice. Coach Leo gets Amelie not just to think about signs of failure but also what she would do to sustain the step if she sees them. By planning this decision-making, Amelie is more prepared.

Improve

Coach Leo explicitly highlights the great work teacher Amelie is doing in this part of the conversation to make sure the step becomes part of her practice using the technique **meta move**: 'By identifying those proxies for success and failure, you know what to look out for to monitor the effect of this step and make sure it works for your students. This monitoring is an important and effective way of ensuring the changes to your practice happen and help.' Highlighting *how* to improve (not just what to change) helps your teacher understand how to think and act in order to make changes stick.

Do this in your coaching

Let's look at how we can use these coaching techniques at the right time for the right reasons in our coaching.

Get started with these foundational techniques

When you're trying something new in your coaching, you need some foundational techniques to adopt. Try these techniques using one of the suggested sentence stems.

Execution plan:

- When, specifically, will you use this step?
- Let's be more specific. When exactly in your lesson?

See signs:

- What signs might suggest the step is supporting learning?
- What signs might suggest the step isn't supporting learning the way we want it to? What will you do?

Seal the gaps:

- Imagine you don't use this step. What has prevented you?
- Imagine you only use this step once or twice. What got in the way?
- How do we make sure this doesn't happen?

Adapt your coaching appropriately using flexible techniques

Have these flexible techniques in your coaching repertoire to use when needed.

Meta moves:

- Your execution plan is really specific. This makes it more likely this action step will become part of your practice.

- Now you'll be able to self-monitor as you implement the step because you know what the proxies of success or failure are.
- That's a really useful barrier to anticipate and plan to overcome. It's less likely this will get in the way of success for you now.

Seesaw support:

- **Seek** the teacher's expertise by asking a question, e.g., how might we overcome this barrier?
- **Scaffold** the question with a narrower focus and more cues if they can't answer well, e.g., is there anything you can do to prompt your memory at the point in the lesson where we want you using this technique?
- **Share** your expertise if they can't answer well, e.g., we could put a reminder on the display board in your eye line to jog your memory.

Notes

1 Sims, S., Fletcher-Wood, H., O'Mara-Eves, A., Cottingham, S., Stansfield, C., Goodrich, J., Van Herwegen, J., and Anders, J. (2025) 'Effective teacher professional development: New theory and a meta-analytic test,' *Review of Educational Research*, 95(2), pp. 213–254.

2 Showers, B. (1985) 'Teachers coaching teachers,' *Educational Leadership*, 42(7), pp. 43–48.

3 Sims, S., Fletcher-Wood, H., O'Mara-Eves, A., Cottingham, S., Stansfield, C., Goodrich, J., Van Herwegen, J., and Anders, J. (2025) 'Effective teacher professional development: New theory and a meta-analytic test,' *Review of Educational Research*, 95(2), pp. 213–254.

4 We are indebted to the work of Steplab in this area who, on their coaching forms, prompt coaches to pre-empt barriers with their coachees and ensure they set concrete reminders so the step is not forgotten.

5 Bélanger-Gravel, A., Godin, G., and Amireault, S. (2013) 'A meta-analytic review of the effect of implementation intentions on physical activity,' *Health Psychology Review*, 7(1), pp. 23–54.

6 Klein, G. (2007) 'Performing a project premortem,' *Harvard Business Review*, 85(9), pp. 18–19.

7 Joyce, B. and Showers, B. (1982) 'The coaching of teaching,' *Educational Leadership*, 40(1), p. 4.

8 Sims, S., Fletcher-Wood, H., O'Mara-Eves, A., Cottingham, S., Stansfield, C., Goodrich, J., Van Herwegen, J., and Anders, J. (2025) 'Effective teacher professional development: New theory and a meta-analytic test,' *Review of Educational Research*, 95(2), pp. 213–254.

9 Goodrich, J. (2024) *Responsive coaching: Evidence-informed instructional coaching that works for every teacher in your school*. Woodbridge: John Catt.

Conclusion

Closing the gaps

Throughout this book, we've explored a question that strikes at the heart of school improvement: how do we coach teachers in a way that improves classroom practice rapidly and sustainably, without compromising teacher agency? We've attempted to solve this problem with a structured, evidence-informed approach that balances rigour with humanity. We have set out a model of coaching that is not woolly or vague. It is clear, concrete, and codified.

This is a book about coaching, but it is also a book about adaptive expertise and the mental models that underpin teacher decision-making. This began by diagnosing the problem: the professional development many teachers receive does not yet help them navigate complexity and close the knowing-deciding-doing gap. Teachers might know what research says and even what their school wants them to do, but still struggle to make wise instructional choices under pressure. We argued that closing this gap is about developing teachers' thinking, not just their actions. This is where coaching for adaptive expertise comes in.

In these pages, we have:

- **Clarified what adaptive expertise means for teachers:** it is not just mastery of technique, but flexibility, judgement, and professional reasoning.
- **Explored agency as a non-negotiable:** it is the belief that teachers must be partners in their development, not passive recipients. They must also be supported to understand how to improve without the coach.
- **Codified the components of great coaching:** from setting purposeful goals, to surfacing mental models, rehearsing decisions and actions, and delivering precise, actionable feedback, readers of this book understand how to improve their coaching and can try this out immediately.
- **Made visible the craft of coaching:** not just what to say, but how to partner and problem-solve with a teacher and to calibrate challenge and support.
- **Created a vision of coaching for everyone:** no teacher is an 'adaptive expert' but always striving for greater adaptive expertise. Coaching is about accelerating the development of situation-sensitive mental models to allow for efficiency and flexibility - something teachers of all levels of experience and expertise can benefit from.

DOI: 10.4324/9781003465850-16

Instructional coaching is not new. But as a profession, we are maturing in how we understand it. The first wave focused on behaviours and routines, which is valuable, but not enough. What we offer here is the next step: coaching that builds internal capacity. After all, if we want teachers to flourish, not just survive, then we need a model that respects their professionalism and builds their expertise. Teachers cannot script their way to excellence, although scripting as we learn can be a useful scaffold. Nor can they rely on charisma.

This book is about developing teachers who can think for themselves, especially when no one is watching. It's about coaching that results in long-term improvement because it focuses on how teachers think, not just what they do. Central to this approach is the concept of mental models, the internal frameworks teachers use to make sense of lesson situations and make instructional decisions. Great teaching isn't just visible behaviour, it's informed by subtle judgements: how to pitch a question, when to adapt a task, how to read the room. Coaches who want to build adaptive expertise in their teachers must work with these mental models. They must surface assumptions, test hypotheses, and reshape thinking.

That's what this book enables. It gives coaches the tools to help teachers reflect deeply, grow confidently, and act purposefully. It replaces vague encouragement with structured dialogue and it creates space for teachers to articulate, test, and refine the thinking that drives their practice. In short, teachers who achieve agency.

Agency is the linchpin of sustainable development. Without it, professional learning becomes something that is done to teachers, not something they own. Agency doesn't mean teachers choosing their own adventure. It means being trusted to think, to decide, and to grow. It means being treated as a professional, not a technician. If we want our teachers to be agentic, our coaching must model that ethos.

In our coaching model, teachers aren't passive, they are partners. We don't tell them what to think. We help them think more clearly. We don't just model moves, we model mindset. We build decision-makers, not dependents. This means coaching also builds culture in the school. Indeed, the practices outlined here are not just tools for coaches, they are levers for culture. Schools that embrace coaching as described in this book are building more than skill. They are building trust, professional dialogue, and a shared commitment to excellence.

When coaching is done well, it becomes part of the fabric of school life. It is not a bolt-on or an intervention. It becomes how we learn, how we reflect and how we improve together.

Of course, some will argue that coaching must remain fluid, intuitive, relational, and of course, those things matter. But our belief is that professional growth deserves structure, not just sentiment. Teachers deserve better than vague platitudes. That's why we've codified what effective coaching looks like. The coaching stages in this book offer clear, repeatable techniques. The Adaptive Expertise Framework is grounded in research, but shaped by practice. It is designed to be practical, not prescriptive, adaptable to context, but firm in purpose. We have made the invisible

visible and in doing so, we hope to have made great coaching accessible to more people, in more schools, more of the time.

So where does this leave us?

It leaves us with a clear challenge and a profound opportunity. You now have the tools. The map is in your hands. The destination is in sight. Now go forth, and be great coaches.

> Be the coach who listens with intention.
>
> Be the coach who sees the teacher behind the technique.
>
> Be the coach who encourages teachers to consider the decisions behind their techniques and help them flex to be adaptive.

We end where we began: with a vision of coaching that is rigorous, respectful, and rooted in the belief that all teachers can improve.

Index

9781032739793